The Life and Times of Jonathan Mitchel Sewall

The Life and Times of
JONATHAN MITCHEL SEWALL
1748–1808
POET – LAWYER – PATRIOT

He was born in Salem, Massachusetts,
educated at Boston Public Latin School,
then he came to Portsmouth, New Hampshire.
The rest is extremely interesting history.

By
Nancy R. Hammond

Peter E. Randall Publisher
Portsmouth, New Hampshire
2022

© 2022 by Nancy R. Hammond
All Rights Reserved. First published 2022

ISBN: 978-1-942155-54-6 print
ISBN: 978-1-942155-58-4 eBook
Library of Congress Control Number: 2022920153

Published by
Peter E. Randall Publisher
5 Greenleaf Woods Drive, Suite 102
Portsmouth, NH 03801
www.perpublisher.com

Book design by Tim Holtz

Printed in the United States of America

If there is a book you really want to read
and it hasn't been written yet,
then you must write it.

TONI MORRISON

Research is formalized curiosity.
It is poking and prying with a purpose.

ZORA NEALE HURSTON

Contents

Preface to *Miscellaneous Poems* by J. M. Sewall, Esq., [1801]   ix

A Parody on the Preface to *Miscellaneous Poems*   xi

Introduction   xiii

Chapter 1. The Patriot Poet   1

Chapter 2. The Early Years   20

Chapter 3. Boston Public Latin School   30

Chapter 4. Apprenticeship, Spain, and Nervous Affections   42

Chapter 5. Law and Portsmouth   53

Chapter 6. Militia, Grafton County, Universalism, Family   69

Chapter 7. Poetry, Sarah March, State Papers, Black Petition   83

Chapter 8. Family, Work, Home, and Entertainment   94

Chapter 9. Ratification, Celebration, Home, and Theater   108

Chapter 10. Celebrations and Demonstrations   122

Chapter 11. Washington, Lawyers, Eminent Men   135

Chapter 12. His Book, His Family, His Friends   150

Chapter 13. Parody, Celebration, and Death   165

Chapter 14. The House on Gates Street   177

Acknowledgements   185

Bibliography   187

Index   195

Preface to *Miscellaneous Poems* by J. M. Sewall, Esq. [1801]

It is with great diffidence that the author submits the following poems to the public eye. The world is already so amply stocked with bad poetry, that a writer should be cautious how he increases the heap: and a real patriot ought to be tenderly jealous, even of the literary reputation of his country.

Many of the original pieces here presented to the public were written at an early period of life—not a few were only momentary effusions, and none of them were composed with much premeditation. But as nothing he can now offer will make them better, he desists from any farther apology, and quietly resigns them to their fate.

The specimens from *Ossian*, are taken from a work more leisurely composed, and therefore, if bad, have less to plead in their excuse. Macpherson's prose translation of these poems fell into the author's hands as early as the year 1770, when they were but little known in this country, they pleased him, and he then attempted to turn a few passages into heroic verse. The work was amusing, and he has from time to time continued it. The greater part of these poems are now completed; and on the favorable reception of the specimens will depend the future publication of the whole version.

Should he meet with the encouragement which every author wishes, he purposes to give his version to the public in two octavo volumes with explanatory notes which he has already prepared, and also to offer some arguments in addition to those urged by Mr. Macpherson, Dr. Blair, and others, in favor of the authenticity of Ossian's poems, against the opinion of Doctor Johnson and his party.

A Parody on the Preface to *Miscellaneous Poems* by J. M. Sewall, Esq. [1801], by N. R. Hammond (2022)

It is with great diffidence that the author submits the following biography to the public eye. The world is already so amply stocked with bad attempts at biography, that a writer should be cautious how she increases the heap; and a real patriot ought to be tenderly jealous, even of the literary reputation of her country.

Most of the original writing here presented to the public was written over a number of years—some of it is little more than momentary effusions, and none of it was composed with much premeditation. But as nothing she can now offer will make it any better, she desists from any farther apology, and resigns this biography to its fate.

The author's acquaintance with Jonathan Mitchel Sewall began some nineteen years ago when his story fell into her hands upon buying the house in which tradition has it that he lived. In 1958, Natalie Fenwick and Dorothy Vaughan published a series of articles in the *Portsmouth Herald* about local houses that should be saved. The Sewall house was one of these and the article was included with the house sale documents. The author was particularly pleased with a quotation attributed to Sarah Sewall, his second wife, "I would rather marry Mr. Sewall drunk, than any other man sober."

Should she meet with the encouragement which every author wishes, she purposes to try her hand at a novel and possibly a time-travel novel to give to the public in two octavo volumes with explanatory notes (sorry, the two octavo volumes were JMS's idea, but there will be nothing in verse), and also to offer some arguments in addition to those urged by Mr. Dishman, that he may well have helped the Black population of Portsmouth in the writing and presenting of their Petition to the New Hampshire Council and House of Representatives in 1780, and also, have been the author of the New Hampshire Bill of Rights as well as much, much more.

Introduction

My introduction to Jonathan Mitchel Sewall (1748–1808) came with the purchase of the house on Gates Street where, according to local tradition, he lived from about 1788 until his death in 1808. It was from here that they took his body to North Cemetery, where he is remembered by this inscription:

Counsellor at law

In vain shall worth or wisdom save
The dying victim from the destin'd grave,
Nor Charity, our helpless nature's pride,
The friend to him who knows no friend beside,
Nor genius, science, eloquence have pow'r,
One moment to protract the appointed hour
Could these united have his life repriev'd,
We should not weep for Sewall still had liv'd.

He was even praised many years after his death in the *Cyclopedia of American Literature* in 1856:

> ...Jonathan Mitchel Sewall is a name that should be better known and cherished, for it was borne by one whose lyrics warmed the patriotism and cheered the hearts of the soldiers of the Revolution in the peril of battle and the privations of the camp. His *War and Washington* was composed at the beginning of the American Revolution and sung by the army in all parts of the country.

Most of what is known about Jonathan Mitchel Sewall comes from obituaries and biographical notes written soon after his death. However, the first thing that I read about him was the

INTRODUCTION

article by Mrs. Marston Fenwick in the *Portsmouth Herald* on December 13, 1958. She and Dorothy Vaughn, librarian at the Portsmouth Public Library, were writing a series of articles on houses that should be saved from urban renewal and this house was one of them. So, here was a more interesting account, but not very contemporary to him, coming 150 years after his death. The article came with the house and immediately made me interested in finding out more about him.

Although he was christened Jonathan Mitchel and spells his name that way, many of the things that have been written about him spell his middle name as Mitchell. I have retained the misspellings in any quotations but have not used [sic] to identify them as there are so many throughout this book.

A word of explanation is needed about some of the language he uses. Jonathan often includes Latin words and phrases and allusions to classical history and literature in his poetry and orations. I found myself beginning to wonder who would be able to understand what he was talking about. He was a very popular speaker for any special occasion in Portsmouth from the 1770s until his death in 1808. His formal education was at Boston Public Latin School from the time he was seven at least until he was twelve, and he studied Latin and Greek and Roman history and literature there. The curriculum bears no resemblance to what is taught in the early years of school today.

Thomas E. Ricks in his recent book *First Principles* explains it well in his first chapter:

> ...Greco-Roman antiquity was not distant to the leaders of the American Revolution. It was present in their lives, as part of their political vocabulary and as the foundation of their personal values. In short, it shaped their view of the world in a way that most Americans now are not taught and so don't see.

George Washington did not receive a classical education, but his favorite play was *Cato* by Addison, about the last days of the Roman senator. He arranged for the play to be put on for his

INTRODUCTION

troops at Valley Forge in May 1778. Enslaved people were given Greek and Latin names. Signers of the New Hampshire Black Petition in 1779 include Nero Brewster, Romeo Rindge, Cato Newmarch, Cesar Gerrish, Seneca Hall, and Cato Warner.

Although some of Jonathan's poetry may be more difficult to understand now, it would not have been for the people of colonial Portsmouth. If there had been a poet laureate of Portsmouth at that time, it would have been Jonathan Mitchel Sewall. Now I am cherishing him and hoping to make him better-known as best I can.

> Nancy R. Hammond
> Portsmouth, New Hampshire
> 2022

CHAPTER 1.

The Patriot Poet

Huzza, huzza, huzza, huzza, for war and Washington!

Jonathan Mitchel Sewall's reverence for George Washington began early in his life. It was June 1775 when Washington took charge of the colonists' troops in Boston. Soon after Washington arrived, Jonathan wrote the words to a song that he called "War and Washington." The words were printed on broadsides and in newspapers. They were widely distributed and sung in all the colonial army camps, when soldiers were marching, and even in taverns and in homes. (Broadsides were large sheets of paper with words printed on one side only and were used much like a poster today.) The copy shown here with the woodcuts was printed in Danvers, Massachusetts. The printer, Ezekiel Russell, moved his office there from Salem in March 1777. An earlier broadside without the woodcuts was

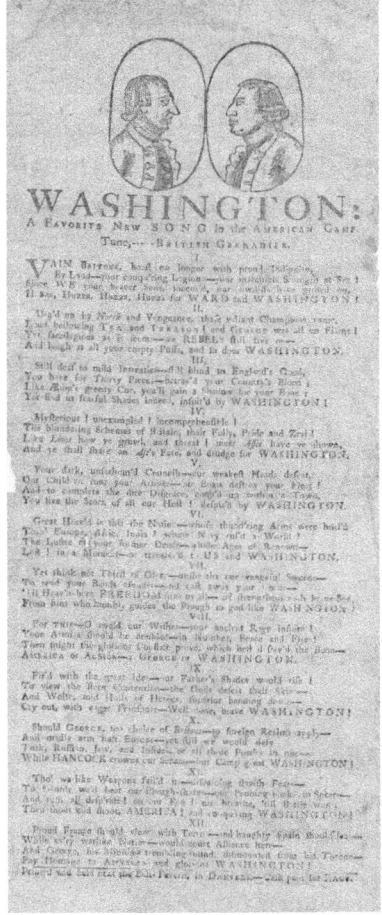

Washington: a favorite new song in the American camp, broadside (Sewall 1777). Collection of the Massachusetts Historical Society.

printed in Salem and is preserved by the Massachusetts Historical Society. Salem is where Jonathan was born, and he visited frequently all his life. The paper is a little over fifteen-inches high and about seven-inches wide. The printer would have printed two on each sheet of paper. At the top is written: "A favorite Song at the Columbian Camp, in the late glorious and victorious struggle for LIBERTY. by Mr. Sewall of Portsmouth, Newhampshire." At the bottom is printed "Written when the British Army were besieged in Boston."

"War and Washington" may have been even more popular during the Revolutionary War than the song we all learned as children, "Yankee Doodle." That was a British song that was sung to make fun of the American soldiers around 1755, during the French and Indian War. It was also sung at that time by the Americans as a song of defiance. It was a bit easier to remember, too!

Jonathan's song ran to twelve verses and it was about what was happening right then. The words to "War and Washington" were set to a very well-known British song, "The British Grenadiers," and so, the song which mocked the British was set to a British tune. It began:

> Vain Britons, boast no longer with proud indignity,
> By land your conquering legions, your matchless strength at sea,
> Since we, your braver sons incensed, our swords have girded on.
> Huzza, huzza, huzza, huzza, for war and Washington.

A story attributed to a British prisoner-of-war in Delaware gives some idea of how the song was received by the British. "Not being able to procure private lodging, we have agreed to live entirely at a tavern. Our most disagreeable attendant is the noise of the American soldiers who vociferate their songs so loud that the whole house rings with *War and Washington*, a favourite ballad" (Spicer 2001, p. 63). Even recently, the song was heard being sung in one of the army camps during an episode of *Turn*, the television series about Washington's spies that ran from 2014 to 2017 on AMC.

THE PATRIOT POET

"Behold he comes! Columbia's pride."

Fourteen years later, Jonathan Mitchel Sewall was standing in front of the State House in the parade in Portsmouth, New Hampshire, on Saturday afternoon October 31, 1789. It must have been one of the most exciting days of his life. George Washington, the new President of the United States, whom he had greatly admired for so many years, was about to appear on the balcony of the State House...and right in front of Jonathan's eyes for the very first time.

There was an official announcement at the end of September in 1789 that Washington would be coming to Portsmouth. The exact date was not known even when he left New York on October 13. During those two weeks and four days, Jonathan would have been extremely busy, writing and perfecting his three Odes to Washington. They were to be proclaimed and sung by the town choir and accompanied by the town band as Washington stood on the State House balcony in what is now Market Square.

He would need copies of the words to the Odes for the chorus and band. Did he spend part of the time making a few copies in his beautiful calligraphic hand? Or perhaps his son Stephen, then fourteen and learning the trade of printer, was able to print or at least help to print copies?

The words flowed easily for Jonathan because he was praising his hero, George Washington. George Sparhawk and William Dame were his good friends, and they would speak and sing the words with him. The chorus and the band were set up on a stage that had been erected in front of Mr. Pearse's shop, opposite

Portsmouth State House. Illustration by William Paarlberg. Permission granted by artist 2022.

the balcony of the State House. You can see the balcony in the drawing on the previous page showing what it is thought the building looked like.

According to the newspaper reports, people were lined up on either side of Congress Street for as far as anyone could see. The men were all arranged by trade. Perhaps his son Stephen was there with John Melcher, who then owned the printing office. Daniel Fowle and Primus, his enslaved man, printed the first newspaper in the state in 1756. Primus might have been standing with them that day. He was nearly ninety years old by then and had been willed to John Melcher when Daniel Fowle died in 1787.

John Barnard Sewall, Jonathan's second son, would have been with the boys from the Latin School, along with Samuel Hale, their headmaster. The children from each school were lined up together and looking very smart in their matching school uniforms. Their hats had colored ribbons that identified each school. Behind all of these "official" people were the masses of Portsmouth residents who had come out for this momentous event. Jonathan's wife Sarah and their four-year-old, Caroline, must have been somewhere in the crowds. In his diary, Washington noted that "The streets, doors and windows were crowded here, as at all other places."

Just before 3 o'clock in the afternoon, a cannon salute by the artillery companies was heard from the far end of the town. It signaled the entry of the procession from out at the Greenland Road. From the other direction, there was a gun salute from the Castle on Grand Island, today's New Castle, and then they arrived. What a wonderful sight this must have been. Washington dismounted his horse in front of the State House and was led up the stairs by the Hon. John Langdon; John Pickering, who was Jonathan's own friend, teacher, and mentor; and the other men who had greeted him at the state border. Washington soon appeared on the balcony overlooking the parade, the throngs of people, the school children, the town band and the poet, Jonathan Mitchel Sewall.

Jonathan and his friends began to sing. The full chorus sang:

> Behold he comes! Columbia's pride,
> And Nature's boast—her favorite Son,
> Of valor—wisdom—truth—well tried—
> Hail, Matchless WASHINGTON.

Then Jonathan spoke out the recitative:

> 'Tis gratitude that prompts the humble lay,
> Accept great Chief what Gratitude can pay.

Then he and Sparhawk and Dame sang:

> Let old and young—let rich and poor,
> Their voices raise,
> to sing his praise,
> And bid him welcome o'er and o'er.

Then the full chorus came in with:

> Welcome matchless WASHINGTON!
> Matchless as the deeds you've done.

Again, Jonathan spoke out:

> From North to South, from East to West
> His fame unrivaled stands confessed.

He and Sparhawk and Dame sang:

> This, this is he—by Heaven designed,
> The pride and wonder of mankind.
> United then your voices raise,
> And all united sing his praise.

And again, they joined the chorus singing:

> Welcome matchless WASHNGTON!
> Matchless as the deeds you've done.

The band joined in for the next two odes. The first was to the tune "He comes, He comes," the hymn written by Charles Wesley.

The three men sang:

> He comes! He comes! Your songs prepare,
> The matchless Chief approaches near,
> Each heart exults! Each tongue proclaims,
> He's welcome to Hantonia's plains.

And then the chorus came in:

> Welcome! welcome! welcome! welcome!
> Welcome to Hantonia's plains.

Sewall, Sparhawk, and Dame again:

> Those shouts ascending to the sky,
> Proclaim great WASHINGTON is nigh!
> Hail nature's boast—Columbia's Son
> Welcome! welcome Washington.

By now the surrounding crowds were singing the chorus:

> Welcome! welcome! welcome! welcome!
> Welcome to Hantonia's plains.

The three men sang out:

> Let strains harmonious rend the air
> For see the Godlike hero's here!
> Thrice hail—Columbia's favorite Son,
> Thrice welcome matchless WASHINGTON.

Now everyone sang out:

> Welcome! welcome! welcome! welcome!
> Welcome to Hantonia's plains.

But then there was a third ode, and this they all sang to the familiar tune of "God Save the King," a song that everyone knew, but of course weren't singing any more. It was good to have some new words to go with the old tune:

> LONG may thy Trumpet, Fame,
> Let echo waft the Name
> Of WASHINGTON;
> o'er all the world around,
> far as earth's utmost bound,
> Thy equal is not found,
> Columbia's Son.
>
> Ye blest of Human kind,
> Columbians, call to mind,
> The deed he's done
> Hark! hark! Those shouts declare,
> That "Heaven's peculiar care,"
> The matchless Hero's here,
> Great WASHINGTON.
>
> Hantonia's sons rejoice,
> Welcome with heart and voice,
> Your country's pride:
> On this auspicious day,
> Drive sorrow far away,
> And sing in rapturous lay,
> "Let joy preside."
>
> Rejoice—let all rejoice,
> And with united voice,
> The HERO hail;
> He stemmed oppression's tide,
> And humbled Britain's pride,
> Is still your matchless guide
> That will not fail.

(Hantonia was the Latin word for Hampshire and Columbia another Latin derivation used to describe the early colonies of the United States, meaning Columbus's country.)

The New Hampshire crowds must have cheered and cheered for the President at the end of the odes. Then the troops—horse, foot, and artillery under the command of Major-General Cilley—passed Washington in review. Every officer saluted as he passed. Finally, the President was led back into the senate chamber. Soon he appeared at the door and was conducted to his lodgings at Colonel Brewster's, which was just down the street from the State House. He was accompanied by the New Hampshire President, John Sullivan; the Council of the State, the Hon. Mr. John Langdon; and Colonel Parker, the Marshall of New Hampshire. (The early governors of New Hampshire were called presidents. In 1791, the title was changed to governor.)

Arrangements had been made for Washington to stay at Brewster's Tavern during his visit to Portsmouth because he did not want to single out any one family's home for his stays. This was true throughout his progression through the states. The tavern had been the home of John Langdon until he moved into his mansion farther up Pleasant Street in 1785. Brewster's was at the corner of today's Pleasant and Court streets where the brick Treadwell-Jenness House now stands. The old tavern burned to the ground in the Great Portsmouth Fire of 1813.

Jonathan, Sparhawk, and Dame would have made their way through the throng of people for a drink. They always enjoyed a drink together. Maybe they went to Brewster's Tavern in hopes of seeing the President there. But there were lots of other taverns in Portsmouth where they could go.

That evening, the State House was beautifully illuminated. According to the newspaper reports:

> ...thirteen rockets were let off the balcony—mutual gratulations took place, and the day concluded without any unlucky occurrence to mar the pleasure excited by so auspicious an event. Thus far for the day—we flatter ourselves it will be remembered so long as patriotism continues to be a virtue, and the name of WASHINGTON to sound grateful to American ears.

On Sunday morning, President Washington was accompanied by New Hampshire President Sullivan; Mr. Langdon; and his two personal secretaries, Tobias Lear and William Jackson. They made their way to the Queen's Chapel on Bow Street for the morning service. Tobias Lear was from Portsmouth and had been tutor to Martha Washington's children since 1784. He became Washington's most trusted secretary. William Jackson had just recently become one of Washington's secretaries, and he too was making the tour with the President.

When they arrived at the church, Colonel John Parker, recently appointed as United States marshal for New Hampshire, and two church wardens escorted Washington to his seat. The seat was a beautiful mahogany chair, which may or may not be one of the two chairs that are now placed near the altar in St. John's Church. (Queen's Chapel was renamed as St. John's Church in 1791.) The Reverend John C. Ogden, the rector, preached and sacred music was played during the service.

In the afternoon, not wanting to show any partiality, the President and his entourage went to another service at the Congregational Church in Market Square, now known as the North Church. The Reverend Joseph Buckminster preached that afternoon. He was known as an "earnest preacher, distinguished for fervent eloquence...adhering to conservative and orthodox principles."

From the newspapers we read:

> The Rev. Messrs. Ogden and Buckminster, in their well-adapted discourses, paid a just and beautiful eulogium, on the numerous virtues of this dignified personage, whose appearance diffused such general joy, and awakened in every breast the most grateful sensations.—Felicitating their numerous hearers on the happy occasion which called them together, to offer up their unfeigned thanks to the Supreme Ruler of the world, for all his mercies, and to implore a continuance of his divine and gracious benediction

> on the head of their beloved chief. On this uncommon
> occasion, both houses of worship were crowded with
> spectators, among whom were a brilliant concourse
> of the fair daughters of Hantonia, whose lovely
> countenances testified the heart-felt joy, the presence
> of their illustrious countryman inspired.

Jonathan used the Latin word for Hampshire, "Hantonia," in his second and third odes to the President, and the language used here is rather grand, like much of what we find in Jonathan's writings. Was he "A Gentleman in this Town" to whom the stories of this momentous event that were published in *The Spy* and *The Gazette* were attributed? Elwin L. Page in his book *George Washington in New Hampshire* thought it most likely was Sewall, and so do I based on everything of his that I have read.

On Monday morning, Washington made an excursion on the Piscataqua River in a barge rowed by seamen dressed in white and accompanied by his usual entourage. He had a short landing in Kittery and from the newspapers we find that "A number of young gentlemen who compose the band in this town, anxious to afford our illustrious and beloved President, all the entertainment in their power, followed him in a barge, and performed several pieces of music on the water, we hope to his acceptance." We can assume that Jonathan was part of this adventure, and because the article says, "we hope to his acceptance," it was most likely someone in the barge that wrote the account. The President's barge landed at Little Harbor where Benning Wentworth's mansion was then occupied by his widow, Martha Hilton Wentworth and her second husband, another Wentworth. (Colonel Michael Wentworth came to Portsmouth from England to visit his friend John Wentworth, the last royal governor, in 1767. He stayed, and after Benning Wentworth died, he married his young widow.) After refreshments with the Wentworths, Washington's party proceeded back to town by land.

That afternoon, an address from the people of Portsmouth was given to the President, probably at Brewster's Tavern. A committee including John Pickering, John Parker, Dr. Ammi

Cutter, Jonathan Warner, and Colonel Joshua Wentworth had been appointed to prepare the address just a week before. The address was signed "John Pickering for the Inhabitants, Portsmouth Nov. 2 1789." Here is a paragraph from the address:

> It is with pleasing emotions, we recognize the dispensations of divine providence towards the United States, in placing the Deliverer of his country at the head of the General Government by the unanimous suffrages of a free and grateful people, at a crisis when none but the man who has long enjoyed, and richly merited, the confidence of America, and the plaudits of an enlightened world, could be found equal to the arduous task.

Did John Pickering write this? He was not known for his way with words. Two of his contemporaries, Jeremy Belknap and William Plumer, both commented on the deficiencies in his literary skills, pointing out that he "writes nothing but in the way of his profession" and "has read more than he has digested; his mind is a vast storehouse, in which the goods are placed in a promiscuous condition. He wants clearness of perception, accuracy of distinction, decision and firmness." Whereas Jonathan, his good friend and colleague, with his literary and poetic skills, was a real wordsmith. Did he help with this address to George Washington "from the Inhabitants" (Belknap 1637–1891)?

That evening, Washington dined with John Langdon in his beautiful new home on Pleasant Street. They knew each other well. John Langdon was one of New Hampshire's delegates to the Constitutional Convention in Philadelphia during the very hot summer two years earlier. Washington was elected the president of the convention, and it was here where they hammered out the final document that became the Constitution of the United States of America. In April of that year, Langdon had attended Washington's inauguration in New York City. He was a senator from New Hampshire and became the first president of the United States Senate soon after the inauguration.

The President notes in his diary that "a large circle of Ladies" were present, so there must have been quite a few guests at the dinner. According to the newspapers, the guests included the President's secretaries and a number of gentlemen of distinction. Unfortunately, there is no record of who they were. Were Jonathan and Sarah there? It is quite likely that they were. John Langdon certainly knew them. During his second term as president of New Hampshire, he appointed Jonathan as attorney general for the state. But Jonathan did not take up the post.

On Tuesday morning, the President was persuaded to sit for two hours for the painter Christian Gullager from Boston to paint his picture. When this was over, he went to call on New Hampshire's president, John Sullivan, at Stavers Tavern. Afterwards, he went on to take tea with Mrs. Mary Lear, the mother of his secretary, Tobias.

Grand Finale

That afternoon, there was a dinner for the President in the Assembly Room that included an address from New Hampshire President John Sullivan, with an answer from President Washington. The Assembly Room was on today's Vaughan Street. It was an impressive building, as Washington wrote that it "is one of the best I have seen anywhere in the United States." Unfortunately, this wonderful building only exists in parts today.

That evening, the gentlemen of Portsmouth were hosts at "an elegant ball," according to the local paper. Washington writes, "At half after seven I went to the assembly, where there were about 75 well dressed and many of them very handsome ladies ..." According to the newspaper account, after the President arrived, "an excellent song was sung accompanied by the band." Afterwards there was dancing, but George Washington notes that he returned to Brewster's Tavern about nine. It is very likely that Jonathan and Sarah and all the other "gentlemen of Portsmouth" and their ladies enjoyed themselves until much later.

The next morning at seven thirty, George Washington left Portsmouth as quietly as possible with his two secretaries and the six other staff who were traveling with him. He had "earnestly entreated that all parade and ceremony might be avoided..." It is hard to believe that many of the people, including the Sewalls, were not on the streets to see him respectfully on his way. What a very memorable time it must have been for all of them.

(Newspaper accounts are from *NH Spy*, Nov. 3, 1789; *NH Gazette*, Nov. 5, 1789.)

"Our firm support and strenuous defence."

Seven years later, in 1796, when Washington was at the end of his second term in office, he chose not to seek reelection. He sent a public letter to the American people to explain this, and it became known as his "Farewell Address." Early in Jonathan's life he decided that rhyming verses were easier to remember than prose, and he never stopped writing in verse. So, he rewrote the entire address in rhyme. His words were published by Charles Peirce in 1798 and made available for sale in his bookstore on Daniel Street. The Portsmouth Athenaeum holds a copy which is shown here.

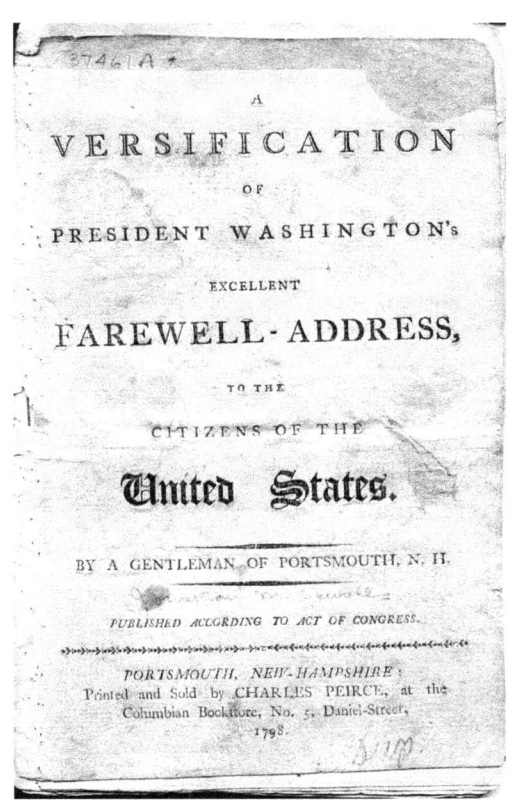

Versification of Washington's Farewell Address (Sewall 1798). Courtesy of the Portsmouth Athenaeum.

In Charles W. Brewster's *Rambles about Portsmouth* #125 he wrote:

> This Versification we have before us. It was written by Mr. Sewall and published, with the author's characteristic modesty, without his name. The poem, if such it may be called, occupies forty-four octavo pages, and is almost a literal presentation of the original in rhyme—the author endeavoring to shun any of the tinsel decorations of poetic ornament, "not indulging to his own fancy on such momentous subjects, handled before with such masterly perfection."

Washington wrote:

> This Government, the offspring of your own choice, uninfluenced and unawed, adopted upon full investigation and mature deliberation, completely free in its principles, in the distribution of its powers, uniting security with energy, and containing within itself a provision for its own amendment, has a just claim to your confidence and your support.

Jonathan wrote it this way:

> This government, our own free choice, unawed
> By force, or fear; uninfluenced by fraud;
> Constructed upon principles most pure,
> On Freedom's broad foundation grounded sure;
> By different parties, through all mediums viewed,
> Discussed, debated, fully understood;
> With jealous circumspection, keenly eyed,
> By calm investigation fairly tried;
> And by a wise enlightened whole at last,
> On full conviction, cordially embraced;
> Most justly claims our highest confidence
> Our firm support and strenuous defence [sic].

Yes! Washington, the great and good—is no more.

George Washington died peacefully between 10 and 11 p.m. on Saturday, December 14, 1799, according to Tobias Lear. The news would have spread quickly through the states, but at a much, much slower pace than it could today. On Friday, December 27, the *Federal Observer*, published in Portsmouth, reported the death. After a short poem we read, "The truth of the melancholy event appears beyond controversy. The information is announced in a New York Paper which is encircled with a mourning border. It is contained in two letters from Alexandria ..." Following this is a notice to the inhabitants announcing a procession from the Assembly Room on Monday proceeding to St. John's Church where "an Eulogy will be delivered by Jonathan Mitchel Sewall esquire." The plan was that those who wished to join the procession should be there at half past ten o'clock. A rain date was given, and because it rained on Monday the event happened on Tuesday.

The local newspaper, *Oracle of the Day*, was published on Saturdays, so the following day its entire third page had a black border around it. It included a poem followed by a long article about George Washington's life. Much of this, and sometimes word for word, is included in Jonathan's eulogy, so the article including the poem was probably all his work.

The newspaper account of the celebration was published on January 4, 1800, in what had become, as of that issue, *The United States*

Oracle of the Day, December 27, 1799. GenealogyBank 2020.

Oracle of the Day. All four pages of the issue were encircled with a black border and almost everything in it was about George Washington.

The account of the celebrations in Portsmouth was on page three. "At an early hour on Tuesday morning, all public offices, stores, and shops, were shut; active life stood still. Business and pleasure paused." The flags of all the ships in the harbor were at half-mast. Mourning crapes were worn by almost every individual. At 11 a.m., a procession formed at the Assembly Room and proceeded to St. John's Church. First were Captain E. J. Long's Artillery Men, then Captain T. Sparhawk's Light Infantry, followed by Captain S. Larkin's Governor Gilman's Blues with their drums muffled and music in crape. They were followed by the Masons of the Grand Lodge of St. John. Then came "The Orator. Jonathan M. Sewall, Esquire, *The pride of Eloquence and power of Verse*," followed by the Rev. Mr. Willard, rector of St. John's, then more military and civic officers, the other clergy from Portsmouth and the vicinity and everyone else who had come to walk with them. As they turned into Congress Street the procession passed through two lines of children belonging to the three public schools. The streets from there to the church were lined six deep with mourners.

The church was "elegantly habited in full mourning. A large branch of an evergreen fir tree, severed from its roots, and hanging perpendicularly as a chandelier, ornamented with a vast assemblage of black plumes. The severed root, and the living branch addressed the heart." Sacred music was performed on the organ by Mr. Stanwood as the procession entered the church. A dirge that had been composed for the occasion was sung by a group of performers from all the different religious societies. It was led by Captain Gookins, the senior church chorister. After Reverend Willard read the prayers and a hymn was sung, Jonathan came forward to proclaim his eulogy. He had composed it "at the request of the inhabitants."

As you can see here in the copy at the Portsmouth Athenaeum, he began:

> Would to God (if I so speak without seeming to blame the Sovereign Will and Wisdom) Would to God! I had not so melancholy an occasion as the present, to address my mourning fellow citizens on their late irreparable loss! But THAT BEING "who doth his Will in the armies of Heaven above, and among the inhabitants of earth beneath," in his holy (though inscrutable) Providence by this last most afflicting dispensation, hath pointed out the melancholy duty.

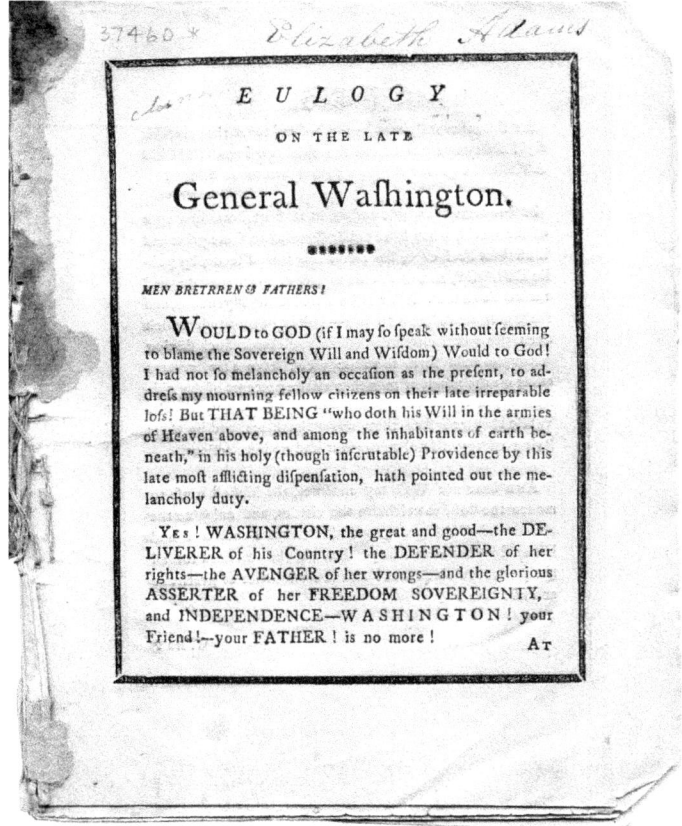

Eulogy of the Late General Washington by Jonathan Mitchel Sewall. Courtesy of the Portsmouth Athenaeum.

He then went on to praise Washington, give a long description of his life, and compare him to Moses. The eulogy must have lasted at least a half an hour. Then Jonathan comes to the point where he says: "But the theme overpowers me—I sink beneath it—A thousand, thousand tender, grateful, ideas rush upon my Soul! My nerves refuse their support!" He then ends with this poem:

> Oh Washington! thy Country's boast and pride,
> In every scene of woe, and peril tried;
> Thou se'est (though throned above yon starry spheres)
> An Empire bleeding! and a world in tears!
> Kindly look down! Oh, mitigate our woes!
> And soothe thy weeping Country to repose!
> Oh, look from Sion's consecrated hill,
> And be Columbia's Guardian-Angel still!
> For sure, if aught below the thrones above
> Can touch thy Spirit, 'tis thy Country's love!
> Revive those counsels thou didst here impart,
> And grave the heavenly precepts on each heart.
> Instruct us where our truest interest lies,
> And lift Columbia's glory to the skies!
> Till heavenly hosts, with earth's vast tribes, agree
> Thy precepts made us Happy, Great and Free!

The long article published in the *United States Oracle of the Day* about the celebration says this about the eulogy:

> The interesting impressive form of the Orator; his
> fine powers of melancholic modulation; the heaving
> bosom and the bursting sigh, would have commanded
> the best applauses, if neither sentiment, genius
> nor taste had been discernable in the Eulogy; but
> it happily combined the depth of thought, elegance
> of expression and the beauties of gentle, pathetic
> [arousing pity, sorrow, or grief] oratory. A Washington

might have heard it without a blush and an Adams will praise it. (*US Oracle of the Day*, January 4, 1800)

This almost sounds like something Jonathan might have written himself. But we know that he quite often did not even sign his name to his writings, much less praise himself, so it seems very unlikely. Maybe his son Stephen, then age twenty-four and working as a printer, wrote these words. After his father's death Stephen printed an "Elegy on the death of J. M. Sewall, Esq." in *The Literary Mirror*, a weekly newspaper that he was publishing in Portsmouth in 1808. It consisted of thirty-four lines of rhyming couplets. For some years after his father's death Stephen continued his father's role of writing poetic verses and proclaiming them at celebrations in Portsmouth.

CHAPTER 2.

The Early Years

Stephen Sewall House, Salem, Massachusetts (Perley 2022).

Salem

When Samuel Sewall wrote in the famous *Diary* that he kept from 1674 to 1729 that he stayed with his brother Stephen and wife Margaret when he came to Salem, Massachusetts, this was the house where he stayed (Perley 2022). It was right in the middle of Salem on Essex Street at the corner of what is now known as Sewall Street and where the YMCA building stands today.

Stephen Sewall built the house soon after he bought the land in October 1681. In addition to the house, there were a barn, a coach house and outbuildings on the property. Stephen died in 1725 and left the house to his wife, Margaret, and their eight living children. Margaret died ten years later. Their eldest son, Samuel, bought the house from his other siblings, and he deeded it to Mitchel, his younger brother.

Mitchel Sewall married Mary Cabot in 1729. Their first child, Catherine, was born in 1731, and Margaret, known as Peggy, was born in 1735. Mitchel and Mary and their two girls moved into his father's house, the house where he was born, in 1735, after his mother's death. Their daughter, Mary, was born, and the girl's mother, Mary, died, probably in childbirth, in 1736 or 1737.

In January 1742 when Mitchel was forty-two years old, he married Elizabeth Price who was just twenty-seven. At that time his daughters were six, seven, and eleven years old. The following year Mitchel and Elizabeth had a daughter whom they named Elizabeth. In March 1746, their son Stephen was born.

By then the family was well established in the house on Essex Street. Mitchel was a lawyer. He had graduated from Harvard College in 1718 and went on to complete a master's degree, which he received in 1721. He served as the librarian at Harvard for two years before returning to Salem and setting up his law practice. In 1733, he was appointed justice of the peace and held the posts of clerk of the Essex County Courts and registrar of deeds for the county from 1727 until his death. In addition to his local offices and law practice, he also taught law to young men who came and lived with the family.

At the end of March in 1748, their son Jonathan Mitchel was born in the house. The following Sunday, March 27, he was christened at the nearby First Church of Salem. The Rev. John Sparhawk was pastor of the First Church from 1736 to 1755. It was the original Puritan church founded in America.

The fate of this family was to take a dramatic turn when Mitchel Sewall died on Thursday, October 13, the same year.

Elizabeth, at the age of thirty-four, now had her own three children; Elizabeth, age five; Stephen, just two and a half; and Jonathan Mitchel, who was less than six months old. Mitchel's three older daughters; Catherine, now seventeen; Peggy, thirteen; and Mary, age twelve, were also living there. In addition to whatever help these teenage girls might have been, Elizabeth had many relatives who would have come to her rescue.

The extended family

Jonathan Mitchel was born into a large extended family who kept in close touch with one another over many years and generations. Many of his relatives lived in Salem and nearby Newbury, Boston, and Cambridge. His great-grandfather, Henry, and his wife, Jane, had ten children. Henry was the first in the family to come to America. By the time of Mitchel's death, his only living siblings were his brother Samuel and his wife Katherine; and his younger brother, Stephen. They all lived in Boston. Jonathan's uncle Samuel owned wharves in Boston and property on Beacon Hill. Many of the other aunts and uncles and great-aunts and uncles' children lived in Salem and Boston and even in York, Maine.

Jonathan's paternal grandmother's family was from Cambridge. His grandmother, Margaret, was the daughter of the famous Rev. Jonathan Mitchell (or Mitchel), the namesake for both Mitchel Sewall and Jonathan Mitchel Sewall himself. The Rev. Jonathan Mitchell came to New England as a child and graduated from Harvard in 1647 (founded in 1636). Although he died quite young, he left many learned writings, sermons, and translations from the Greek Bible. He was highly respected and praised by his contemporaries.

Jonathan's mother's family were all from Salem. Her father, Walter Price, had been a prosperous merchant. Jonathan's mother's sister, Sarah, was married to Dr. Joseph Bartlett, a physician in Salem. Their son, Walter Price Bartlett, was just five years old in 1748. Elizabeth's mother, Freestone Turner, was one of the daughters of John Turner who built the House of Seven Gables in 1668. Her uncle, Captain John Turner, was a wealthy merchant who owned wharves, warehouses, schooners, houses, and land, and was also an influential councilor in Salem. Captain John and his wife, Elizabeth, had three sons and four daughters who were alive in 1748. Most of them lived in

Salem and had sons and daughters of their own. Many of their families lived there, too. Captain John died only six years earlier in 1742, and his estate went to his son John III.

In 1748, when Jonathan Mitchel was born, John Turner III lived in the house with his wife, Mary; their daughter, also Mary, who was five; and their son, John IV, age four. Another son, Edward, was born in 1751. Over the next thirty years, John III managed to squander the family fortunes, and by 1782 he had to sell the House of Seven Gables to help pay his debts. He died four years later. (The House of Seven Gables is one of the oldest surviving timber-framed mansion houses in continental North America, with seventeen rooms and over eight thousand square feet including its large cellars. In 1851, Nathaniel Hawthorne made it famous with his novel of the same name.)

The Probate and Inventory

Because Mitchel died without a will, Jonathan's mother was required by law to have an inventory of everything in their house taken for her husband's probate record. Mitchel Sewall died on October 13 and the inventory was filed on November 10, 1748. Epes Sargent, John Nutting, and Samuel Barton were the three men who came to carry out the inventory.

The five-page list of their furniture and belongings is extensive and contains a page and a half of the books that Mitchel owned.

ALL Perfons who are indebted to, or have any Demands on the Eftate of *Mitchel Sewall*, Efq; late of *Salem*, deceased, are defired to bring in their Accounts to *Elizabeth Sewall*, Widow, Administratrix on the faid Eftate.

Notice of the Estate of Mitchel Sewall.
Boston Evening Post, November 21, 1748.
GenealogyBank 2020.

The note at the end of the inventory states "shown to us by Elizabeth Sewall." The house is large, with four bedrooms and a guest chamber. There is an office, presumably where Mitchel taught his law students, a living room, and a kitchen all "lavishly furnished." Among the many other things that are enumerated are a horse and a cow in the barn. Mitchel also had two common rights of land in the Great Pasture. The whole was assessed at nearly £6000 but with £2440 worth of debt (NEHGS 2005, pp. 2289–91). How much was this worth today? Historians do not agree on a formula to work out a current value. Professor John J. McCusker wrote: "£750 in Massachusetts during 1750 is worth roughly $48,000 in [the year] 2000" (McCusker 2001). If this is correct, then all these figures would be multiplied by sixty-four and their pewter would be worth over $2000. However, others believe that a pound was worth about $5 at that time. There is no way that we will ever know the true value.

After the inventory was filed, Elizabeth had to appear and make an oath that it was correct in front of Thomas Berry, the judge of probate for Essex County. On June 6, 1749, at the Ipswich court "Eliza Sewall made oath to the foregoing inventory and if any thing further appeared it should be added before Thos. Berry" (*Essex County Probate Records*, file 25084).

Guardianship

On June 5, 1750, the daughters of Mitchel's marriage to Mary Cabot signed this letter written to the Honorable Thomas Berry, Esq., judge of probate for the County of Essex:

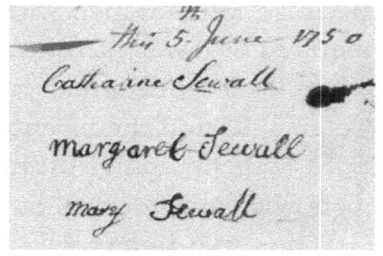

Signatures of daughters of Mitchel Sewall. *Essex County Probate Records*, file 25084.

> Catherine Sewall, Margaret Sewall and Mary Sewall, minor children of Mitchel Sewall Esq. late deceased, Humbly shew That they have no Guardian, nor have had any since their Father deceased, and pray that Messrs. Stephen Higginson and Francis Cabot may be appointed Guardians.
>
> Witness their Hands this 5th of June 1750.

In 1750 guardianship papers were drawn up for Mitchel's children. Stephen Higginson is the first person that the three daughters asked to have as a guardian. He was the son of their aunt Margaret and uncle John. Margaret was their father's oldest sister. She married John Higginson in 1714. He was a lawyer and a merchant and held the office of registrar of probate from 1698 to 1702. By 1750 their son, Stephen Higginson, was one of the most influential merchants in Salem. He held the principal offices in the town, was justice of the Court of Common Pleas and a representative. His wife, Elizabeth Cabot Higginson, was the sister of Francis Cabot.

Francis Cabot was the second person that the girls asked to be their guardian. He was the brother of Mitchel's first wife, Mary, and their sister Elizabeth Cabot Higginson. Francis was one of the wealthiest and most distinguished Salem merchants of his generation. His commercial operations extended to the West Indies, Great Britain, Bilbao, Cadiz, Lisbon, Gibraltar, and the various American colonies. His business was in association with his brother, Joseph, until Joseph died in 1767. Francis had little to do with public affairs and held no offices of importance, but in 1761 he was made coroner of Essex County, and in 1768 he was appointed a justice of the peace.

When Francis and Joseph's father, John, died in 1741, he left £1000 to be divided amongst his three granddaughters: Catherine, Margaret, and Mary Sewall. When Francis's brother, Joseph, died in 1767, he left his house to his wife. When she died in 1781, she left the house to Francis who lived next door (*Essex County Probate*

Francis Cabot House, Salem, Massachusetts (Perley 2022).

Records, Case 4435). Both houses were opposite the Sewall home on Essex Street.

The guardianship papers for Elizabeth's children state, "Elizabeth Sewall Nominated and Allowed to be Guardian unto Elizabeth, Stephen and Jonathan Mitchel." There is a separate document for each child. The obligation stipulates that the proceeds of Mitchel's estate will be divided amongst Elizabeth and Mitchel's children when they come of age.

Mitchel Sewall died without a will and his estate was finally settled on April 15, 1751. It is signed by Elizabeth Sewall; Stephen Sewall, her brother-in-law; and John Higginson. On April 16, 1751, the family's home was conveyed to William Lynde (Perley 2022). It included the house, a barn, a coach house, and the land. The house was torn down in 1830. What is now seen as one of the finest Classical Revival buildings in Salem was built on the site in 1898 for the Young Men's Christian Association. It remains today on the corner of Essex and Sewall streets.

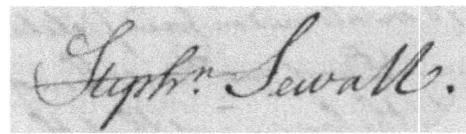

Stephen Sewall signature. *Essex County Probate Records*, file 25084.

All biographical accounts of Jonathan Mitchel Sewall state that he and his brother, Stephen, were adopted by their uncle Stephen who lived in Boston. No document establishing this has been found. However, their uncle Stephen was named and signed the obligation paper with their mother in April 1751. In January that year Stephen Sewall had been appointed as chief justice of the Massachusetts Superior Court of Judicature, the highest court in the colony. When he graduated from Harvard College in 1721, he became a schoolmaster in Marblehead, Massachusetts where he taught for seven years. In 1728 he became a Tutor at Harvard College, where he remained until he was appointed to the Massachusetts Superior Court in 1739.

Education

The first school board in Salem was established in 1712. The five-member board included Stephen Sewall, Jonathan's paternal grandfather; John Higginson, his uncle; and Walter Price, his maternal grandfather. Obviously, education was extremely important in this family.

There "was no parallel to them [early schools] in English speaking America, let alone in Europe" (Monaghan 1988). Boys began school after they had been "breeched." This was often a family ceremony at home when boys were about four and were given their first male clothing. Until that time, they wore dresses. Boys began to wear breeches with stockings and buckle shoes along with a muslin shirt and vest or waistcoat. To this they added a jacket and hat to wear outdoors.

Even before boys began school, they would begin to learn their letters at home. Jonathan had four older sisters and even though they may not have attended school, by 1750 Catherine, Margaret, and Mary were all able to write their names. This was seen on the letter about their guardianship. As their father was a Harvard graduate, he would have taught them their letters himself or employed someone to teach them. Reading and writing were equally as important. Parents sometimes taught children as young as three to read some Latin words almost as soon as they could read English ones. The story was related of a boy of five who each morning read Latin to his father while he shaved. The

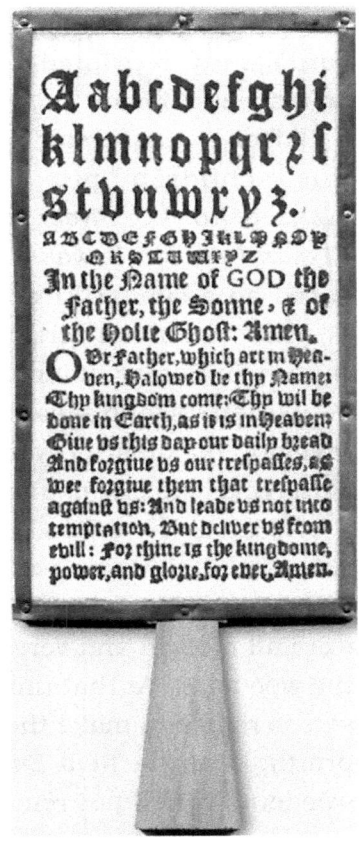

Hornbook (Tuer 1897).

boy and his father each had a copy of the same book so that the father could correct the child's errors (Earle 1889).

Because very young children would find it difficult to cope with a quill pen, their first years consisted mainly of learning to read. They would begin using a hornbook, a wooden paddle with the alphabet and the Lord's Prayer printed on a sheet of horn.

After mastering this, children progressed to the *New England Primer*. It was

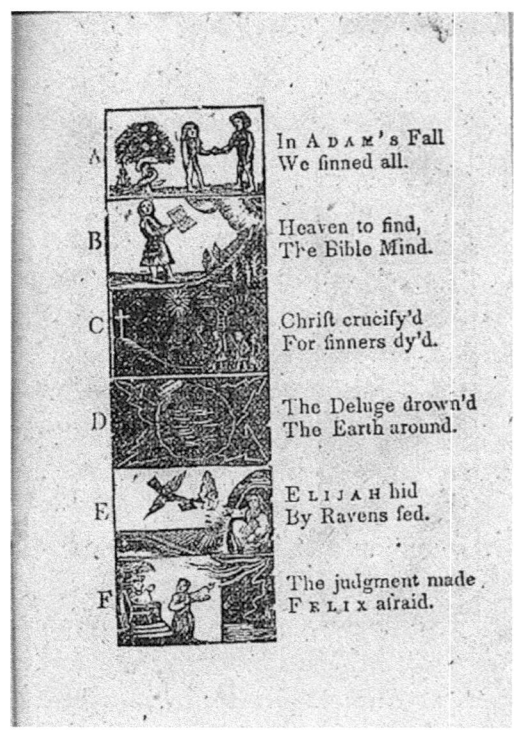

New England Primer, 1777. Author's copy.

based on a similar English book entitled *The Protestant Tutor*. The first American version was printed in the late-seventeenth century in Boston. It included the alphabet, vowels, consonants, double letters, and syllables of two-to-six letters. There were also religious maxims, prayers, woodcuts, alphabetical assistants, acronyms, catechism answers, and moral lessons.

Because there was a terrible shortage of paper in colonial America, all this was printed in a book that measured 4½ by 3¼ inches. This example shows how tiny the print was. The verses were all biblical and very somber. Perhaps most interesting are the woodcuts. At that time few books had any illustrations. The verses rhyme to make them easier to remember. Over the many printings of the *New England Primer* some of the verses and woodcuts varied but remained rather joyless.

Jonathan's brother Stephen, who was now six years old, would surely have begun school in Salem. The Salem Latin School had been established for over a century by this time. Their cousin, another Jonathan Sewall, was the schoolmaster from 1749 to 1757. School was attended all year. The school bell rang at 7 a.m. and 5 p.m. from March 1 until November 1. From November to the end of February it rang at 8 a.m. and 4 p.m. There were few holidays.

CHAPTER 3.

Boston Public Latin School

In 1755, at the age of seven, Jonathan and his brother, Stephen, entered the Boston Public Latin School. The boys attended what was known as a grammar school because they were there to prepare for college. Some of the things required for admission to Harvard College in the 1760s were: read a classical author in English, be able to speak and write true Latin in verse as well as in prose, and show that you knew how to decline nouns and verbs in Greek.

Where did they live?

We do not know when the boys left Salem and came to Boston to live with their uncle Stephen Sewall. They may have arrived in 1751 after their house in Salem was sold or stayed on and attended the Salem Latin School where their cousin was schoolmaster. By the time that they entered the Boston school in 1755, their uncle was well established as the chief justice of the Supreme Court of the Massachusetts Bay Colony. He had never married and lived "in the westerly part of Town." He never owned any property himself but the "house had a large Garden, Yard, Well, Barn, etc." (*Boston News Letter*, Sept. 4, 1760).

At this time Boston was a peninsula with the State House in the middle and the wharves in the east. What is now known as Back Bay, just west of the Public Garden, was literally a bay until the middle of the nineteenth century. Even what was known as the Sewall Mansion would have been in the western part of town. Today, its location seems right in the middle of the downtown. This had been the home of Samuel Sewall, the diarist, and his wife, Hannah Hull, and had been willed to their children. It was Hannah's family home and was on what is now the southern corner of Summer and Washington Streets where Macy's stands today. The property was extensive. It had accommodations for two families and many house guests.

Their uncle Stephen's probate record enumerates his belongings but there is no mention of real estate. The notice about it in the *Boston News Letter* states "in the occupation of the Honorable Stephen Sewall, Esq.," indicating that he did not own it. The furniture is from a living room, bedroom or bedrooms, kitchen, garret, and cellar. Listed separately are one "Green China Bed" worth £2 and "two bedsteds and two feather beds" worth nearly £12. The silver is valued at more than £27. The books are not listed separately as they were in Mitchel Sewall's inventory. They account for less than £20 of his whole estate, but they number over two hundred in the various sizes, plus an additional 397 pamphlets. His pew in Dr. Mayhew's West Meeting House was worth £10.

Going to School

Jonathan and Stephen could easily make their way to the school even if they lived farther west, as there was little that was settled

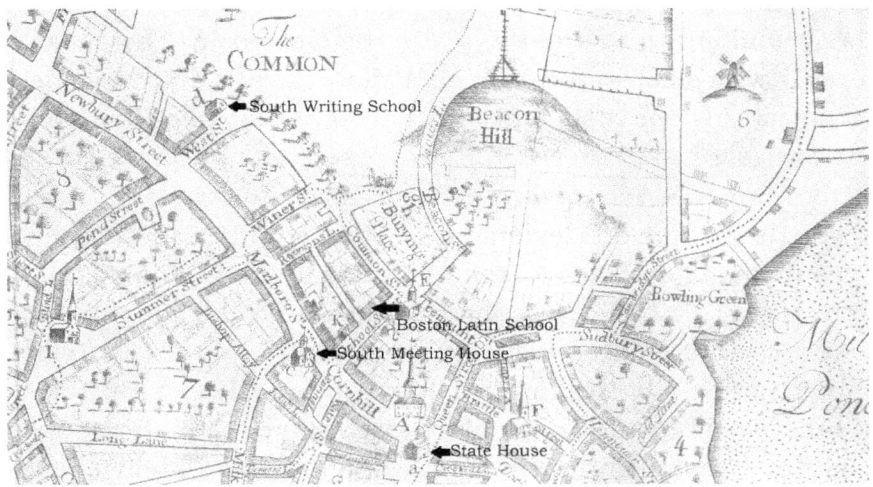

Based on a section of the 1728 Map of Boston by William Burnet. Reproduction courtesy of the Norman B. Leventhal Map & Education Center at the Boston Public Library.

west of the Common. Even then the name of the street where it was situated was School Street. If the boys were coming from the Sewall mansion they would just walk down Marlborough Street (renamed Washington street in 1788) past the South Meeting House and turn left into School Street.

When Boston Public Latin School opened in 1635 the building was behind the King's Chapel. It was rebuilt across the street from its original location in 1748 and the space behind the King's Chapel became part of its burying ground. Today the Parker House Hotel towers above the spot where the boys went to school.

First School House on South Side of School Street, 1748–1810 (Fitch 1866).

The school was housed in a one-story brick building with an attic above the classroom. There was a cupola with a bell at the front as is shown in this drawing. There was just this one room for boys of all ages from about six and a half or seven to fourteen or fifteen. A separate bench known as a form was allotted to each of the classes. The older boys were given desks. The only examination to be admitted to the school was reading a few verses from the Bible to the headmaster at a meeting in his home. It is inconceivable that the adopted sons of the celebrated chief justice of the Massachusetts Bay Colony would not have been admitted, but they would have been able to do this easily as well. In colonial New England the Bible was read daily at morning and evening prayers in almost all households.

Although it was called a "public" school that meant it was a democratic, public institution and it was not restricted to any special class of children. However, it was not free. There were entrance fees and fees for keeping the school warm known as "firing," as well as general town taxation that supported all the schools. Wealthy citizens and others from towns beyond Boston who sent their children there gave contributions and income from property, wharves, ferries, and house rents. (The term "public" school is still used today in England to refer to the exclusive, private, fee-paying schools like Eton College and others.)

John Lovell was the master of the Boston Public Latin School from 1742 until April 19, 1775 when war was declared. He was remembered as a stern, rough man, and a Loyalist. After declaring on that day "War's begun—school's done." he moved to Halifax, Nova Scotia, and died there only three years later. He had graduated from Harvard College in 1728 and had an excellent reputation for teaching. John Lovell was also well-known as a rigid disciplinarian, and he was totally feared by the boys. He sat at a desk directly opposite the entrance to the schoolroom, presumably so he had the best location to view everything that was going on, including the comings and goings of the boys. James Lovell, the school master's son, was sub-master during the time that Jonathan and Stephen were pupils. He sat at the opposite side of the room and was an equally strong Patriot.

John Lovell, Master of the Boston Public Latin School 1742–1775 (Butterworth 1886).

School began at 7 a.m. in the summer and at 8 in the winter. It closed at 11 a.m. and began again at 1 in the afternoon. School was over at 5 p.m. These hours applied nearly all year around. Every day, all the forms were dismissed at various times and went to Abiah Holbrook's South Writing School on West Street.

From the school the boys would just turn the corner onto Tremont Street and walk along the street opposite the Common that had been established in 1634. After a few streets they crossed West Street, and the Writing School was there opposite the Common. They learned to write and to cipher at this school, what we would call handwriting and arithmetic.

We know the date when Jonathan and Stephen entered the school because of a list that John Lovell kept, which his son wrote out. A copy of the original manuscripts made by Dr. Jonathan Homer is preserved at the Boston Public Library in their Rare Books and Manuscripts' Division. Henry F. Jenks used this to compile his list in *The Catalogue of the Boston Public Latin School established in 1635 with an Historical Sketch* in 1886. It lists when Jonathan and Stephen entered the school but does not include when they left, despite this information being given for many of the other students.

Students admitted to Boston Public Latin School in 1755 (Fitch 1866).

What did they study?

The curriculum was planned as a seven-year course of study. What they studied is almost unbelievable when we consider what a seven-year-old child might be learning today. The first three years were spent "Learning by heart & then acc[ording] to their capacities understanding the Accidence and Nomenclator in construing & parsing acc[ording] to the English rules of Syntax...and *Aesop's Fables*."

The books the boys used in their first year were *Cheever's Accidence*, a small nomenclature, and *Corderius' Colloquies*. The content of these books is interesting to look at and they were described by George Emery Littlefield in his book *Early Schools and School-Books of New England* published in 1904.

Ezekiel Cheever was headmaster of the school from 1670 until his death in 1708. He wrote the *Accidence, A Short Introduction to the Latin Tongue*. It was a reinterpretation of the earlier *Lily's Grammar* that was made compulsory in England by Henry VIII in the early sixteenth century. Cheever's textbook is probably the earliest schoolbook written in America. It was published in Boston in 1709 after his death. The rest of the title page reads "For the Use of the Lower Forms in the Latin School. Being the Accidence Abbridged[sic] and Compiled in that most easy and accurate Method, wherein the Famous Mr. Ezekiel Cheever taught; and which he found the most advantageous by Seventy years' experience." In an article about Cheever and the book published in *The Classical Weekly* in 1950, John F. Latimer writes, "Memorizing by rote was not abolished, but in learning forms and grammar a teaspoon was used instead of a ladle."

The nomenclature was a collection of words and phrases. The one that was used at the school then was written by William Hamilton, a teacher at a private school, and originally published in Dublin in 1751. Its full cover page is *"Hermes romanus anglicis Dni. Johannis Garretsoni vertendis exercitiis accommodatus*: or, A new collection of Latin words and phrases, for the more ready and exact translating of Garretson's English exercises into Latin. The whole being done in a most complete method: shewing how

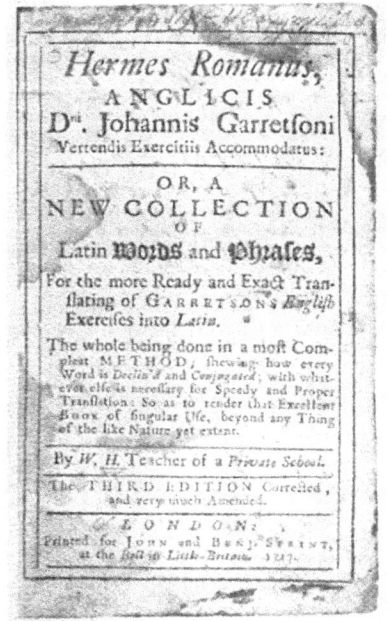

Title page of *Garretson's Hermes romanus* (Hamilton 1727).

every word is declined and conjugated; with whatever else is necessary for speedy and proper translation: so as to render that excellent book of singular use, beyond any thing of the like nature yet extant." They also used Dr. John Garretson's book of exercises and Hamilton wrote this nomenclature to help young students with the translations.

Corderius' Colloquies were written by Mathurin Cordier in Switzerland in the sixteenth century. There were innumerable editions of these that were used in schools for three centuries after he died. The editions printed in London included the conversations in Latin translated into English. It was somewhat like a phrase book we might buy today when we are traveling, only much more complex.

In the second year they added *Aesop's Fables* in Latin and English and a Latin phrase book. Later in that year they began using *Ward's Latin Grammar* and reading *Eutropius*, which they continued to study the following year.

It is disputed exactly who Eutropius was. However, it is known that he wrote a summary of Roman history entitled *Breviarium Historiae Romanae*. It covers the history of Rome from its foundation into the fourth century. It was translated into English as early as the seventeenth century. At this young age the boys must have read it in English.

One of the most popular elementary Latin phrase books was entitled *Gradus Ad Parnassum* by Paul Aler, a member of the Society of Jesus. It was a thesaurus of synonyms, epithets, and poetical verses and phrases. The one used during the time that Jonathan and Stephen were students was published in 1709 in London.

Along with the Latin language and Roman history they also studied oration. Littlefield describes his own copy of the eighth edition of John Clarke's *Formulae Oratoriae* published in London in 1659. It has the undated autographs of Nathaniel Gookins, John Higginson, and Jonathan Mitchell Sewall. There is no list of the early students who attended the school, but we can guess that this John Higginson was one of the Higginsons that lived in Salem and was related to Jonathan through his half-sisters.

Benjamin Dolbeare Jr. attended the school for seven years from 1752 to 1759 beginning three years before the Sewalls. He made a list of the textbooks that he bought which cost him just over £6. It contained *Accidence, Corderius, Aesop's Fables,* Nomenclatur, Clark's *Introduction, Eutropius,* a dictionary, a grammar, Castatio's Latin Testament, Garretson's *Exercises,* Tully's *Epistles,* Ovid's *Metamorphoses,* Greek grammar, Virgil, *Caesar's Commentaries,* Greek Testament, Latin Testament, Terrence, Greek lexicon, Horace's *Delphi,* Tully's *Orations,* King's *Heathen Gods, Gradus ad Parnassum,* and Homer. Why did we begin with *Dick and Jane*?

Later in life when Jonathan was ill, one of the things he did to forget about his pain and divert himself from melancholy was to attempt to describe eminent men in acrostic verse. Each line had to begin with a letter in the man's name. Among these many "Profiles of Eminent Men" are Ovid, Virgil, Horace, and Homer. Here are two examples of the results of this diversion that he found so helpful.

OVID

O'er fancy's fairy fields thou lov'st to range,
Vast thy invention! wond'rous ev'ry change!
In Love's soft school, unrival'd skill inspires,
Dame Venus prompts thee, and young Cupid fires!

HOMER

High as the heav'ns, sublimely tow'rs thy muse,
O'er earth expatiates, and all nature views!
Men, heroes, monarchs, gods, thy spirit warms,
Earth shakes! seas roar! heav'n trembles! nature arms!
Revere thy awful nod, and thunder with alarms!
(Sewall 1801)

The South Writing School

Abiah Holbrook was master of the South Writing School for twenty-seven years from 1742 until his death in 1769. "He was looked upon by the Best Judges as the Greatest Master of the Pen we have ever had among us...He was indefatigable in his labours, successful in his Instructions, an Honour to the Town and to crown all an Ornament to the Religion of Jesus" according to his death notice in the *Boston Gazette*.

He instructed his pupils by making demonstration pieces for them to attempt to imitate in their own copies. Learning to make and repair their goose-quill pens was not easy and he had to teach them that as well.

The Houghton Library at Harvard University houses a beautiful collection of his work and the copies made by some of his pupils. One of the best-known signatures in America is that of John Hancock, who entered the Boston Latin School in 1745. This

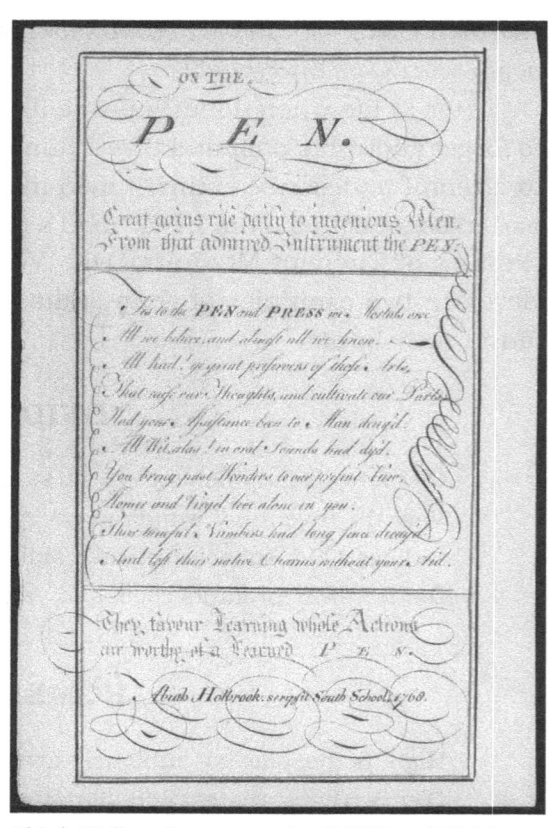

Abiah Holbrook manuscript (MS Typ 473.22, SWS (3)). Courtesy of Houghton Library, Harvard University.

clear "gentlemanly" style became known as the Boston style of writing. There are many handwritten documents that Jonathan wrote that can be seen today. The Portsmouth Athenaeum has a manuscript book of Jonathan's poetry. Some of the petitions he wrote to the state for various reasons are held at the New Hampshire State Archives in Concord. In one of them we see this lavish rendition he made of his initials.

Jonathan Mitchel Sewall initials on petition, 1801. Courtesy of the New Hampshire Division of Archives and Records Management.

Arithmetic was not taught until the pupils were about ten years old. There were few arithmetic textbooks and usually only the master had a copy. He would make cyphering books for each of his pupils. The students worked out the answers separately and then copied them neatly into their own cyphering book. They learned addition, subtraction, multiplication, division, fractions, simple interest, and the "Rule of Three" which solved proportions.

The loss to them was irreparable.

On May 17, 1758, when the boys were in their third year at the school, their mother died in Salem. The date was found in the records of the First Church of Salem but no further information about her death is known. She was only forty-four years old.

Just as tragic was the death of their guardian a little over two years later on September 10, 1760. John Eliot in his *Biographical Dictionary of New England* writes of the chief justice: "No one's death ever excited a more general sympathy. He was as much beloved for his good qualities, as admired for his superior wisdom. His polite and elegant manners gave a charm to the virtues of his life. It was remembered, likewise, how much he had dispersed and given to the poor! He was so kind to his relations and friends, and all who applied to him for help, 'that he outdid his proper capacity.' Two orphan children of his brother, Mitchel Sewall, Esq. were under his immediate care. It was his intention to give them every advantage of education. The loss to them was irreparable."

The *Boston Post Boy* on September 18 adds this: "He was a bright, penetrating genius, a fine scholar, a knowing lawyer, an upright judge, a wise and faithful counsellor, an accomplished gentleman, and an exemplary Christian. It may be added...that the republic of letters, the law, and the courts of justice, the common wealth, and the church of God, could not have sustained a greater loss in the death of any one person in the province, than in that of chief justice Sewall."

Stephen Sewall, Chief Justice of Massachusetts by Benjamin Feke (c. 1755). Courtesy of Harvard Law School Library, Historical & Special Collections.

The Rev. Dr. Jonathan Mayhew gave a discourse in the West Meeting House on the Sunday after Chief Justice Sewall's death. It may well have continued for at least an hour and can be read in full as it was published soon after. Mayhew retold the life of Samuel in the Old Testament and compared it to the life of Stephen Sewall. Toward the end of his speech he gave some biographical details and then said, "The relatives of the Deceased, those of them that are present, will allow me to exhort them while they sorrow, not to 'sorrow as those that have no hope:'—And also, while they mourn the Dead, to live as he lived; in expectation of a joyful meeting with him another day; when the times of refreshing shall come from the presence of the Lord" (Mayhew 1760).

The *Boston Gazette* reports on Monday, Sept. 15, that on the previous Saturday evening the funeral cortege was "longer perhaps, than was ever known amongst us upon the like occasion; and in which there was not a countenance, but what seemed to be that of some particular friend to, and mourner for, the deceased."

Stephen Sewall died intestate with the inventory of his estate worth less than £200. His executor appealed to the General Court for a grant to save the estate from the disgrace of bankruptcy, but it was not granted. It may be that he lost what little money he had not already given away "probably through involvement in his brother's speculations" according to a letter written by John Adams (Graves 2022, p. 586). He was the last of the children of Jonathan's paternal grandparents, Stephen Sewall and Margaret Mitchell Sewall.

The two boys would have been part of all of this—his death, the cortege, the burial, and the laudatory event at the West Meeting House. What an affect it must have had on their young lives that week and in the years to come. At the ages of twelve and fourteen they were now truly orphaned.

Chief Justice Stephen Sewall was praised for his effect on Jonathan's own character in a biographical sketch of Jonathan Mitchel Sewall in the *Early State Papers of New Hampshire* (Batchellor 1893, p. 845). From his uncle "the young orphan… imbibed that firmness of moral principle, honor, and integrity for which he was eminently distinguished, and a love for the belles lettres and elegant literature, which afforded him the most rational, refined, and sublime pleasures." Another characteristic that they shared was "an excessive self-diffidence" as reported in an obituary in the *Boston Post Boy* on September 18, 1760. Many of the poems and other writings of Jonathan's were not signed.

CHAPTER 4.

Apprenticeship, Spain, and Nervous Affections

Jonathan should have been on his way to Harvard College when he left the Boston Latin School or even after he finished his studies at the Salem Latin School. A good many of his relatives had graduated from Harvard. His father received his A.B. in 1718 and his master's degree in 1721. His great-grandfather, the Rev. Jonathan Mitchell, was one of the early graduates in 1647, only eleven years after the founding of the college in 1636. His guardian, Chief Justice Stephen Sewall, received his first degree in 1721. His cousin Jonathan Sewall of Boston, the one whose first job after graduation was at the Salem Latin School, graduated in 1748. This Jonathan's parents had also both died when he was young. When his cousin Jonathan was ready to go to Harvard, part of his expenses were paid for by his uncle, Chief Justice Stephen Sewall.

Jonathan Mitchel Sewall's entry in the *Dictionary of American Biography* states: "He is said to have entered Harvard College, but he did not graduate and no trace of him can now be found in the college archives." He is not mentioned in *Colonial Collegians* which includes men who enrolled but did not graduate. Surely, he wanted to go to Harvard College and probably never thought that he would not be headed there, but it was not to be.

Apprenticeship

In Jonathan's biographical notice in the *Early State Papers of New Hampshire* (Batchellor 1893, p. 845), we read that: "He was apprenticed to the mercantile business..." Apprenticeships in

APPRENTICESHIP, SPAIN, AND NERVOUS AFFECTIONS

colonial times were the way that most boys learned a trade. Lawyers studied law with another lawyer, not at college. Jonathan's father taught law from their home. His father taught William Pynchon, who became Jonathan's brother-in-law, and Pynchon went on to teach others in his home as well. Boys who became mercantile and professional apprentices were those who were destined to become merchants themselves or doctors or lawyers. They were the sons of gentlemen.

Although Jonathan had relatives in Boston he most likely went back to Salem because he had many close family ties there. And they were almost all in the mercantile business in some way. Perhaps the only immediate family relative who was not a sea captain or a merchant was William Pynchon, the husband of his stepsister, Catherine. Catherine and William were married in 1751. William Pynchon kept a *Diary* from 1776 until his death in 1788. It details all the times that his brother-in-law, whom he always referred to as "Brother Mitchel" or "Mitchell" visited them from Portsmouth during that time. They most likely called him Mitchel because there were so many other Jonathan Sewalls in their family. The entries in the *Diary* show his continued close links with his family in Salem (Oliver 1890).

His two other stepsisters, Peggy and Mary, could have still been living with Francis Cabot and his wife in the early 1760s. Mary married Nathan Goodale in 1765. He graduated from Harvard in 1759 and was the master of the Salem Latin School from the time that their cousin Jonathan Sewall left the school until 1770 when Nathan started working in his father's shop and became a merchant, and eventually a very wealthy one. Jonathan's stepsister Peggy never married. The stepsisters' other guardian, Stephen Higginson, had died in 1761, but Stephen's wife Elizabeth was Francis Cabot's sister.

There is no record of Jonathan's sister Elizabeth after the guardianship papers in 1750. His brother Stephen is next found in 1769 as a merchant in Marblehead, just a few miles from Salem. Perhaps the brothers went back to Salem together and were both apprenticed to family merchants there.

The population of Salem in 1764 was about 4,500 people. There were about 100 shops, 30 wharves, and 40 warehouses in the town. By the end of the eighteenth century, it was the sixth-largest city in the country, and it was second only to Boston in New England. It was an exciting place for a young man to begin his career. Boston was about twice its size, but Salem was next to it in wealth and importance among all the New England seacoast towns.

The merchants in Salem either owned their own ships, invested in the ships of other merchants, or sometimes both. This way they shared the risk as well as the profits. They employed the ship captains and purchased the goods to export. The exports included such diverse items as salted codfish and mackerel, cedar shingles, wax candles, beaver skins, cranberries, and other commodities. These were sold in Europe where they would fill their ships for the return journey with items needed in the West Indies and the American colonies.

Francis Cabot, as was noted before, became one of the wealthiest and most distinguished Salem merchants of his generation. The seventh-wealthiest man in Salem in 1759 is recorded as Joseph Cabot (Morris 2000). Joseph and Francis are brothers, and they built the business together. Joseph died in 1767, some years after Jonathan would have begun his apprenticeship. On Francis's death in 1786, his probate records included the brigantines *William*, *Leopard*, and *Hannah*, and the schooners *Sebastian*, *Francis*, and *Benjamin* in his ownership.

Jonathan's step-grandmother Anna Orne Cabot was Captain Timothy Orne's sister. He was recorded as the wealthiest of all the Salem merchants in the mid-eighteenth century. Jonathan's niece Elizabeth Pynchon married Timothy Orne, the son of this wealthy merchant in 1771. The families must have been close. Jonathan's cousin John Turner III, from his mother's side of the family, was a merchant sea captain. Jonathan had so many family connections to the mercantile trade in Salem it was certainly the most likely place for him to become "apprenticed to the mercantile business..."

APPRENTICESHIP, SPAIN, AND NERVOUS AFFECTIONS

An apprentice lived in the home of the merchant and the merchant was responsible for the training of his apprentice in addition to his food and lodging. Mercantile training included helping to keep the accounts, providing regular day-to-day assistance in taking care of the goods, and generally helping to run the business. The merchants often kept shops in their warehouse and an apprentice would also wait on customers.

The merchants in cities like Salem were involved in a wide variety of activities. They worked as middlemen and had to coordinate the buying and selling of the goods that came in and went out in the ships that they owned. When the ships returned, the merchants would sell the items they imported to the local shopkeepers, as well as to shopkeepers and farmers who lived outside of the city. There would have been considerable detail for the merchant and an intelligent apprentice or apprentices would have been a great help.

Ships sailing east to Europe were aided by the Gulf Stream and prevailing westerly winds which cut approximately two weeks off the length of the return trip back to America. Such a voyage normally took at least six weeks to get to Europe (Bryce 2014). They usually made two roundtrips a year and might stay weeks or even months in the foreign ports. On their way back they used the easterly trade winds, might sail as far south as the Azores, and then across to the West Indies. They stopped there for sales of some of the items they had purchased and might spend some time there as well. More items produced there were purchased to sell at home. From the West Indies, they sailed up the East Coast to their home port.

In 1755, there was a fleet of thirty-five vessels sailing out of Salem. They were owned and manned by Salem men. These trading ships went to Gibraltar, Spain (mainly the port of Bilbao), Portugal, the wine islands (specifically Madeira) and frequently came home by way of the West Indies. The largest ship owners at that time were Timothy Orne, Benjamin Pickman, Richard Derby, and Francis and Joseph Cabot. There were also sixty to seventy part-owners. By 1765, there were eighty-eight ships owned in Salem (Phillips 1937).

The types of goods that they purchased from Europe and the West Indies included dry goods—sieves, hooks, shot, nails, tobacco pipes, scythes, knives, needles, lead, chairs, books, cotton, and silk—as well as sugar, molasses, cotton, rum, salt, oranges, sweetmeats, and chocolate. One of Timothy Orne's schooners, *Caesar*, with Joshua Grafton as its master, sailed to Gibraltar from Salem on November 21, 1757, and returned in May 1758. It returned with cargo including nine casks of wine, Malaga, Sherry, French red wine 2¼ hogsheads (about 158 gallons), 89 casks raisins, 35 chests of oil, soap, and 25 bolts duck (canvas) (Essex Institute Historical Collections, vol. 37-1901, p. 78).

Malignant fever

Continuing in the *Early State Papers of New Hampshire* (Batchellor 1893, p. 845), we read that: "some years before his [apprenticeship] term expired he was attacked with a fever of a malignant type, which reduced him so low that a voyage to a milder climate was considered as the only means of restoring his health."

Among the imports into Salem during Jonathan's apprenticeship, there must have been a disease or some type of bacteria that caused him to become extremely ill. American colonists were not aware of what caused a sickness, they only saw the symptoms, such as the fever. In their minds the symptoms of a disease were the disease itself. Yellow fever and smallpox were the most common diseases and yellow fever seems to be the one most likely to have affected him. It is referred to elsewhere as a "malignant fever" and was often brought into a seaport on ships arriving from the West Indies or southern ports in the colonies.

The doctors of the day would have prescribed strong medicines which may have included purgatives, opium, cinchona or Peruvian bark (quinine), camphor, potassium nitrate, and mercury. These were among the most widely used drugs. Colonial New England doctors used over 200 preparations that they made up out of approximately 100 different active raw ingredients (Estes and Goodman 1986).

APPRENTICESHIP, SPAIN, AND NERVOUS AFFECTIONS

The types of drugs that were available from the Lyon and Mortar, a Salem shop, are seen in this advertisement placed in the *Boston Gazette* in 1764. (No newspaper was published in Salem until 1786.)

Continuing in the *Early State Papers of New Hampshire* (Batchellor 1893, p. 845) we read that: "He embarked for Spain…"

He embarked for Spain.

Whatever medicines they tried were obviously not resulting in Jonathan's restoration to health. Both Joseph and Francis Cabot and Timothy Orne had ships that regularly sailed to Bilbao in Spain. It seems likely that this was the place where Jonathan was sent to try to recover from his illness.

Samuel Gardner, a young man from Salem, kept a diary in 1759 that gives some idea of what this trip might have been like (Essex Institute Historical Collections, vol. 49, pp. 1–23). Samuel graduated from Harvard College that year and his health was poor, so he came home to Salem. He went to Gibraltar on one of his father's ships whose Captain was Richard Derby. He tells of the highs and lows of a sea voyage in the mid-eighteenth century. Included here are some of the entries.

> Aug 3 - Trade flourishes at Salem, foreigners bring their Goods here. There is in our harbour 6 or 8 Topsail vessels besides a great number of other vessels.

Salem apothecary advertisement. *Boston Gazette*, January 23, 1764. *GenealogyBank* 2020.

> Oct 10 - Determined to go to Sea with Cap. Derby quite sudden as well as unexpected. Preparing for it. We wait for nothing but a wind.
> Oct. 19 - Fine fair wind at NW Sailed from Salem. May I be in the care of God throughout this voyage. Very Sick. Cap. Josiah Orne sailed the same day.
> Oct. 20/21 - prodigious Sick.

Interestingly they spoke with others from ships they pass as they travel.

> Oct. 31 - Fair pleasant weather.
> Nov. 1 - Roast ducks for dinner.
> Nov. 8 - Quite sick again.
> Nov 12 - Saw a sail standing to the SW We fired a shot at her. She then hoisted Dutch Colours. I am quartered at the aftermost gun and its opposite on the Quarter Deck, with Cap. Clefford. Apple dumplings for supper.
> Nov. 13 - I have entertained myself with a Romance, the History of the Parish Girl.
> Nov 15 - Saw another ship that chased then It fired 3 shot at us which we returned. She proved to be the Ship Cornwall, from Bristol bound to the Coast of Africa.
> Nov. 22 - Just as the sun set the Captain discovered land.
> Nov. 23 - At 2PM came to anchor in Gibraltar Bay.

Various people came on board the ship, but Samuel does not go on shore until the 26th. He visited people, all of whom have English names. Gibraltar was part of the Spanish kingdom until 1713 when Spain ceded the territory to Britain.

> Nov. 29 - Cap. Darby begins to sell his cargo.
> Dec. 8 - Capt. Clefford came off to us this morning and invited Capt. Derby and myself to dine at his brothers. Also the first and second lieutenants and the doctor of the regiment. Accordingly, we went and were entertained with an elegant dinner. The dinner consisted of very fine fish boiled with fish sauce and butter, boiled fowls and

bacon, boiled leg of mutton with caper sauce, greens, potatoes, etc. A very fine roast turkey, cranberry tarts, etc., etc., etc. We had likewise very good Liquors, viz. Madeira, sherry, Bristol Bear and Punch. The whole of the entertainment was very gentil.

The diary ends Dec. 11, 1759 with them still in Gibraltar. Despite Samuel's sickness, he was fortunate in one way because the crossing took them less than five weeks.

Though Gibraltar and Bilbao are on opposite ends of Spain, the trans-Atlantic journey that Jonathan embarked on might have been comparable to that of Samuel Gardner. Being "prodigious Sick" does not seem like a helpful remedy to recover from a malignant fever, even if you are eventually going to arrive in a warmer climate.

Bilbao is seven miles inland from the Bay of Biscay on the northern coast of Spain in the Basque Country. During the eighteenth century it had about 200 merchants and nearly 300 ships that entered and left its very sheltered harbor each year. It imported large quantities of dried, salted codfish from Newfoundland and the American colonies. This accounted for 26% of total Spanish imports of cod during the 1770s (Lamikiz 2008, p. 86). The merchants and ship owners of Salem, Francis Cabot and Timothy Orne, accounted for some of this. One of the reasons for the harbor's popularity was that it was a free port and a distribution center that linked the American colonies with those in northern Europe.

Ship captains were like seagoing postmasters of the eighteenth century. "Captains were a conduit of information for shipowners, merchants (local and foreign), and other captains, and crews and their families" (Lamikiz 2008). In William Pynchon's *Diary*, he often notes news that has been brought in by ships that arrive in Salem.

As early as the 1730s, more than a third of all the imports into Bilbao were controlled by six companies owned by foreigners. "The Irishman Lynch, one of the town's wealthiest merchants, traded in textiles, fabrics, sugar, iron, cod, sardines, cacao, rugs, sugar, cinnamon, vegetables, hardware, copper, tin, wax, cheese, hides, flour, candles and hardwoods" (Uriarte 1998, p. 153).

Whereas the population of Salem was only around 4,500 in 1764, Bilbao's population was 6,000 in 1700 and rose to 11,000 by 1800. Most of this expansion was between 1746 and 1768. Jonathan would have arrived there near the end of this expansion. Even John Adams visited Bilbao in 1780. It was not quite as populous a city as Boston, but it was very much older, as it was founded in 1300. The city was surrounded by two small mountain ranges of about 1,300 feet which would have been quite a change from the surroundings of Salem or Boston. The elevation of Bunker Hill in Boston is only 110 feet.

When Jonathan was well enough to have a look around, he would have marveled at the churches that were found all over the city, some of them already several hundred years old. The Cathedral-Church of Bilbao was dedicated to St. James the Apostle, the patron saint of Bilbao since 1643. It was built in the fifteenth century in a Gothic style. Another Gothic basilica dating from the sixteenth century is on the top of a hill that dominates the entire city. In the 1700s it was surrounded by the steelworks which provided one of the main industries in the Basque country.

The convent of the Incarnation was built between 1513 and 1526 to serve the Dominican nuns. The seventeenth-century Parish Church of St. John is a Baroque church founded by the Jesuits. There were other older churches, but the San Nicolás of Bari Church was very new, built in 1756. It has a Baroque façade that is topped by two towers. It became a meeting point for sailors before they went to sea. These stone churches would have been quite an amazing site for a young man who grew up attending the plain wooden puritan churches of New England:

> [T]he salubrity of the climate produced a favorable effect on his system in general, yet the violence of the fever and the strong medicines which the physicians

administered to him when sick, afterwards subjected him to exquisite nervous affections and the keenest mental suffering approaching delirium. (Batchellor 1893, p. 845)

Exquisite nervous affections

The medical description of "affections" is a neurological disorder describing an illness affecting the nerves or an acute or chronic disorder to characterize an illness. Here are some quotations from various sources about the effects of Jonathan's illness on him.

William Pynchon noted Jonathan's visits from Portsmouth to Salem in his *Diary* and among them are these:

> 6 August 1783 find Bro. Mitchel ill at my house.
> 22 September 1785 Bro. Mitchell comes; is deeply disordered.
> 21 December 1785 Bro. Mitchell comes in Portsmouth stage; a dark cloud over his visage, his eyes wild... (Oliver 1890, pp. 158, 207, 227)

Additional sources include the following:

> ...the necessary use of extremely powerful medicines, rendered him the future subject of exquisite nervous affections, and at times a prey to the keenest sufferings, which deprived his friends of the pleasure of his company, and the delight his fascinating and instructive conversation afforded. (Obituary in *The Literary Mirror*, April 16, 1808)

> In later years he suffered from nervous problems and hypochondria and found solace in what one writer delicately called "stimulating beverages." (Heard 2006)

> Mr. Sewall's health suffered as he increased in years; and to relieve his nervousness and hypochondria, he resorted to stimulating beverages, which of course only afforded temporary alleviation, although they fixed upon him habits that he never overcame. But

his friends loved him none the less and appear never to have lost respect for him. The lady who became his second wife, when remonstrated with on her engagement to a man of his habits, replied, "I would rather marry Mr. Sewall drunk than any other man sober." One who inspired such sentiments could never have been regarded as a victim of sensuality." (Bell 1894, pp. 629–630)

In Jonathan's own book published in 1801 he writes this:

The following sketches . . . of eminent men, &c. were produced while the Author was confined by sickness, laboring under the worst of maladies, nervous affections. As his own physician he prescribed the task, to divert his attention from himself. And to overcome indolence, he contrived to render it difficult, and even servile, by confining himself to the letters of the respective names, while at the same time he wished to preserve the spirit and likeness of the original characters. How far he has been successful, others must judge. But the prescription succeeded with himself. It alleviated his pain, and diverted his melancholy. (Sewall 1801)

CHAPTER 5.

Law and Portsmouth

To avoid confusion at the beginning of this chapter, "Jonathan Mitchel" is used rather than "Jonathan."

Continuing with the biographical note in the *Early State Papers of New Hampshire* (Batchellor 1893, p. 845): "The uncertain and frequent ill state of his health did not prevent him, soon after his arrival from Spain, from engaging in the study of law. He commenced his legal studies with his kinsman, Jonathan Sewall, an eminent lawyer at Boston…"

Cousin Jonathan Sewall of Boston

Jonathan Sewall of Boston was Jonathan Mitchel Sewall's first cousin. Their fathers were brothers, Jonathan Sewall (1693–1731) and Mitchel Sewall (1699–1748). During the time that Cousin Sewall was the schoolmaster at the Salem Latin School he studied law with their uncle John Higginson. By the time Jonathan Mitchel returned from Spain, he had obviously decided he was not going to be a merchant or possibly ever go to sea again. He would follow in the footsteps of his father and his

Jonathan Sewall, Attorney General of Massachusetts (Wilson 1900).

guardian and become a lawyer as many other members of the Sewall family had done before him.

His cousin was well-established in the Boston area by the time Jonathan Mitchel came to study with him. Cousin Sewall had met Judge Chambers Russell of Charlestown through their uncle John Higginson. He moved into Russell's home and studied law with him and eventually took over his law practice in Charlestown when Russell moved to Concord. Sewall attended the supreme court in Worcester and spent his evenings in Colonel James Putnam's law office with John Adams. Putnam also taught law and Adams studied with him and lived in his home.

His cousin's good friend John Adams

Cousin Sewall and John Adams became great friends as attested to by Adams in his *Works*:

> Here commenced between Mr. Sewall and me a personal friendship, which continued, with none but political interruptions, till his death. He commenced practice in Charlestown, in the county of Middlesex; I, in that parish of the ancient town of Braintree... We attended the courts in Boston, Cambridge, Charlestown, and Concord; lived together, frequently slept in the same chamber, and not seldom in the same bed. Mr. Sewall was then a patriot; his sentiments were purely American. (Adams 1856, vol. 4)

Adams says of his friend:

> He possessed a lively wit, a pleasing humor, a brilliant imagination, great subtlety of reasoning and an insinuating eloquence...I know not that I have ever delighted more in the friendship of any man...He had virtues to be esteemed, qualities to be loved, and talents to be admired. (Adams 1856, vol. 4, p. 7)

They remained close personal friends. Sewall frequently stayed with the Adams family in Braintree over weekends during the time when he was courting Esther Quincy. This courtship went on for over five years until she finally became his wife in 1764. (Her sister Dorothy married John Hancock and her sister Mary married Portsmouth merchant Jacob Sheafe IV.) By 1766, Cousin Jonathan and Esther Sewall were living in Cambridge at the corner of Brattle and Sparks Street. Their first son, another Jonathan Sewall, was born that year and baptized at Christ Church in Cambridge (NEHGS 2005, p. 5399). The picture of the house shown here was taken around 1900. Today it is barely visible from the street. The property was confiscated by the state in May 1778. Cousin Sewall became a Loyalist and moved to England at the outset of the Revolution. In 1785 he changed the spelling of his name to Sewell. He said the fact that his ancestors had emigrated to America proved that they did not know enough to spell their own name (NEHGS 2005). John Adams was in London as the American minister in 1787 before "Sewell" left to take his post as a judge in the Vice Admiralty Court of Nova Scotia. Adams and "Sewell" renewed their old acquaintance and "embraced each other as cordially as ever."

Jonathan Sewall House, Cambridge, Massachusetts (Crawford 1902).

Attorney General and the Study of Law

In 1767, Jonathan Sewall became the attorney general of the Massachusetts Bay Colony. He adjudicated in many of the cases between British soldiers and the citizens of Boston after the soldiers arrived in 1768. He personally conducted the prosecution of every criminal case. It was said that he knew how to assert the independence of a judge over and above any political bias. He was involved in the defense of blacks in at least three cases. In two of these, Margaret vs. Muzzy in 1768 and James vs. Lechmere in 1769, he managed to procure their freedom. These cases involving the defense of enslaved people were likely heard during the time Jonathan Mitchel studied with his cousin.

Jonathan Mitchel would have come to this house on Brattle Street when he returned from Spain. Sewall took in law students much in the same way as many other lawyers did at that time. In the years before the Revolution a liberal university education was desirable for a lawyer, but law was not seen as the sort of subject that you would study at college. Actual training was acquired through a clerkship because legal education was the responsibility of the profession.

Most colonial lawyers in Massachusetts had a college education. They then went on to study for at least three years as a clerk with someone who also had such an education. During this time the clerk would have access to the legal forms and abstracts and notes the lawyer made about his own cases. He also copied out the documents that the lawyer prepared, which included petitions, wills, and other types of legal papers. Clerks also traveled around the countryside following the judges on their circuits. These happened four times a year and provided the opportunity to meet people from all over the colony. Massachusetts at this time included what became Maine in 1820. Part of the circuit traveled to York and any judge from there would travel to all the courts in the rest of the colony.

"The wealthiest [lawyers] might have an enormous collection of 50 to 100 books, and most of the best collections were owned by Tory lawyers. A collection of this size would include nearly every legal work available in the colonies" (Consalus 1978, pp. 295–310). The English lawyer William Blackstone was the first to reduce the common law to a system and to put it into writing. His book *Commentaries* sold thousands of copies in America, and it was the most important law book used for many years. Cousin Sewall wrote to John Adams in September 1759 "Your account of Mr. Blackstone's lectures is entirely new to me. I am greatly pleased with it." Jonathan Mitchel's cousin would have had an extensive library and perhaps he was also guided to study some of what he might have learned at Harvard College if he had been able to attend.

Cousin Sewall was obviously very learned, but also witty, and must have been an entertaining person to be with at times. He had known Jonathan Mitchel for his entire life as he was working in Salem and studying with their uncle from the year Jonathan Mitchel was born until he was nine years old. All sources show that the Sewall family kept in close contact over the years. In addition to studying law, perhaps this was where Jonathan Mitchel began working on his poetical skills, and maybe he thought he could certainly do better than Cousin Sewall. In Sewall's biographical entry in *Colonial Collegians,* we read that "His correspondence is larded with tags from better poets and gaily bad verse of his own" (NEHGS 2005, p. 5397). This was part of a very long poem illustrating his "gaily bad verse" written to his cousin Thomas Robie in 1757.

> They tell me Tom, you mean to wed,
> (I wish they'd told me you were dead,)
> Nor can you think my Wish uncivil,
> Unless you're influenc'd by the Devil,

Poem in Letter to Thomas Robie from Jonathan Sewall 1757. Collection of the Massachusetts Historical Society.

When he began studying law Jonathan Mitchel wrote a long poem entitled "On Music and Poetry; addressed to a Lady." In one of the stanzas he writes:

> But I, alas! whom humbler thoughts inspire,
> Untrain'd in verse, unskill'd to strike the lyre,
> In silent rapture on each genius gaze,
> Nor feel their spirit, tho' I love their lays.
> Or if one kindling spark should faintly gleam,
> A cold, dull * science damps the generous flame.
> And while the fav'rite themes my bosom warms,
> I'm charm'd myself, yet want the pow'r to charm.

At the bottom of the page it reads, "* The author was then beginning the study of Law."

Chroust notes that there was only one competent lawyer in New Hampshire in the seventeenth century, John Pickering (1640–1721), and only three during the eighteenth century. The youngest of these was John Pickering (1735–1805), a distant relative of the earlier man of the same name. The younger John Pickering graduated from Harvard in 1761. "Practically all of the early Massachusetts lawyers of standing and repute were Harvard graduates" (Chroust 1957).

Ossian

Much later in his life Jonathan tells us that it was during this time that he acquired a copy of the book of poems of Ossian. In the introduction to his own book *Miscellaneous Poems* he writes, "Macpherson's prose translation of these poems fell into the author's hands as early as the year 1770, when they were but little known in this country, they pleased him, and he then attempted to turn a few passages into heroic verse. The work was amusing, and he has from time to time continued it."

James MacPherson was a Scottish writer, poet, literary collector, and later in life a Scottish politician. In December 1761 he published *Fingal, an ancient Epic Poem in six books: together with Several Other Poems composed by Ossian, the son of Fingal, translated from the Gaelic Language* in which he purportedly translated these poems which dated from the third century. He said that he had collected the poems and some ancient manuscripts in the Scottish Highlands. In 1765, he published a compilation of his work as *The Works of Ossian*.

This book must be the one that Jonathan owned as early as 1770. It was not published in America until 1790, so his copy would have come across the Atlantic. All of MacPherson's books about Ossian were first published in Edinburgh. The work has been described as written in "musical measured prose rather

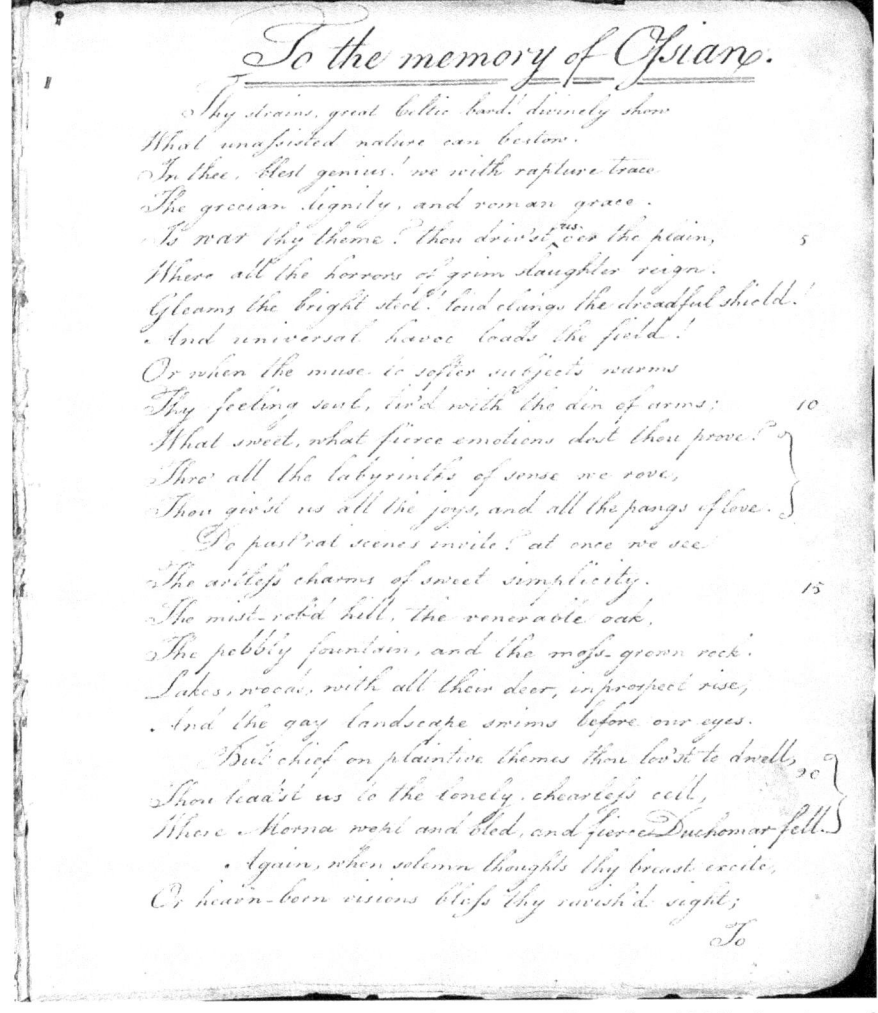

Manuscript book of the *Poems of Ossian* in verse (Sewall c. 1800). Courtesy of the Portsmouth Athenaeum, Portsmouth Historical Society Collection.

than in verse." From time to time during the next nearly forty years, Jonathan rewrote the entire book in rhyming verse. He also included some arguments for its authenticity, which had been disputed since its publication. His manuscript copy was donated to the Portsmouth Historical Society and is now part of the Portsmouth Athenaeum's collection.

MacPherson's book became extremely popular in colonial America. Even John Adams records this about a letter he received from his wife. He quotes her first: "'Mr. Adams you are going to embark under very threatening Signs. The Heavens frown, the Clouds roll, the hollow Winds howl, The Waves of the Sea roar upon the Beech,' and on she went in such a Strain that I seemed to be reading Ossian" (Adams 1778, part 2).

Portsmouth connections

There are various connections that come to light in attempting to work out why Jonathan Mitchel Sewall came to Portsmouth to study with John Pickering. One of the reasons not to stay in Massachusetts was that there were many better qualified young men because they did have college degrees.

David Sewall of York was one of Jonathan's second cousins. Their grandfathers were John and Stephen Sewall. Two of John's children, Nicholas and Samuel, moved from Salem to York in the early 1700s. David was Samuel's son and he studied law in Portsmouth with Judge William Parker and married the judge's daughter Mary in 1762. The couple settled in York. David Sewall was justice of the Superior Court of Massachusetts from 1777 to 1789 as well as a delegate to the Massachusetts Constitutional Convention that was held in 1779–80. In William Pynchon's *Diary*, that he kept from 1776 until 1789, he writes that Judge Sewall was in Salem over the weekend of the 7th to the 9th of November in 1778. He called on the Pynchons Saturday evening and spent the day with them on Sunday before setting out for York on Monday (Oliver 1890, p. 58). Apparently, David Sewall had a continuing relationship with his Salem relatives and with the family of Jonathan's sister Catherine and her husband William Pynchon in particular. In a letter dated May 22, 1821 from John Adams to David Sewall he begins, "As we have been friends for seventy years..." (Adams 1856, vol. 10, p. 399). They were classmates at Harvard, graduating in 1755 along with John Wentworth, who became the colonial governor of New Hampshire in 1767.

Another Salem and Portsmouth connection was with the family of the Reverend John Sparhawk who baptized Jonathan in Salem First Church. Reverend Sparhawk was related to the Sewalls by marriage. His wife Jane's mother was Jonathan's aunt Susannah, the one who married George Atkinson in Portsmouth. Reverend Sparhawk's brother Nathaniel married Elizabeth Pepperell of Boston and Kittery. Elizabeth was also related to Jonathan's family. She is his second cousin through her grandmother. Her father, Sir William Pepperell, had the beautiful mansion, known as Sparhawk Hall, built for Elizabeth and Nathaniel as a wedding present. It still stood in Kittery, Maine, until it burned in 1967. Their son William Pepperell Sparhawk became Sir William Pepperell. He left the country at the start of the Revolution, but when he was a child, he entered the Boston Latin School the same year as Jonathan in a class of about thirty boys. In January 1784, William Pynchon notes in his *Diary* that "Bro. Mitchell comes with N. Sparhawk and Jno. Sparhawk in the stage." The stage from Portsmouth to Boston first began running in 1761 and stopped in Salem by this time. Pynchon mentioned people visiting and leaving for Portsmouth frequently throughout his diary.

Pickering connections

John Pickering's grandfather, Thomas Pickering, was born in Salem in 1645 and came to Newington, New Hampshire, soon after he married Mary Gee in 1679. Their thirteen children were all born in New Hampshire. Their son Joshua was John Pickering's father. Joshua and his wife Deborah had seven children, the youngest of which was John who was born in 1737. Deborah died that same year. There are also various Pickerings mentioned frequently in Pynchon's *Diary*.

John Pickering's early education and preparation for Harvard, where he graduated in 1761, was with the Reverend Joseph Adams of Newington Town Church. Joseph Adams was a Harvard graduate in the class of 1710 who first taught school at Bloody Point, which became Newington. He became minister of the church there. The town is just five miles northwest of Portsmouth. Reverend Adams' nephew was John Adams. Adams stayed at the Newington parsonage as a child and returned to visit his uncle in later years. In John Adams' diary he writes that John Pickering was a "very sensible and accomplished lawyer" (Adams 1961, vol. 2, p. 40). John Pickering married Abigail Sheafe in 1769. She was the sister of Jacob Sheafe IV, who had married Mary Quincy, the sister of Cousin Sewall's wife. There were many connections.

Another John Pickering and Timothy Pickering were contemporaries of Jonathan and they were born in Salem in 1740 and 1745. Their mother was from Hampton, just south of Portsmouth. John graduated from Harvard in 1759, and although he was happy to be a farmer, the town elected him to public office. He became a representative in the Massachusetts House and was speaker in 1778 among other duties like register of deeds for many years (NEHGS 2005, p. 6603). Timothy attended the Salem Latin School and graduated from Harvard in 1763. "He described the teaching [at Harvard] as wretched and found that his own preparation had been so good that the college work was a bore..." (NEHGS 2005, p. 7158). He read law with William Pynchon in Salem. John Adams on first meeting him remarked, "He treated me with great politeness, and seems a very sensible and well accomplished lawyer" (Adams 1856, vol. 2, pp. 283–4). George Washington made Timothy Pickering postmaster general in 1791 and he remained in the cabinet for nine years into the beginning of John Adams' presidency, becoming secretary of war and then secretary of state. He and Adams had many disagreements, and he left the Adams' cabinet only to return to Washington later as representative for Massachusetts from 1812–1817.

It is interesting to speculate that it could have been John Adams who suggested that Jonathan come to Portsmouth to study with John Pickering.

A spirited performance by the American Apollo J. M. Sewall, Esquire

Shown here is part of an article published in the *Salem Gazette* about the birthday celebrations for President Adams in Portsmouth in 1799.

Select Companies.—At 3 P. M. a large and respectable company of private citizens met at the Assembly Room, and partook of a very elegant entertainment. Many excellent songs heightened the joys of the hour, and among them we recognize with pleasure a spirited performance by the American Apollo, J. M. SEWALL, Esquire,

Whose lyre to raptures extatic is strung
When ADAMS, when WASHINGTON, dwells on his tongue.

The American Apollo. *Salem Gazette*, November 8, 1799. *GenealogyBank* 2021.

In Jonathan's own book of poetry "Song for President Adams' Birth-Day" finishes with:

> Then let Adams be sung
>
> By each Patriot tongue,
>
> And Columbia's loud lyre
>
> be to exstacy [sic] strung!

Jonathan's poem "Anniversary Song" ends:

> Then shout great Adams! Freedom's son!
> Immortal heir of Washington!

John Pickering

John Pickering read theology after his graduation from Harvard but then changed to law. He opened an office in Greenland which is adjacent to Newington, but soon moved to Portsmouth. In 1769, when he married Abigail Sheafe, he became a pillar of the South Church. Early in his career in Portsmouth John Adams met him and spoke well of him. A. P. Peabody described him to the Massachusetts Historical Society: "He was always

John Pickering. Courtesy of the New Hampshire Historical Society.

spoken of as not only the foremost man of his State and time as a lawyer and a jurist, but as pre-eminent in all qualities appertaining to a good citizen and a Christian gentleman. I can say with confidence that there was no name of his time held in equal honor with his in the memory of the community" (NEHGS 2005).

In *Bench and Bar of New Hampshire* we read: "His native powers were trained to their best by assiduous study and exercise; he was witty, eloquent, and judicious; his opponents—he had no enemies—could speak only good of him, and in spite of the fact that his profession was cordially disliked by the mass of the people they all liked him. He was a reader and a scholar." William Plumer tells us that Pickering was a very religious man and believed that he should do all that he could for his fellow man (Plumer 1857). One of the ways that he practiced this in his life was to give legal counsel to the poor without any compensation. Historian Charles Bell said that "though one of the most eminent practitioners of his time, he realized from his business little more than required for the support of his family" (Bell 1894).

When Jonathan came to Portsmouth in the early 1770s to study with Pickering he probably lived in John and Abigail Pickering's house, which was on Market Street on the northern corner of Commercial Alley where the Kennedy Gallery stands today. The house was described by Charles Brewster in his *Ramble #31* as "a large two-story house, gable end toward Market street, with an entrance on the street, also a front entrance on the court." In *Ramble #62* he tells us that "Judge Pickering's house came next, end to the street, with an office in it." The office door was on Market Street and the house extended down Commercial Alley from there. In *Ramble #74* Brewster describes the house as Pickering's "mansion": "...next north of Dearborn's combined shop, house and academy, was the mansion of Judge John Pickering. Connected with the Penhallow mansion, which came next, was a large garden extending back over the land now bearing the name of Penhallow street." The office of the *New Hampshire Gazette*, often claimed to be the first newspaper in the United States, was across the street. Market Street was then known as Paved Street because it was the only street in the town that had been paved. The paving was paid for by a public lottery in 1762. The Pickering's mansion house was destroyed in the fire of 1802.

In the early 1770s, Portsmouth was similar in many ways to the town of Salem where Jonathan was born and many of his relatives lived. The population was about the same and they were both seaports with ships coming and going constantly. The major businesses were ship building and trade with the other American colonies, the West Indies, Europe, Africa, and beyond. They were seaport towns predominately of merchants and shipbuilders. Ralph May writes in *Early Portsmouth History* that "Portsmouth from 1770 to 1780 was more than ever a civic and social center of importance." The first newspaper had begun publication in 1756. John Staver's Flying Stagecoach started traveling to Boston in 1761. By the 1760s there were passenger ships between Portsmouth and Boston.

Portsmouth and New Hampshire

John Wentworth, a Portsmouth local, became the new royal governor of New Hampshire in 1767. He was quite popular with the people and Portsmouth was the seat of the government of the colony. Wentworth was responsible for much of New Hampshire's early road construction, so it was becoming easier to get around in the state.

The first of four "highways" had been completed in 1764. By 1771 there were over two hundred miles of road in the state. That year Wentworth established five counties which he named after English friends. Grafton and Strafford counties were less densely populated so they were annexed to Rockingham County, which included Portsmouth and Exeter. They remained so until the governor declared them competent to exercise their own jurisdictions in 1773. These original counties were created to care for the roads, record land transactions, administer the courts and penal system, and enforce the laws of the colony. Jonathan's biographical sketch in *Bench and Bar of New Hampshire* states, "In 1773 he was appointed by Governor Wentworth Register of Probate for Grafton County, and major in the militia..."

The second deed in the *Grafton County Registry of Deeds*, dated 27 June 1772 (Book 1, Page 2), was for the sale of land in the township of Dartmouth (renamed Jefferson in 1796) that was owned by a number of prominent men from Portsmouth which included John Parker, Esq.; Joshua Wentworth; John Langdon, who became governor; Jacob Sheafe; Daniel Fowle, the printer; and Jonathan M. Sewall; among various others. Colonial governors rewarded relatives, friends, and others by making direct grants of land to them or by placing their names among those of grantees of new townships. Few, if any, of the original grantees would have visited their land grant and taxes were levied on them but they often were not paid (Hoefnagel and Close 1995). The townships of Percy, Northumberland, and Jefferson are in the northern part of what was Grafton County and became Coos County in 1803. All lands in these townships were granted to private shareholders or "proprietors" before they were settled (Garvin 2002). Jonathan was one of the proprietors, and his name appeared often in the newspaper as someone who owed tax.

Likeness

John Wentworth obviously knew Jonathan Mitchel Sewall by this time. It is interesting to wonder if Wentworth observed that his new register of probate looked like someone that he had met during his time in England. One of Jonathan's locally published obituaries states that "In his person, manner, gesture and look it is a striking fact he had a resemblance to Edmund Burke" (*Intelligencer*, April 21, 1808).

How could someone in the United States at the time of Jonathan Mitchel Sewall's death know what Edmund Burke not only looked like, but even what he was like in "his person, manner, and gesture"? Edmund Burke was an Anglo-Irish orator who is famous for saying many things, probably the most memorable is, "The only thing necessary for the triumph of evil is for good men to do nothing."

John Wentworth went to England as a young man and became friendly with the English Wentworths. He frequently visited their palatial home in Yorkshire, which is known as Wentworth Woodhouse. Edmund Burke became the personal secretary of Lord Rockingham, Charles Wentworth of Wentworth-Woodhouse, the year before John Wentworth left to return to New Hampshire. He named Rockingham County for his friend Lord Rockingham. Another Wentworth "cousin," Michael, also related to Charles Wentworth, was born in Yorkshire. He and John became great friends during John's time in England. Michael came to Portsmouth to visit him in 1767 and stayed. He married the widow of Benning Wentworth and lived at the Governor's House at Little Harbor until his death in 1795.

And then there was John Adams, who was in London

Edmund Burke in 1774, from a painting by Sir Joshua Reynolds. National Galleries of Scotland. Creative Commons CC by NC.

from May 1785 until March 1788. Edmund Burke was a member of Parliament from 1766–1794. He had expressed his support for the grievances of the American colonies under the government of King George III. It seems likely that John Adams met him when he was in England.

Jonathan's resemblance to Edmund Burke must have been public knowledge as many of these men who would have met Burke were not alive when Jonathan died.

CHAPTER 6.

Militia, Grafton County, Universalism, Family

Jonathan Mitchel Sewall's biographical sketch in *Bench and Bar of New Hampshire* states, "In 1773 he was appointed by Governor Wentworth Register of Probate for Grafton County and major in the militia..." This appointment in Grafton County was going to greatly change his life.

Militia

In 1771:

> With the exception of a few exempted groups, all males between sixteen and sixty years of age were obliged to bear arms and to perform military drill on four days each year. Each man or boy had to provide himself with a musket and other necessary military equipment, and each town must keep a store of supplies on the basis of a barrel of powder, two hundred pounds of bullets, and three hundred flints for every sixty men of military age. (*Acts and Laws of New Hampshire* 1771 ed., Chapter 67)

Two provincial regiments were created when Governor John Wentworth organized the northern counties in the state. The Eleventh Regiment had its headquarters in Plymouth in Grafton County. John Fenton, who had been appointed judge of Probate and Clerk of Court for the county, was its colonel. David Hobart was the lieutenant-colonel and Jonathan was the major. In 1774

Jonathan resigned (Stearns 1906, pp. 395, 468). This appears to be the end of his military career.

Register of Probate

The two main towns in Grafton County were Haverhill and Plymouth. Plymouth was about halfway along the Province Road, and Haverhill was the next-to-last stop on this road which ran from Durham to North Haverhill. The Province Road was the first "farm to market" road in New Hampshire. It was planned in 1763 to divert crops from being shipped down the Connecticut River from the Haverhill area and instead have them brought to the Durham area (Federal Writers' Project 1938, p. 63). The road was finally completed around 1773–1774. It was the only "highway" to the west of the state that was "passable for wheeled vehicles. It is not contended that this was a good road, but that it was so passable, doubtless requiring very careful driving in some places" (Upham 1920, p. 440).

A few years later, Jonathan wrote a poem lamenting the death of his horse in which he cries:

> Poor hapless steed! the truest, best,
> That e'er by luckless weight was prest;
> How oft in dirtiest, vilest road,
> O'er roots, and stumps, thro' mire and mud;
> 'Midst cold, thirst, perils, and fatigues,
> no barn within a dozen leagues.
> Tho' wearied, hungry, parch'd, and faint,
> Has thou, despising all complaint;
> And only studious to approve
> Thy strength, speed, diligence and love;
> Bore thy sad lord, with many a pack,
> A pleasing burthen; on thy back. (Sewall 1801)

According to an article in the *Boston Evening Post* on January 17, 1774, Grafton County had grown from no families in 1760 to about six hundred families: "…the principal increase has been under the auspices, and by the encouragement of his Excellency the present Governor Wentworth." It also reports that during the previous seven weeks Haverhill had built a county house forty-eight feet by thirty-eight feet, "the heaviest and stoutest timbered building perhaps in New Hampshire." On the second floor, there were two lobbies and a room fourteen feet in height and thirty-six-feet square for the use of the Courts of Justice.

The *History of Plymouth* (Stearns 1906, p. 443) records that Jonathan was the first lawyer there and that he was in active practice in the town, but that he never lived there. "Jonathan Mitchell Sewall, the poet lawyer, was made register of probate in 1773, presumably with a view to his location in the county, but he soon resigned the office and continued in practice at Portsmouth" (Child 1886, p. 39).

This notice in the *New Hampshire Gazette* announced a court in Plymouth in January 1774 and the next one to be in Haverhill in April that year:

> THE HONORABLE
> # JOHN FENTON, ESQ
> JUDGE of *Probate* for the County of *Grafton*.
> NOTICE is HEREBY GIVEN, That a COURT of WILLS and PROBATE will be held at *Plymouth*, on the 24th Inftant, at 11 o'Clock, A. M. at the Houfe of Mr. *Samuel Emerfon* ;——
> ALSO, at the Houfe of Mr. *Andrew S. Crocker*, at Haverhill, in faid County, on the 25th Day of April next, at 11 o'Clock A,M.
> By Order of the JUDGE,
> JONATHAN MITCHEL SEWALL, *Reg.*
> *January* 6, 1774.

John Fenton, Judge of Probate for Grafton County. *NH Gazette*, January 7, 1774. *GenealogyBank* 2019.

> The first term of the Court of Common Pleas in Haverhill was held at Haverhill April 21, 1774. The session lasted for three days. John Fenton was Judge of Probate and Clerk of the Court. There were twenty- three cases on the docket of which fifteen were disposed of, and of these fifteen, six were tried by a jury. Eight were continued to the July term. The counsel in the cases whose names appear on this first docket were Jonathan M. Sewall of Portsmouth...who appeared for the plaintiff in each case, and Simeon

Olcott of Charlestown who was entered for the defendant in two cases. (Whitcher 1919, p. 274)

One of these cases was the probate for Daniel Gerrish Wood which was filed on April 24, 1774. Wood married Sarah Thurston on December 6, 1772. He lived in Haverhill at that time, and she was from Newbury. Whether this was Newbury, New Hampshire, Vermont, or Massachusetts is not known. Wood did not leave a will when he died in November 1773. Sarah, along with Jonathan Hale, also of Haverhill, were the administrators of the estate. They had to make an inventory of all the "Goods, Chattles, Rights and Credits" of the deceased and present it for the registry of the Court of Probate before the last Wednesday in July. This obligation is witnessed by Simeon Olcott. The inventory is provided on May 6 and includes his house and the meadow that he was buying from Moses Titcomb from Wenham, Massachusetts, a cow, two pair of oxen, wheat, and corn among all the household items. Sarah appears before Justice of the Peace John Hurd to swear that the list is correct on May 9 (*New Hampshire Wills and Probate Records*, 1643–1982, image 675). Much of the business at this time appears to be conducted with signed notes for whatever was bought or sold rather than cash. There are many of these small pieces of paper included in the probate records.

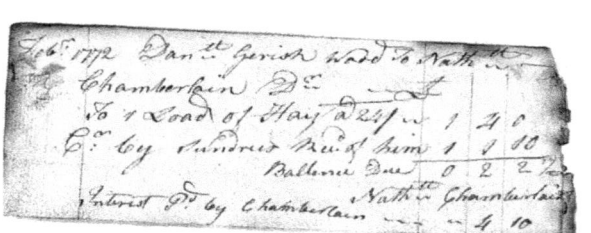

Signed note from Nathaniel Chamberlain to Daniel Gerrish Wood. 1772. Image #696. *Ancestry.com* 2021.

On July 19, Moses Titcomb signed a declaration that he had received payment for the meadow and the house lot and that the administrators were discharged from any obligation to him. This was signed and sealed in the presence of Asa Porter and Jona M. Sewall. The final document for this probate was not signed until November 1781.

The next document that comes to light is the probate for Captain John Hazen on October 22, 1774, which is again signed by Jona M. Sewall.

The last document signed by him in the records for Hazen, on November 4, has this lavishly rendered signature.

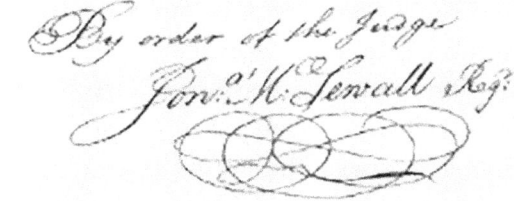

Signature from Grafton County Probate records 1774. (*NH Wills and Probate Records* 2020).

Marriage and Universalism

Ten days later, on November 14, Jonathan married Sarah Wood in Haverhill.

The population of Haverhill in 1775 was 365 (Whitcher 1919). It seems unlikely that there was another Sarah Wood there at the time.

The previous November Rev. John Murray had come to Portsmouth. He was from England and had been traveling along the eastern seacoast of New England since 1770. As a Calvinist Universalist, he preached that God is the father of all of mankind and that salvation is promised to everyone without fear of hell. It was not necessary to be in communion with one of the established churches. He caused quite a stir in Portsmouth because he was such a wonderful preacher, and his gospel message was so cheering to the people. He was made welcome by all the churches at that

Reverend John Murray. (Murray 1816).

time because his message had not completely split from the already established churches. He made it so clear that his views of religion were biblical that it was not easy for any clergyman to find him unacceptable.

The story most often told about Mr. Murray's time in Portsmouth was a visit he made to the home of Mr. Drown. The brick oven at the home was heated for baking and when it was opened Mr. Murray looked in and asked what they were going to cook. Mr. Drown replied that they were going to bake bread. Then Murray said he had been wondering if they had intended to bake the children. Mr. Drown was obviously horrified. Murray said that it would not be much worse for him to roast his little children, than for the "Infinite Father" to burn millions of unconverted souls. It is said that from that moment Mr. Drown rejected the doctrine of endless punishment (Craig 1966).

Before the Rev. Murray left Portsmouth, he had gathered a large number of followers who became the nucleus of the church. According to an address given on the centennial of the founding of the church, his congregation "embraces a considerable portion of the wealth, talent, culture and social influence of the town. Sewall the Poet [Lawyer], and [James] Sheafe the United States Senator, and Walden, and [Jeremiah] Libbey [Lawyer], and Blaisdell, and [Captain Peter] Coues, and Melchers and the brothers Simes and many other names prominent in the annals of that time, early associated themselves..." They asked him to stay but he felt that he needed to continue his missionary work. Eventually, he settled in Gloucester, Massachusetts, but was able to visit Portsmouth frequently (Patterson 1873).

Jonathan's poem "On Fanaticism; A Parody" ends:

> But should these methods all united fail,
> Take M_____ for thy model, and prevail.
> Snatch from his hand the scourge, defy all rules,
> Out-roar his roaring!! be the Fool of Fools!

War and Family

Of course, much was happening in all the American colonies during this time. New Hampshire sent Nathaniel Folsom and John Sullivan to the First Continental Congress in Philadelphia which met from September 5 to October 26, 1774. By the end of the meeting the delegates had decided to impose a boycott on British trade. They also wrote a petition to King George pleading with him to understand their grievances and to repeal the acts that were imposed on the Massachusetts Bay Colony after the Boston Tea Party.

The very first armed resistance to Great Britain took place in Portsmouth on December 14, 1774, a month after Jonathan and Sarah were married. There had been rumors that British troops from Boston were headed to reinforce Fort William and Mary on New Castle Island which was then a part of the town of Portsmouth. It was said that the troops were coming to take the gunpowder and arms that were stored in the fort because of the unrest in Boston after the Tea Party.

Four months before his more famous ride in Massachusetts, Paul Revere rode from Boston to Portsmouth to sound the alarm. On December 13 he rode the sixty-six miles into town and found Samuel Cutts, a local merchant whom he knew was a patriot. Cutts was able to convene the Committee of Correspondence so that Revere could explain what had been heard in Boston. Quickly the patriots from New Castle attempted to take the gunpowder from Fort William and Mary, but they were unsuccessful.

As this was happening John Langdon was making his way through Portsmouth with a drummer collecting a crowd to descend on the fort. About four hundred men set out on the Piscataqua River some in small boats while others marched through the snow to get to the Fort. They easily stormed the fort, which only had six British soldiers in its garrison, and took one hundred barrels of gunpowder that was stored there. The next day patriots led by John Sullivan again raided the fort and seized the rest of the powder, muskets, bayonets, cartouche boxes, and sixteen cannons. Everything they had taken was then dispersed through several New Hampshire towns to hide it from the British. The plan was that these supplies would be available for patriot troops if it came to war.

Soon after this happened Stephen Sewall was born to Jonathan and Sarah in Haverhill on January 1, 1775. Sarah surely must have remained there after their marriage. We know that the road from Haverhill through to Portsmouth was only just passable. It would have been a perilous trip for her as she was nearly eight months pregnant at the time of their marriage.

Jonathan resigned his job as register of probate to continue with his practice in Portsmouth and perhaps leave the scene of what must have been an embarrassing incident. How soon Sarah and the child were able to come to Portsmouth is not known. Jonathan was now twenty-seven years old and he had a wife and son to support.

1775

In May 1775 a cargo of timber for masts for the Royal Navy on the ship *Bochacheco* was seized. Edward Parry, the agent for John Durand who held the contract to provide the masts, was imprisoned. Governor John Wentworth also held the title of Surveyor General of the Woods, in charge of marking the tall white pines for use by King George for masts for the Royal Navy. The seizure of the ship was just weeks before the Wentworths fled their home on Pleasant Street. Parry was paroled to Portsmouth in June 1776 and in August he filed a suit in the Portsmouth Maritime Court, but the court found against him. It awarded the ship *Bochacheco* and its cargo of masts to the state to be sold at public auction (Walsh 1996, p. 141). In April 1777 the state paid Jonathan £9 for "libelling and prosecuting" the *Bochacheco*.

On June 13 Colonel John Fenton, whom Jonathan worked with in Grafton County, visited Governor and Mrs. Wentworth at their home in Portsmouth. He was a staunch Loyalist. A Portsmouth mob was enraged by his presence in town. In the words of Mrs. Wentworth, they "stove at the House with clubs, brought a large Cannon and placed it before the Door, and swore to fire through the house" (Frances Wentworth's letter from Fort William and Mary to Mary Wentworth-Woodhouse, June 24, 1775). Fenton surrendered. The Wentworths left the house that night and never returned to Portsmouth, or soon after to New Hampshire, for the rest of their lives. John Fenton was imprisoned and then released to leave for Great Britain.

What became known as the Battle of Bunker Hill took place in the middle of June in 1775. It was originally known as the Battle of Charlestown Heights. After the news of this battle reached Portsmouth, Jonathan wrote "A Poem, On the burning of Charlestown" in which he asks:

> Unhappy victims in the noblest cause!
> Was it too little, my brave country-men!
> But once to perish, spurning impious laws?
> Must ye be hack'd and butchered o'er again?

Congress appointed George Washington "General & Commander in chief of the army of the United Colonies and of all the forces raised or to be raised by them," and instructed him on June 22, 1775, to take charge of the siege of Boston. Jonathan wrote about this in a poem he composed in 1776:

> Thus the Grand Council of our land,
> The reas'ning power of state,
> Gave WASHINGTON supreme command,
> And made his edicts fate.

Another poem written in 1775 is his "Paraphrase of the 80th Psalm":

> Return, O God of hosts! return!
> Let thy fierce wrath no longer burn,
> But pity and forgive.
> Look down from heav'n, thy dwelling place,
> Vouchsafe one beam of heav'nly grace,
> That we may see and live.

War and Washington

It was after Washington arrived in Boston that Jonathan composed the words for the song entitled "War and Washington" that was sung through all the military camps during the Revolutionary War. As early as February 2, 1776 the words were printed in the *Massachusetts Spy*. The newspaper had recently moved to Worcester because of the situation in Boston where it had been published. Again, on February 24 the words were printed in the *Virginia Gazette*, a newspaper published in Williamsburg, Virginia.

It is interesting to look at some of the first-hand accounts about the poem being sung. For instance, on December 14, 1777, in the diary of Dr. Albigence Waldo, a surgeon at Valley Forge, he wrote "See the poor Soldier, when in health—with what cheerfulness he meets his foes and encounters every hardship—if barefoot—he labours thro' the Mud & Cold with a Song in his mouth extolling War & Washington—" (Waldo 1897).

A Narrative of Joshua Davis published in 1811 tells Davis's story as an American citizen who was captured and served on board of six ships of the British Navy. On his twenty-first birthday in 1781 he got some gin to celebrate the day and wrote: "Eight of us were confined together by the feet...I drank round to them, until the gin was gone; and feeling pretty merry, told them I would give them a song..." There are six verses to his song "Washington." He does not start with Jonathan's first verse which begins "Vain Britons," obviously for very good reasons. But his first three verses are nearly word for word from "War and Washington." "The song was overheard by the master at arms, who said to me, 'you d—d rascal, how dare you sing such a rebel song on board of his majesty's ship?'"

Broadsides of this poem were published over a number of years. The first one that we know of was printed in Salem where Jonathan was born. He visited Salem from Portsmouth on April 5, 1776. This is recorded in *William Pynchon's Diary* (Pynchon was Sewall's brother-in-law). But as the diary begins in 1776, Jonathan may have taken it there to be printed even earlier. This

A favorite Song at the Columbian Camp by Mr. Sewall of Portsmouth. Collection of the Massachusetts Historical Society.

broadside has the inscription, "A favorite Song at the Columbian Camp, in the late glorious and victorious struggle for LIBERTY. by Mr. Sewall of Portsmouth, Newhampshire." At the bottom is printed "Written when the British Army were besieged in Boston." The Columbian Camp refers to the American colonists' military camps. Jonathan often referred to America before the Revolution as Columbia.

Another verse from the song:

> Yet think not thirst of glory unsheaths our vengeful swords,
> To rend your bands asunder, or cast away your cords,
> 'Tis heaven-born freedom fires us all, and strengthens each brave son.
> From him who humbly guides the plough, to god-like Washington.

The New York Historical Society has a manuscript book with patriotic songs by a Henry Brown dated about 1789. It includes the tune for "The British Grenadiers" with the opening lines of "War and Washington."

The song is referred to in a book entitled *Questions d'hier et d'aujourd'hui* by Alphonse Gagnon that was published in 1913 in which he describes the poem as "dans le style pompeux" particular to that time. He translates the first verse beginning Vain Britons as "Orgueilleux Britons, ne vous vantez plus, dans un présomptueux dédain..."

In October 1775 the ship *Prince George* that had come from Bristol, England, to Boston came into Exeter harbor and was boarded by Lieutenant Thomas Pickering. The ship contained 1,892 barrels of flour for General Gage's army. The New Hampshire Committee of Safety wrote to George Washington, and he asked that the flour be sent to him for his army. The final decision was that 600 barrels be kept for Portsmouth because they were concerned that the British fleet might come into the harbor (New Hampshire Committee of Safety 1775). They brought the ship to Portsmouth and suggested that 100 barrels of flour be used to support the state's own soldiers and those who were helping with fortifications being erected on the harbor islands. They proposed to sell 500 barrels to the people of Portsmouth and save the money until they had directions from Congress. In November they petitioned the Provincial Congress for men and ammunition to defend Portsmouth (*New Hampshire State Papers*, v. 13, pp. 279–280). In April 1777 the state paid Jonathan £9 for "libelling [sic] and prosecuting" the *Prince George*.

1776

On January 5, 1776, the Congress of New Hampshire met in Exeter and voted to establish a civil government. They agreed on the manner and form that the government would have. In doing this New Hampshire became the first state to establish a government that was independent of England.

Jonathan continued writing his poetry and in the poem "On the gloomy prospects of 1776; Written with allusion to part of the 11th chapter of Job," he implored:

> Oh, then learn wisdom, much-enduring land!
> Implore thy God to stay his wasting hand!
> He'll not be deaf, if humbly thou prepare
> Thine heart, and stretch thine hands in fervent prayer,
> If in them wrath or wickedness be found,
> If fraud, extortion, violence, abound,
> Far, far remove them, let no guilty stain,
> The tabernacle of thy God profane.

His "A Song Written in 1776—in imitation of the 'Watry God,'" was published in the Boston newspaper *Independent Chronicle* on December 19, 1776. Later, it was reported as a song by the "gifted New Hampshire poet, Jonathan M. Sewall, Esq.," in which we find these lines:

> Michael! go forth! (the Godhead cry'd,)
> Wave thy dread Ensign o'er the Tide,
> And edge Columbia's Sword!

1777 Law and Grief

By 1777 Jonathan was well-established as a lawyer. His biographical note in the *Early State Papers of New Hampshire* (Batchellor 1893, p. 845) summarizes his work:

> As a lawyer he was distinguished for the clearness of
> his views, for honor and integrity. Tho' not deficient
> in his knowledge of the principles of law, he was more

indebted to his eloquence for his reputation as an advocate than to his legal science. In one particular sphere he was destined to shine with unrivalled honor. The humane and sensibilities of his feelings deplored the commission of crimes, but his pity and compassion induced him to defend the accused. This he did with great success, and of all the capital cases he advocated, and they were many, he never lost one. His efforts were ardent, but his principal fee was the gratitude of his clients.

On Wednesday, January 1, 1777 the *State Papers* record:

> Voted to choose a Committee to draw up & bring in a Bill for the Trial & punishment of Persons who shall by any misbehavior in word or deed be adjudged Enemical [opposed] to the Liberty & Freedom of the States of America (not within the Act against treason) and directing how such Trial shall be had, and how judgments thereon shall be executed, and that John Wentworth jun. Esq, Jonathan Mitchell Sewall, Esq., Samuel Gilman jun. & Col. Peabody, be the Committee for that purpose. (*New Hampshire State Papers, v. 8, p. 450*)

The record of "Accounts, petitions, bills, &c. passed on by the House and concurred by the Council, from Jan. 9th to 18th, 1777, Account of Jonathan M. Sewall for drawing Bills for the Assembly, pd. £8" (*New Hampshire State Papers*, v. 8, p. 541) show at least he accepted money from the state government.

On February 17, 1777, a second son was born in Portsmouth. The boy may have been stillborn or died soon after his birth. There is no record, and this could be because there are no official records for the Universalist Church in Portsmouth until the early 1800s. February 19, two days later, Sarah died. Jonathan's thirtieth birthday was in June that year. He was now a widower with his son, Stephen, who had just had his second birthday.

CHAPTER 7.

Poetry, Sarah March, State Papers, Black Petition

IN JONATHAN'S BOOK *MISCELLANEOUS POEMS*, PUBLISHED IN 1801, most of the poems appear to be arranged chronologically, with some slight variations possibly due to how they would fit on the page. There are many poems on an extremely wide variety of subjects written around 1777 and 1778. He continues to praise George Washington in his song "Shout, Shout America 1777":

> Still Union bind our land,
> Our councils Wisdom sway,
> Great WASHINGTON command
> And FREEDOM's Sons obey.
> Then Britain, Russia, Europe rise;
> Your rage untied we despise.
>
> We laugh at war's alarms,
> Its toils and arts we know;
> And how to wield our arms,
> And when to charge the foe.
> Fam'd Britain, in the trade complete,
> Excels us only in—retreat.

Other titles include the one about the death of his horse quoted in the last chapter along with "An Elegy on two female Steeds." Another is entitled "To S. S. Esq. on joining the American Army in 1777" and some are addressed to ladies. As a young, widowed lawyer with a two-year-old son, he needed a wife.

John Pickering's friend
Dr. Clement March of Greenland

The March family was an important family in Greenland, New Hampshire, in the early years of the state. Greenland was originally a parish of Portsmouth but became a separate town in 1706. From the center of Portsmouth, it is about five miles to the center of Greenland and even less to the March Farm, which is on the northern side of Greenland on the road to Portsmouth. Dr. Clement March was born in 1707 and became a physician. In 1739 he married Eleanor Veasey, and they had twelve children. Eleanor died in 1774 and Dr. Clement three years later at the age of seventy. He had served as a justice in the Superior Court and represented Greenland in the New Hampshire legislature for more than twenty years. He would have known Jonathan Mitchel Sewall, who studied and worked with his friend John Pickering. Jonathan would most certainly have known Dr. Clement March. His will is signed a few days before his death on May 25, 1777. It appears that he wrote most of the will much earlier and signed it on May 21 in the presence of his "trusty friends" John Pickering and Joseph Pierce.

Dr. March was a very wealthy man at the time of his death and one of New England's largest landowners. He left money, land, and all his possessions to each of his many children. He appointed John Pickering and Joseph Pierce to be overseers of his will. It begins, "In the Name of God. Amen. I, Clement March of Greenland in the County of Rockingham in the State of New Hampshire, Esq. being weak in Body, but of perfect sound mind and Memory thanks be given to God Do make and ordain this my last Will and Testament and first I commend my Soul to God hoping for eternal Life thru Jesus Christ..." The bequest for each child is specified and then Martha, Elizabeth, and Sarah are each to be given £50 within a year or two after his death. As long as they remain unmarried, they are allotted rooms in his house which he has left to one of his sons. The executors, who are his sons, are to have accommodation built for the unmarried girls on the farm. In addition, they were to have use of the barn, have a cow and the use of a horse kept by the executors. Dr. March's best side saddle was available for their use and was to become the property of the last daughter to be married. The three daughters are bequeathed most of the furniture in the house as well. Each of his children receive parcels of land throughout the state. Sarah and Elizabeth, the two youngest daughters, are given in "equal shares divided all my farm or Land in Allenstown so called in the State of New Hampshire containing about six hundred Acres" where the tenant Samuel Bow lives (*New Hampshire Wills and Probate Records*, images 1114-1117).

Sarah March was Clement and Eleanor's eighth and youngest daughter. In addition to her seven older sisters, she had two older brothers and two younger ones. Her sister Martha had died the same year as their mother in 1774. Her sister Elizabeth had married Captain John Salter in April 1777, the month before their father died. Elizabeth and John Salter lived near the corner of Washington and Court streets in Portsmouth. Their son John was born in January 1779 and died in March 1781. Their son Joseph March Salter was born in April 1781 and died in 1837. Elizabeth died in childbirth and her husband remarried on November 1, 1781.

So, it was Sarah March who inherited rooms in the house, use of the barn, a cow, and a horse. Four years later when her sister died, the saddle and all the land in Allenstown would have been hers too. By this time in his life Jonathan appears to have gained a reputation for drinking to treat his continuing "nervous affections." This year in particular he must have been quite disconsolate after the death of his wife and their baby. The story according to Jonathan's entry in *Bench and Bar of New Hampshire* (Bell 1894) is that "The lady who became his second wife, when remonstrated with on her engagement to a man of his habits, replied, "I would rather marry Mr. Sewall drunk than any other man sober." Sarah's mother's obituary states that "Her Temperance was such as must render the longest Life agreeable..." (*NH Gazette,* July 22, 1774). So, perhaps it is no wonder that people were concerned for Sarah. Jonathan must have known Sarah for some time because he had been working with her father's friend John Pickering for about seven years by then. Sometime, possibly the following year, Jonathan and Sarah were married. There is no official record.

State Papers

"Thursday Feb. 19th, 1778 Voted, That Jonathan Mitchell Sewall Esq by & hereby is chosen & appointed Attorney General for this State" (*New Hampshire State Papers,* v.8, p. 771). William Plumer adds in his biographical note about Jonathan that he "immediately declined the appointment. He said he had been so long a constant defender of the accused, and found so much satisfaction in that course, that he could not assume the character of a public accuser. In civil suits he promptly devoted his time and talents to aid the poor, the widow, the fatherless, and strangers, and that without the prospect or even hope of reward" (Batchellor 1893, p. 845). Was he too busy performing as well?

Epilogue to Cato; Written in 1778

On March 31, 1778, Jonathan's "Epilogue to Cato" was published in the *New Hampshire Gazette* with the note that it was "Spoken at a late Performance of that Tragedy." It was also reproduced in the Hartford *Connecticut Courant* and the Boston *Continental Journal and Weekly Advertiser* in April 1778.

The play about Cato for which Jonathan wrote his *Epilogue* was written in England in 1713 by Joseph Addison and was very popular in colonial America. One of the earliest presentations was at the New Theatre in Charleston, South Carolina, in November and December of 1735 (Willis 1924, pp. 29–30). It was particularly popular in the south and one of George Washington's favorite plays from which he often quoted.

Cato is a dramatization of the last days of the Roman Senator Marcus Porcius Cato (95–46 BCE). Addison felt that Cato was an excellent example of republican virtue and opposition to tyranny. When Caesar tells Cato that he will spare his life but not give him freedom, Cato declares that death is preferable to slavery. Cato held out against Caesar at Utica in Northern Africa and became friends with Juba, the king of the ancient region of Numidia there. Juba falls in love with Cato's daughter and in the final address Cato allows Marcia to marry Juba and says he considers Juba to be a brave and virtuous Roman.

On May 11, 1778, General George Washington defied a congressional ban on theatrical productions which had been enacted in 1774 to discourage "shews, plays, and other expensive diversions and entertainments." A production of Joseph Addison's tragedy *Cato* was performed for the entire company based at Valley Forge after the terrible winter there. Colonel William Bradford Jr. wrote to his sister from Valley Forge: "Last Monday *Cato* was performed before a very numerous & splendid audience." Jonathan's "Epilogue" equated Cato with Washington, Juba with Lafayette, and Caesar with King George. His epilogue was published before the performance at Valley Forge. Had the players seen his epilogue? If they had, surely, they would have used it for that performance. Some verses include these:

> Did Rome's brave senate nobly strive t'oppose
> The mighty torrent of domestic foes?
> And boldly arm the virtuous few, and dare
> The desp'rate perils of unequal war?
> Our senate too, the same bold deed has done,
> And for a Cato, arm'd a WASHINGTON!
> A chief in all the ways of battle skill'd,
> Thy scourge O Britain! and Columbia's boast,
> The dread, and admiration of each host!
> Whose martial arm, and steady soul, alone
> Have made thy legions quake, thy empire groan,
> And thy proud monarch tremble on his throne.

Just before the end of his epilogue Jonathan wrote this:

> Rise then, my countrymen! for fight prepare,
> Gird on your swords, and fearless rush to war!
> For your griev'd country nobly dare to die,
> And empty all your veins for Liberty.
> No pent-up Utica contracts your pow'rs,
> But the whole boundless continent is yours!

The final two lines in this stanza have been repeated by many people over the years throughout the country and have been quoted and misquoted innumerable times.

The New World was a weekly literary newspaper in New York published from 1839 to 1845. The paper was founded and edited by Park Benjamin Sr. and its masthead read: "No pent-up Utica contracts our powers: The whole unbounded Continent is ours!" changing "your powers" to "our powers," "boundless" to "unbounded," as well as "yours" at the end to "ours." Although it was not a word-for-word quotation, there is no doubt that it came from Jonathan's *Epilogue.*

Masthead of the *New World* newspaper. 1839–1845.

In the August 24, 1908, *Pittsburgh Post* there is an article about James S. Sherman who was the Republican nominee for vice-president and also belonged to the House of Representatives Gag Committee. Because he resided in Utica, New York "L. C. M." reports that "In past days about everybody has used the lines — times, more or less." He explains the lines and ends: "How rich the verses quoted are in suggestive material touching on and appertaining to Mr. Sherman must be left to others to discover. It may be that the people will pen him up in Utica, though he now protests suspiciously too much that he is heart and soul for Roosevelt's policies, which as a gagster he was an accomplice with Cannon Dalzell in defeating. Certainly the people will rule, and they know that 'No pent-up Utica' can long contract their powers when they rise up on their hind feet."

An article in the *Montgomery Advertiser* (Alabama) on June 22, 1911, is a column *Talks with Girls,* entitled "'No Pent-up Utica Contracts Your Powers.' - - J. M. Sewall" by Marie Bankhead Owen. She explains the origin of the quotation and about the story of Cato and then says, "In reading these lines, and recalling the sad story, the thought has occurred to me to speak to you today about the moral responsibility resting upon each of us to cheer the discouraged and to stir the ambition of those about us." She concludes: "Many a hero has been on the brink of despair and was saved to the world and great usefulness by the persuasive voice of some friend who cried: 'No pent-up Utica contracts your powers.' See if you can speak these words today."

General Frank W. Miller, the Centennial Historian for New Hampshire at the Philadelphia Exhibition, collected things from colonial times that could be found in the state. There was a call for articles to send to the exhibition in the *Portsmouth Journal of Literature and Politics* on Saturday April 29, 1876. Miller was going to send Daniel Fowle's old wooden and stone printing press that he himself owned and: "Gen. Miller has also the old arm chair in which Jonathan Mitchell Sewall, the Portsmouth poet of the Revolution, wrote the famous couplet. 'No pent-up Utica contracts your powers, but the whole boundless continent is yours.'" Where is that chair today?

Jonathan's entire "Epilogue to Cato" is reprinted in a wide variety of newspapers during the 1870s and '80s to celebrate one hundred years since the time when it was written. The excerpts come from "the whole boundless continent" and include the *Louisiana Democrat*, the *Wisconsin Republican*, *Jamestown Journal* (New York), the *True Flag* (Boston), and the *Sacramento Daily Union* among many others, as well as being reprinted in several New Hampshire newspapers.

The Petition of Nero Brewster and friends

Perhaps writing and thinking about Cato convinced Jonathan that as a lawyer he could be trying to help the enslaved people of Portsmouth. Cato had declared that death was preferable to slavery, and he had also decided that the Black King Juba was a brave and virtuous Roman whom he had no objection to marrying his daughter Marcia.

As noted previously, Jonathan was studying with his cousin Jonathan Sewall in Cambridge when Sewall managed to procure the freedom of two enslaved people in Margaret vs. Muzzy in 1768 and James vs. Lechmere in 1769. A few years earlier, his cousin David Sewall of Wells, Maine, who studied law in Portsmouth, and met both of his wives there, "brought down the resolve which passed the House yesterday, forbidding the sale of two negroes..." (Massachusetts 1919-1990, Sept. 14, 1776). The article shown here is from the *New Hampshire Gazette* in May 1774. It tells the story of a Negro slave who had run away and said that he had "obtained the opinion of David Sewall, Esq. respecting Slaves which he calls a Pass, and often shews to People as such." Years before Jonathan was born, his famous great-uncle Samuel Sewall wrote the earliest protest against slavery published in colonial America. It was entitled *The Selling of Joseph: A Memorial* and was printed in 1700.

RAN away from his Master Benjamin Littlefield of Wells, a NEGRO SERVANT called POMPEY. Had on when he went away, a short Jacket, a pair of Moose Skin Breeches ; he says he was baptized in London, and that he is become a Free Negro, having obtained the Opinion of David Sewall, Esq; respecting Slaves, which he calls a Pass, and often shews to People as such. Masters of Vessels and others are cautioned not to entertain him or carry him off. And any Person who shall apprehend the said Pompey, and return him to his said Master, or commit him to his Majesty's Goal in York, or any other of his Majesty's Goals, and notify his said Master thereof, so that he may obtain said Negro again, shall have two Dollars Reward, and all necessary Charges paid by   BENJAMIN LITTLEFIELD:
Wells, May 5th. 1774.

Ad for capture of Pompey, a Negro Servant. *NH Gazette,* May 20, 1774. GenealogyBank 2021.

Before the petition was written Jonathan had denounced slavery in some of his poems. "On the gloomy prospects of 1776: Written with allusion to part of the 11th chapter of Job" includes this couplet:

> Then faith shall triumph, envy rave in vain,
> Oppression tremble, slavery drop her chain,

In "A Song written in 1776—in imitation of the 'Watry God'" he writes:

> To burst vile slavery's iron band,
> Guard sacred freedom, save your land,

During 1779 a group of enslaved Negroes in Portsmouth wrote a petition asking for their freedom. Several similar petitions had been written and submitted in Boston in previous years. Valerie Cunningham writes about the Portsmouth petition that "The document is an eloquent, respectful, yet earnest plea to legislators to 'restore us that state of liberty of which we have been so long deprived'" (Cunningham 2003).

"In New Hampshire what became known as 'the petition of Nero Brewster and others,' addressed on November 12, 1779, to the 'Council and House of Representatives…now sit[t]ing at Exeter,' was not read and considered until April 25 the following spring. At this time arrangements were made for 'the Petitioners [to] be heard thereon before the General Assembly' on June 9" (Dishman 2010, p. 77). When the legislature met on June 9, the petition was "read, Considered and Argued by Counsel on behalf of the Petitioners" (*New Hampshire State Papers*, v.8, p. 861). One thing that was needed, that the petitioners themselves could not do, was someone to present it in court. No record can be found detailing what arguments were used or who presented the petition for Nero Brewster and his friends.

Dishman makes the case that a lawyer was needed to present the petition and he needed to be one who would "plead the case with passion and conviction, and preferably one who would give his services *pro bono publico.*" Dishman believed that person was Jonathan Mitchel Sewall for some of the previously stated and following reasons.

Jonathan was an established lawyer in Portsmouth by 1779, and he was known to speak and write eloquently and to give his services for free. Both he and John Pickering were known for not charging for their services. One of Jonathan's obituaries states: "The widow, the fatherless, and the stranger, also found in his talents a never-failing resource; for without even the hope of reward, he devoted his great abilities to their service" (*The Literary Mirror,* April 16, 1808).

There were two other lawyers who were possible candidates for helping with the petition who were senior members of the New Hampshire bar at the time. William Parker had represented three "freedom suit" litigants in the 1740s, but by 1775, Judge Parker was confined to his home and no longer taking part in politics. He was the father of Jonathan's cousin David Sewall's wife, Mary.

Jonathan's mentor, John Pickering, although also known for never refusing aid to someone if they could not afford it, was not known for his literary skills or his eloquence (Belknap 1637–1891).

If the enslaved people needed help stating their case as well as defending it, Jonathan would have been able to do both. The men had the Boston petitions of 1773, 1774, and 1777 as models for their petition. Otis Hammond wrote in the *Granite Monthly* in 1880 that some of the wording is similar but the New Hampshire petition was more sophisticated in its "organization and rhetoric, its compelling expression of libertarian concept, its relatively standard orthography, and its professional quality penmanship." He had studied the handwriting in the old papers at the State House but had been unable to decide whose it might be. The Portsmouth Athenaeum holds a manuscript book written by Jonathan and there are copies of various petitions that he wrote. The handwriting is very similar but there are a number of differences that indicate that the "professional quality penmanship" was probably not his.

A few things that happened later continue to indicate Jonathan's feelings about slavery. In 1788, he delivered one of his many Fourth of July orations in Portsmouth. The final section is delivered in verse and contains the lines,

> Oh! Stretch thy reign,
> fair Peace from shore to shore,

Till conquest cease,

and slav'ry be no more.

At the time that Daniel Fowle's enslaved pressman Primus died in 1791, Jonathan wrote an epitaph for Primus. If Jonathan's own reputation for "the cheerful dram" was not known, this might not seem respectful. If you do know it, it sounds like he was a friend and he himself may be the "neighbour."

> Epitaph on the Death of PRIMUS.
>
> UNDER thefe clods, old *Primus* lies
>   At reft and free from noife,
> No longer feen by mortal eyes
>   Or griev'd by roguifh boys ;
> The cheerful *dram* he lov'd 'tis true
>   Which haftened on his end.
> But *fome* in *paved*-ftreet well knew
>   He was a *hearty* friend,
> And did poffefs a grateful mind
>   Though oft borne down with pain,
> Yet where he found a neighbour kind
>   He furely went again ;
> Too often did the mirth of fome
>   His innocence betray,
> By giving larger draughts of rum
>   Than he could *fwill* away,
> But now he's dead, we fure may fay
>   Of him, as of all men,
> That while in filent graves they lay
>   They'l not be *plagu'd* 'agen.

"Epitaph for Primus." *NH Gazette*, May 26, 1791. *GenealogyBank* 2019.

CHAPTER 8.

Family, Work, Home, and Entertainment

Attorney Generals

On Thursday, February 19, 1778, it was recorded in the *Journal of the House* that "Voted That Jonathan Mitchell Sewall Esq by & hereby is chosen & appointed Attorney General for this State" (*New Hampshire State Papers*, v. 8, p. 798).

In Jonathan's biographical note, William Plumer wrote: "On the 19th February 1778, he was appointed attorney of the state, but immediately declined the appointment. He said he had been so long a constant defender of the accused, and found so much satisfaction in that course, that he could not assume the character of a *public accuser.*" Back in 1767 his cousin and law teacher, Jonathan Sewall of Boston, became Attorney General of Massachusetts and remained so until he fled the country in 1776. This decision was an intriguing one for anyone to turn down such a high office in the state government.

Children Born and Mourned

Jonathan and Sarah's first child was born on May 3, 1779. The boy, named Jonathan Mitchel Sewall, was baptized privately on May 19 by Samuel Parker. A private baptism was usually performed at home when a child was near death. There are no further records for this child. Parker was born in Portsmouth and taught school there until he was called to the ministry and became rector of Trinity Church in Boston in 1774. Sometime later he was appointed the bishop of Massachusetts. His father was the Portsmouth lawyer and judge William Parker. It was

Samuel Parker's sister Mary who was married to Jonathan's cousin David Sewall. Perhaps other members of the family were there for the baptism. Tragically Jonathan's brother Stephen and his wife Nabby, who lived near Salem where the brothers were born, also had a baby that was baptized the previous month on April 11. This boy was named Jonathan Mitchel Sewall too, and there are no further records for him either.

The "Scituation" in Portsmouth

At a Portsmouth Town meeting on June 13, 1780, "The Freeholders & Inhabitants of the Town...taking into consideration the very large and disproportionate Tax laid on them by Government, for the present Year, and being fully Conscious of their utter Inability to discharge it, beg leave to lay before your honors a true State of their Present unhappy Scituation, and leave it with your honors to Judge how, & in what manner you can best Alleviate & redress their sufferings." They enumerated the losses to shipping and trade and the depreciation of the currency. One of their examples was that "Many suffered extremely & some were ruin'd by the Regulating Act—Vast quantities of Rum & other Merchandise were sold at the Stipulated Prices," while in a month or two afterwards, five times the sum would not replace the same articles. "These, and many other causes which it would be tedious to mention, have reduc'd this once flourishing Town,—to its Present low & distress'd Scituation—A Scituation—more deplorable than that of any Sea-Port Town on the Continent, that has not been Actually in the hands of the Enemy—Multitudes are reduced from easy Circumstances, to want & beggary, and half the Inhabitants at least have frequently been without Bread or Fuel—" The report was accepted and it was voted that "John Pickering & J. M. Sewall Esq be a Committee to enforce the same at the General Court in behalf of the Town."

Although the first battle of the War for Independence may have been fought in Portsmouth, that was the last battle in the town as well as in most of the state. However, the war obviously had serious effects on the people, and they were very much involved in the war effort in many ways besides joining up to fight:

> During the Revolutionary war, Dr. Haven, [minister of the South Parish from 1752 until his death in 1806] was a genuine "son of liberty," giving the whole weight of his character, influence and exertion to the American cause. When the news of the battle of Lexington reached Portsmouth, he sat up a good part of the night with his family making bullets. And when, in the course of the next year, an alarm was given in the night that the enemy were approaching, he shouldered his fowling piece, and went with his parishioners to share in the toils and dangers to which they might be exposed. (Brewster 1869, p. 324)

Family and Home

In September of 1780 Sarah Sewall gave birth to their son John Barnard. Stephen, Jonathan's son by his first wife, was five years old when his brother was born. Stephen had obviously been named for Jonathan's uncle Stephen with whom he lived early in his life. His grandfather was also named Stephen. John Barnard may have been named for a friend of his uncle Stephen. John Barnard was his uncle Stephen's tutor at the North End Latin School in Boston, and they had remained friends through the years. He died a few years before Jonathan's uncle during the time that Jonathan and his brother were living in Boston and attending the Boston Public Latin School.

Now that the family included two children, where did they live? The "bill for confiscating the Estates of sundry persons" would have included that of John Fisher. When Governor John Wentworth's sister Anna married John Fisher, their father Mark Hunking Wentworth gave her the house on Pleasant Street that is now Wentworth Senior Living. At the time that the last colonial governor John and his wife Frances Wentworth moved into the house, John Fisher had taken a post in Salem, Massachusetts, and the house was rented to the New Hampshire Assembly for the new governor.

It was from this house that the Wentworths fled at the beginning of the hostilities. After they left the house, it was used as a barracks for the militia for a short time. Even a small room in the house was used as a prison for some of the Loyalists. When the war began John and Anna Wentworth Fisher left New Hampshire on the *Scarborough* man-of-war with her brother and his wife. John Fisher was named in the Proscription Act of 1778 but not in the Confiscation Act, so he was banished from the state, but his property, including this house, was not taken. Nine years later an advertisement appeared in the *New Hampshire Gazette* on three occasions in February and March of 1787. The properties mentioned are all those of John Fisher and although they were not sold at that time, it shows that the Sewalls were living in this "Mansion-House" then. When the Sewall family moved into it is not known, but it could have been as early as 1778, when the Fishers left for England.

> TO BE SOLD,
> The late Manfion-Houfe of Governour Wentworth, with the Stable and appurtenances, now in the occupation of Jonathan M. Sewall Efq. alfo, the late elegant Manfion Houfe of Nathaniel Adams, Efq. deceafed, with its appurtenances, now in the occupation of Richard Champney, Efq. alfo, the Houfe & land adjoining north of the laft mentioned premifes, now in the occupation of Mr. James Greward.
> Apply to JOHN PEIRCE.
> Portfmouth, February 13, 1787.

Governor Wentworth's Mansion House to be Sold. *NH Gazette*, March 3, 1787. *GenealogyBank* 2020.

On Tuesday, November 3, 1778, it was recorded in the *Journal of the House* that "Voted, That the Committee appointed in May last together with Mr. John Smith & Jonathan Mitchell Sewell [sic], Esq. with such as the honourable board shall join to be a Committee to Draft & bring in a bill for confiscating the Estates of sundry persons therein to be named, and lay the same before this House" (*New Hampshire State Papers*, v. 8, p 798). Did Jonathan get to choose from the properties?

In June 1781, one of his petitions to the state was for Mary Traill, whose husband was a Loyalist and had fled to Bermuda.

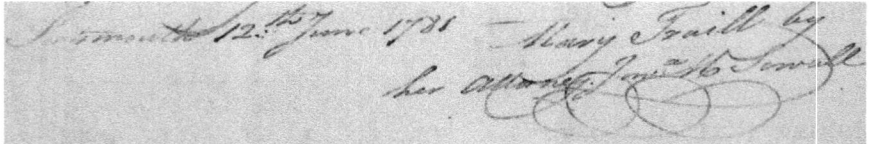

Mary Traill petition 6/12/1781. Courtesy of the New Hampshire Division of Archives and Records Management.

She wanted to join him but also to be able to return to Portsmouth to visit her family. She was the sister of William Whipple who was one of the signers of the Declaration of Independence for New Hampshire.

In 1780 the Universalist Church congregation moved to the recently vacated Sandemanian meeting-house on Pleasant Street near the corner of Richmond Street quite close to this "Mansion-House." Charles Brewster writes in his *Rambles* (1st series, p. 321) that "It was a story and a half building, occupying half as much again ground as the barn now does. It had no pews but was provided with seats. I have heard Noah Parker preach there and seen J. M. Sewall scattering the hymns of his own composition among the audience." The society had grown in strength and numbers and the parish was firmly established. It worshipped at this meeting house on Pleasant Street until 1784, when it built a new and larger place on the west side of Vaughan Street not far from the corner of Congress Street (Craig 1966). So, it is possible that Jonathan and Sarah and the boys lived almost across the street from the home of the Universalist Church at that time. It would have been very easy to go over there and scatter your own hymns on the seats before others arrived.

Constitutional Conventions and Diversions

During the early 1780s Jonathan was deeply involved in New Hampshire's attempt to write a constitution and bill of rights that would be acceptable to the people. The original "Plan of Government" had been drawn up by the state when its representatives signed the Declaration of Independence. This plan had only been enacted for the duration of the fighting with England. The war was finally coming to an end, and something needed to be done urgently. An attempt had been made to write and enact a constitution in 1778, but it was unsuccessful.

On March 28, 1781, the House of Representatives voted to call another convention to "settle a Form of Government." A committee was appointed "to join a Committee of the Board, to form and issue a suitable Precept to the towns, for that purpose; which vote was concurred by the Board on the 6th of April, 1781, a joint resolve was adopted that the said Convention should meet at Concord, the first Tuesday of June, next" (*New Hampshire State Papers*, v.9, p. 842). On May 26, 1834, an article appeared in the *New Hampshire Patriot and State Gazette* asking for information from anyone "especially the family of J. M. Sewall, Esq. of Portsmouth who was the Secretary" because the journal of that convention had not been found. Fortunately, according to the *State Papers*, a Mr. G. Parker Lyon had a list of delegates which was presumed to be correct. Also, it was found that in 1845 when Daniel Lancaster wrote the *History of Gilmanton*, he had the information and included the names of the delegates. Those from Portsmouth were George King Atkinson, who was married to Jonathan's cousin Susanna; John Langdon, who became president/governor of New Hampshire; Dr. Ammi Ruhamah Cutter, an eminent local physician; John Pickering, Jonathan's mentor, friend, and colleague; and Jona. Mitchell Sewall (*New Hampshire State Papers*, v.9, p. 842).

George Atkinson was president of this June 1781 convention, and Jonathan was the secretary. Jeremy Belknap, who lived in Dover for twenty years as minister of the town's First Church, wrote in a letter to his friend Ebenezer Hazard in 1781: "The *hen* sat once, she was not so large, not so speckled as

---

THE SECOND CONSTITUTIONAL CONVENTION.

NOTE.

On the 28th of March, 1781, the House of Representatives voted to call another Convention to "settle a Form of Government," and that a Committee be appointed, to join a Committee of the Board, to form and issue a suitable Precept to the towns, for that purpose; which vote was concurred by the Board; and on the 6th of April, 1781, a joint Resolve was adopted that the said Convention should meet at Concord, the first Tuesday of June, next (1).

The Journal of that Convention has not been found; but fortunately the late Mr. G. Parker Lyon obtained a list of Delegates, which is presumed to be correct: (see N. H. Reg. 1852, pp. 22-25). The names of the Delegates chosen are as follows:

Towns.	*Delegates.*
Portsmouth,	George Atkinson
"	John Langdon
"	Ammi Ruhami Cutter
"	John Pickering
"	Jona. Mitchell Sewall

Second Constitutional Convention. *New Hampshire State Papers*, Vol. 9, p. 842.

heretofore. There is a prospect of something being not only laid, but hatched, that will be clever in itself. Whether it will suit the taste of the people is uncertain" (Belknap 1637–1891, fifth series ser. 2, p. 103). John Pickering and Jonathan were appointed to prepare a draft. The "Form of Government" was to be prepared by John Pickering and Jonathan's job was to draft a Bill of Rights (Lancaster 1845, p. 101).

Despite this job and his own work as a lawyer, in January 1782, Jonathan had time to visit his family in Massachusetts for a few days, at first staying with his half-sister Catherine and her husband William Pynchon. Jonathan spent the evening of the fifth with his half-sister Mary, her husband, Nathan Goodale, and their children. The next day he had tea with William Wetmore, who was his niece Catherine's husband. Tragically, she had died at the age of twenty-four in 1778, just a year and a half after their marriage. Jonathan then went to visit his brother Stephen and his wife Nabby who lived in Marblehead which is just a few miles away, and he stayed with them. On the ninth they all came to Salem to dine at the Pynchons. "We spend a very merry evening at Mr. Goodale's and have musick and diversions the whole evening" (Oliver 1890, pp. 113–4).

By the spring of 1782, Pickering and Jonathan had produced their drafts. Pickering's constitution was based on the one which had been passed in Massachusetts the previous year, which was the work of John Adams. Robert Dishman writes: "For his role Sewall deserved more credit than he has so far received because New Hampshire's Bill of Rights is more simply and less repetitively written than Massachusetts's" (Dishman 2010, p. 82). The draft included a lengthy address to "Friends and Fellow Citizens" which was also most likely compiled by the two of them. It went out to the town meetings for ratification, but the constitution was overwhelmingly rejected.

By August 1782, they had redrafted it and resubmitted it to the town meetings. Jeremy Belknap wrote to his friend again: "Our hen has laid again…We have a constitution as often as we have an almanac, and the more we have the worse" (Belknap

1637–1891, fifth series ser. 2, p. 161). In order to vote for this draft one way or the other, the House required an oath of allegiance from the voters in their town meetings and many refused to sign it, so not enough people voted.

This must have been very frustrating for Jonathan and Pickering as well as all the members of the Constitutional Convention. Early in December Jonathan made another family visit to Salem and this time he took his seven-year-old son Stephen with him. Pynchon describes Stephen as "a sweet youth." According to Pynchon, on the ninth, a cloudy and extremely cold day, Jonathan visited the club held at Mr. Goodale's "and shews [Samuel] Johnson to be wrong as to his criticism on Addison's simile of the Angel." One of Jonathan's "Profiles of Eminent Men" (each line must begin with a letter from the person's name) includes Johnson:

> **J**ust, yet despotic, deck'd with awful rays,
> **O**'er the vast realm of wit proud Johnson sways,
> **H**is will the law, his dictates absolute,
> **N**or dares the haughtiest slave his nod dispute.
> **S**tern monarch! tho' thy greatness all revere,
> **O**ld time, at last, shall pluck thee from thy sphere,
> **N**o throne can e'er be stable, built on fear.
> (Sewall 1801, p. 265)

Samuel Johnson wrote the *Lives of the English Poets* between 1779 and 1781, and they were published in the English literary and society journal the *Tatler*. The club Pynchon mentions was composed of the leading professional men of Salem who met in one another's homes to discuss literary and philosophical subjects. Even though there appeared to be little time to think about poetry, it was obviously never far from Jonathan's mind, and he seems to have impressed his brother-in-law (Oliver 1890, pp. 138–9).

The third draft of the constitution was the same as the one that had been submitted in August but did not require the voters to take an oath of allegiance. It was sent out in the spring of 1783, and when the convention met in June, they realized that they needed to make further amendments, but it was finally accepted by the requisite number of towns. When the convention met again at Concord on October 31 that year, Nathaniel Folsom was president in the absence of Atkinson, and Jonathan continued as the secretary. It was declared that "The Returns from the several towns being examined, and appearing that the foregoing Bill of Rights and Form of Government, were approved by the People; the same are hereby agreed on and established by the Delegates of the People and declared to be the Civil Constitution for the State of New-Hampshire to take place on the first Wednesday of June 1784." This is signed by Folsom and attested to by J. M. Sewall, Secretary (*New Hampshire State Papers*, v. 9, pp. 918–9).

The Bill of Rights and Slavery

Perhaps Jonathan felt that the passing of his bill of rights did once and for all free the enslaved people when he wrote: "All men are born equally free and independent" (Article 1) and "All men have certain natural, essential, and inherent rights; among which are—the enjoying and defending life and liberty—and in a word, of seeking and obtaining happiness" (Article 2). In the *State Papers* a note from Otis G. Hammond, the editor, "respectfully submits the opinion, that the first and second Articles in this Bill of Rights virtually, and in effect, abolished slavery as it existed in New Hampshire" (pp. 896–7). The editor goes on to give various reasons, but some argued that it only freed those who were born after the constitution became law. Nathaniel Bouton in his *History of Concord* (1856, p. 253) states that "The adoption of the State Constitution was regarded as abolishing slavery within the State." Some of the Black petitioners were freed during this time, but others waited another fifteen or twenty years and a few waited for sixty years, and a very few died as enslaved people (Sammons and Cunningham 2004, pp. 65–6).

Nervous Affections and a Daughter in 1785

During the year of 1785 Jonathan visited his family in Salem on several occasions, and according to his brother-in-law, when he arrived in February he was "deeply disordered." He came again in March and was well enough to attend another meeting of the Social Library but he "sets out for Portsmouth without notice" a few days later.

On October 22, Caroline Storer Sewall was born. She was most likely given the name Storer for a close relation to her mother. Sarah's sister Hannah had married Joseph Storer of Kennebunk, Maine, in 1753. Joseph died in 1777 at the Battle of Saratoga. They had two sons, Joseph and Clement who were Sarah's nephews. Clement studied medicine in Portsmouth and married Dorothy Cutter, the daughter of Dr. Ammi Ruhamah Cutter. Clement and Dorothy did not have any children of their own and were most likely close friends with the Sewalls. Clement even might have been their physician.

Sadly, we read in William Pynchon's diary for December 21, "Brother Mitchell comes in the Portsmouth stage; a dark cloud over his visage; at evening he goes to Mr. Goodale's to lodge." On the thirty-first "I called in at Mr. Goodale's; Mitchell was gone forth to musick." It is not until Friday, January 13 that he set off for Portsmouth with someone Pynchon refers to as his "servant." Did they send someone from Portsmouth to bring him home? It is possible that during this time he composed some of his "Profiles of Eminent Men" that are included in his *Miscellaneous Poems* book. He writes that they were "produced while the Author was confined by sickness, laboring under the worst of maladies, nervous affections. As his own physician he prescribed the task, to divert his attention from himself." He also continues to write his poetic rendition of Ossian and his "sketch" for him is:

> **O** Bard divine! to thee each grace was giv'n,
> **S**elf-taught, or like great Homer, taught by Heav'n,
> **S**ublimely tow'ring, soars thy lofty song,
> **I**mpassion'd, tender, nervous, bold, and strong.
> **A**pplauding bards shall deify thy lays,
> **N**or fail to crown thee with eternal praise.

Obviously, his wife and young family spent over three weeks without him. If he was ill, this may have been for the best. Fortunately, Sarah not only had friends like the Storers, but she had many brothers and sisters who lived locally. Her nephew George Weeks, one of the children of her eldest sister Eleanor, even left money in his will to Jonathan and Sarah's daughters.

During the rest of 1786 Jonathan visited Salem again in March, July, and November, but Pynchon makes no mention of Jonathan being disturbed. When he was there for a few days in November Jonathan went to Boston and when he returned on the eleventh, he dined that evening at the Pynchon's with Mr. Goodale and their cousin David, then Judge Sewall of York, Maine, justice of the Superior Court of Massachusetts.

Theater in Portsmouth

In the following year the theater returned to Portsmouth. "Let him be Caesar!" an article by Michael Dobson, gives an interesting look at the theater in colonial America. He says, "The War of Independence ended British imperial control over these violent and unpredictable territories, but it did not evict Shakespeare from them, despite the fact that one of the things the Puritan Pilgrim Fathers had emigrated from England to escape was Shakespearean theatre." British military authorities had taken over the John Street Theatre in New York during the war and staged various plays between 1777 and 1783, but "their local enemies were already getting in on the act. The rebels mounted *Coriolanus* at Portsmouth, New Hampshire in 1778." Jonathan's "Epilogue to Coriolanus" is also among his 1777 and 1778 poems.

Various reference books on the history of theater in Portsmouth state that there was no theater during the war until 1787, and then only after the building of the Bow Street Theatre in 1791. But some of the "Gentlemen of Portsmouth" were obviously putting on quite serious plays much earlier. *Cato* and *Coriolanus* appear to have been staged in 1778. The Assembly House in Vaughan Street was built in 1771 and some of the taverns had large rooms where people could congregate for musical and dramatic productions.

George Washington commented on the beauty of the Assembly House when he visited Portsmouth in 1789. Mrs. Ichabod Goodwin described it in 1870 when she was the wife of the governor at the time:

> The house was of wood, large, long, and painted white. There were on the lower floor three great parlors, a kitchen, and an immense hall and staircase. This hall ran through the house and opened upon a garden, decorated by a summer-house, octagon in shape, of two stories, with large glass windows. The assembly-room took the whole front of the second story, and was about sixty by thirty feet, with large windows and an orchestra over the entrance. Back of it were two dressing-rooms. (Ellis 1899)

Portsmouth certainly had a venue for the performance of Addison's *Cato* and Shakespeare's *Coriolanus*. Another of Jonathan's poems is "Verses Written in a Summer-House"*:*

> ....still the *sick mind* no consolation knows,
> But nourishes in secret, cureless woes.
>   So when th' unhappy parents of mankind,
> By bold transgression lost sweet peace of mind,
> Each whisp'ring zephyr fill'd them with alarms,
> And paradise itself lost all its charms;
> Till heav'n, in pity, doom'd them each to toil
> In rougher regions, and a fitter soil.

Jonathan wrote a "Prologue to Portsmouth Plays" in 1787 when another season of plays was staged in Portsmouth. The "Prologue" begins:

> What various ways has man's poor fancy wrought
> To ease him of that painful burthen—*Thought*?

> Cards, dice, and wine, the coffee-house, the inn,
> And tea, and scandal, fill the tedious scene.
> "Midst such dull vanities, what praise is due
> To him who brought the DRAMA first to view?
> Taught strains of heav'nly eloquence to roll,
> And wak'd up ev'ry passion of the soul;
> Call'd from the murderer's eye a tender show'r,
> And sighs from flint that never felt before.
> Made dulness' self to feel the players rage,
> Or unextinguish'd laughter shake the stage.
> Feelings! which give proud atheism the lie,
> And prove the spirit's IMMORTALITY!

The General Court was in session in Portsmouth, beginning January 23 and most of the members were present at the theater (Sewall 1801, p. 131). The final verse of the Prologue is directed at them:

> Oh, might th' illustrious *House* their vote confer,
> Pass ev'ry act tonight, without demur,
> And the *fair Senate* happily concur.
> Back'd by your suffrage, we'd the stage assert,
> With grateful pride the gen'rous *bill* report,
> And quote your *Statutes* in each *critic's court*!

April 5 was the final night of the theater season in 1787. An article about it was published in the *Essex Journal and New Hampshire Packet* a few weeks later (April 25, 1787):

> Several Gentlemen of Portsmouth in New-Hampshire, associated in company for the purpose of entertaining the inhabitants in the evenings of the past Winter, with Theatrical Amusements—in this is said they succeeded to admiration—but what redounds more to their honor is, the money which was raised by the sale of tickets, they have generously given for the benefit of the poor. The evening of the 5th inst. The West-Indian, A Comedy, was brought on the

Stage, which was the last for the present season, and concluded with the following valedictory EPILOGUE,
>Written and spoken by
>Jonathan M. Sewall, Esquire

To soothe the rigors of th' inclement year,
From stern-ey'd winter force th' unwilling tear,
To pour gay humour forth in copious tides,
While unresisting laughter holds your sides;
Arrest the precious drops from pity's eye,
Or from the tender virgin steal the sigh;
The tragic, comic, muse (instructors sage!)
Have with alternate beauties grac'd this stage.

Now the gay season checks this new delight,
And other scenes, and other sports, invite.
Nature, a lovelier carpet soon will spread,
The glowing heav'ns a brighter splendor shed,
Blossoms, and fruits, and flowers, their sweets display,
The feather'd songsters crowd each leafy spray,
In strains sincere, repeat more artless loves,
While boundless music fills the echoing groves.

Jonathan's "Epilogue" continues with allusions to each one of the season's plays, a fitting conclusion to this Portsmouth season.

CHAPTER 9.

Ratification, Celebration, Home, and Theater

Ratification of the United States Constitution

The United States Constitution had finally been agreed upon by the Federal Convention on September 17, 1787. After a brief debate in Congress, it was submitted to the thirteen states. A requirement in Article VII stated that at least nine states had to ratify it for the new Constitution to become law. The *New Hampshire Spy* printed it on September 29. It appeared in the *New Hampshire Mercury* on October 4 and the *New Hampshire Gazette* on October 6. The state's ratifying convention met at Exeter on February 13, 1788, one week after it had been ratified in Massachusetts. Many people in the state thought that New Hampshire would be the next state to approve it, but it did not work out like that. South Carolina became the eighth state to agree. Both New York and Virginia as well as New Hampshire had conventions that were meeting in June. New Hampshire finally ratified the Constitution at a convention held in Concord on June 21. New Hampshire had become the ninth and necessary state for it to become the law of the land.

There were many celebrations in all parts of the state, but they culminated in a grand celebration in Portsmouth on Thursday, June 26. The *New Hampshire Gazette* begins its coverage with this wonderful cartoon and states "whereby we have, in effect, laid the top stone to the grand FEDERAL EDIFICE, and happily raised the NINTH pillar." It was on Sunday when the people of Portsmouth heard what had happened and public thanks was given in all the churches. Then the first of the celebrations began on Monday when New Hampshire President John Langdon arrived back in town. Bells rang out and citizens paraded the streets with music. Colonel Wentworth's corps of independent horse, Captain Woodward's company of artillery, Colonel Hill's company of foot, along with a large number of gentlemen in carriages and on horseback met Langdon at Greenland and paraded from there into the town, where he was honored by a federal salute. "What added greatly to the brilliancy of the scene was the appearance of a great number of ladies, whose smiling countenances bespoke that congeniality of sentiment, which ever ought to subsist between the sons and daughters of Adam" (*NH Gazette*, June 26, 1788). Could this be Jonathan's writing?

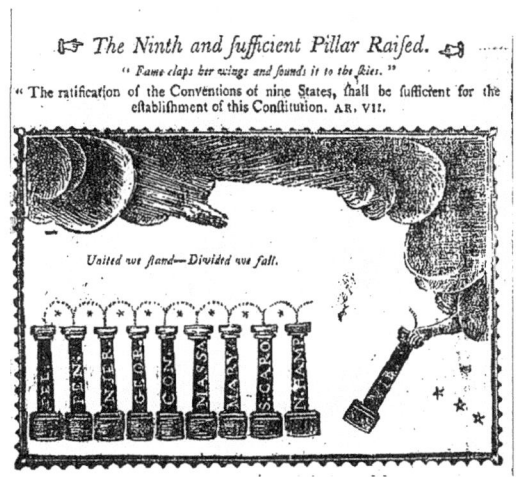

Ratification cartoon. *NH Gazette*, June 26, 1788. *GenealogyBank* 2020.

Thursday had been appointed as the date for special celebration and people from Portsmouth and the surrounding towns assembled on the Parade in the center of town about 11 in the morning. The procession soon began with a musical band in an open coach with six decorated horses. This was followed by all the separate trades in great numbers with "Printers, preceded by two lads with open quires of printed paper, followed with Cases and Apparatus decorated, Compositors at work; Pressmen, with Mr. Benjamin Dearborn's new invented Print-Press employed during the whole procession, in striking off and distributing among the surrounding multitude, songs in celebration of the ratification of the Federal Constitution by the State of New-Hampshire." The list of tradesmen goes on and on and includes the ship *Union* which was mounted on a carriage and drawn by horses. Finally, the clergy, physicians and surgeons, judges, "Gentlemen of the Bar supporting the Federal Constitution," the president of the state, members of the convention, the legislature and lastly militia officers in uniform filed through. The procession went along all the main streets of the town with the band playing and singing the Federal Song.

The picture here shows part of the broadside that was printed and passed out to be sung as the parade progressed. There were thirteen verses to correspond with the number of states that had ratified the Constitution. There is no indication of who wrote the words for this song, but Richard Spicer suggests that although "Neither broadside nor newspaper account credits the author...it appears most likely the work of the town's most talented bard at the time...Jonathan Mitchell Sewall" (Spicer 2001, p. 18). At Union-Hill, a "cold Collation was provided with the band continuing to play. After dinner, many toasts were given with the Artillery firing a salute each time followed by three cheers. Celebrations went on into the evening at the State-House" (*NH Gazette*, June 26, 1788, p. 2).

> To the Tune,—*He comes, he comes*,"
> I.
> IT comes! it comes! high raise the song!
> The bright procession moves along.
> From pole to pole refound the NINE,
> And diftant worlds the chorus join.
>
> II.
> In vain did Britain forge the chain,
> While countlefs fquadrons hid the plain,
> HANTONIA, foremoft of the NINE,
> Defy'd their force, and took Burgoyne.
>
> To the tune,—" *Smile, fmile, Britannia*."
> III.
> When PEACE refum'd her feat,
> And Freedom feem'd focure,
> Our patriot-fages met,
> That Freedom to infore:
> Then ev'ry eye on us was turn'd,
> And ev'ry breaft indignant burn'd.

"It Comes" broadside. Courtesy of American Antiquarian Society.

A week later, on the Fourth of July, they celebrated again, and Jonathan played a big part. The *New Hampshire Gazette* describes the day:

> The twelfth anniversary of the Independence of America, and her emancipation from the shackles of slavery forged by the minions of despotism,

RATIFICATION, CELEBRATION, HOME, AND THEATER

was celebrated in this town...with the most lively testimonials of joy due to so auspicious an era. At eleven o'clock in the forenoon, a most elegant and animated oration was delivered by J. M. Sewall, Esq. at Doctor Haven's meeting-house, to a brilliant and respectable audience, who received it with the highest plaudits.

Jonathan mentioned the ratification of the Constitution in these words: "At length Heaven has again graciously smiled upon us...A Federal Constitution of government is now ratified by nine, which is, in effect, by all the United States. A Constitution which no earthly power short of our own, will ever be able to frustrate or violate!" He ends his lengthy address with a poem. The first section is a direct quote from the poem "Windsor-Forest," written by Alexander Pope in 1713 in England:

> Oh! Stretch thy reign, fair PEACE from shore to shore,
> 'Till conquest cease, and slav'ry be no more,
> 'Till the freed Indians, in their native groves,
> Reap their own fruits, and woo their fable loves.
> Peru, once more, a race of kings behold,
> And other Mexicos be roof'd with gold.
> Exil'd, by thee, from earth to deepest hell,
> In brazen bonds shall barb'rous discord dwell:
> Gigantic price, pale terror, gloomy care,
> And mad ambition, shall attend her there:
> There purple vengeance, bath'd in gore, retires,
> Her weapons blunted, and extinct her fires:
> There hateful envy her own snakes shall feel,
> And persecution mourn her broken wheel:
> There faction roar, rebellion bite her chain,
> And gasping furies thirst for blood in vain!

Jonathan finishes the poem inserting the next two lines (in italics) of his own:

> Whilst thou, immortal Love, fair Liberty,
> And dove-winged Peace, and heav'n-born Charity!
> Your office, nature, essence, still the same,
> Lasting your lamp, and unconsum'd its flame,
> Shall still survive ------
> Shall stand before the host of heav'n, confest,
> Forever BLESSING, and forever BLEST!

Perhaps because the ratification happened so close to the Fourth of July, he had already written an "Ode for the celebration of American Independence, 1788." It is included in his own book and ends:

> Hail America, hail! the glory of lands!
> To thee those high honors are giv'n.
> Thy stars still shall blaze till the moon veil her rays,
> And the sun lose his path-way to heav'n!

An oration delivered at Portsmouth, New-Hampshire, On the Fourth of July, 1788 Being the Anniversary of American Independence by One of the Inhabitants was printed by George Jerry Osborne the editor of *The New Hampshire Spy* with the "Ode" appended to the publication. The preface with the declaration shown here shows that Jonathan was requested by the people to compose and deliver it and then have the oration printed. It is published "for the Subscribers," which meant that people paid for their copy before its publication.

"In honor of the day Colonel Wentworth's corps of independent light horse and Capt. Woodward's company of

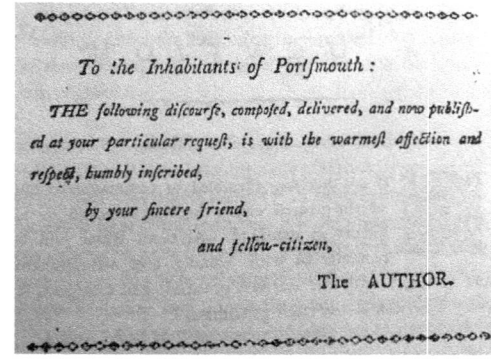

An Oration delivered at Portsmouth, New-Hampshire, On the Fourth of July, 1788 (Sewall 1788). Author's copy.

artillery formed on the parade, and, at twelve o'clock, after performing several evolutions with a celerity and precision which reflects great honor on both corps, a federal salute was fired by the artillery, which was answered by the light horse, and a salute from the Castle." Colonel Wentworth's corps then proceeded to President Langdon's house on Pleasant Street. They were joined by Langdon, "the French Consul, and several respectable and patriotic characters, whom they escorted to Mrs. Knight's, at Newington, and being there joined by an additional number of gentlemen from this and the adjacent towns, they partook of a dinner provided on the occasion." After dinner there were thirteen federal toasts "given by his Excellency John Langdon and several federal songs were sung, in a masterly manner, by Major Flagg, J. M. Sewall, Esq. and other gentlemen, accompanied by a band of musick." After all this they were escorted back to town by the light horse and at 8:30 Langdon and "several other gentlemen assembled at Greenleaf's Inn, where a grand exhibition of fire-works commenced." The fireworks continued until "half after eleven o'clock" (*NH Gazette,* July 10, 1788) when they must have all lurched home to their beds.

The account in the *New Hampshire Spy* (July 5, 1788) concludes with: "Long, very long, may the memory of this important day be engraven upon the hearts of the citizens of United Columbia—and may it ever be celebrated in such a manner, as will best tend to inculcate the principles of order and good government; then shall we see the golden age return'd, and Americans become independent indeed."

Home at Last

An article about Jonathan published in the *Portsmouth Times* in 1910 states that: "Jonathan M. Sewall, one of the most noted lawyers of his day, and a poet-writer of eminence, resided in the house on the south side of Gates street, the first house from Washington street. This dwelling was erected in 1788... It retains much of its original identity and particularly so in the interior." In October 1779, a deed from Samuel Odiorne, a mariner, records the sale of land and buildings to Elisabeth Pascal of Portsmouth. She paid £1682 for the property. Details of it are not described in the document. It is signed in the presence of Joshua Wentworth, Sarah Pray, and Samuel Odiorne Jr. The property must have been a part of a much larger piece of the land that she inherited from her first husband Daniel Wentworth. On December 23, 1789, Elisabeth Pascal sold land and buildings to Joshua Wentworth for £30. Around this time there are various transactions that describe the purchase of parts of Samuel Odiorne's Estate. Some of these include fractions as small as twenty-one-hundredth when Jacob Walker sells his fraction on the south side of Gates Street. He bought it at auction and paid John Peirce £1 and 8 shillings "silver money" for it. When Sarah Sewall purchased the property on Gates Street in 1791, she paid £45. It is most likely that the Sewalls rented it from Pascal and then from Joshua Wentworth, the colonel of the corps of light horse that was part of all the local celebrations. The house is about a two-minute walk from the Wentworth Mansion where they had been living.

Gates Street was known as the "Highway" when it was first laid out through the south end of the town, and that area was originally known as Pickering's Neck. All the land between the South Mill Pond and Puddle Dock and the river was owned by the first and later John Pickerings, relatives of Jonathan's friend of the same name. One deed of 1778 describes Gates Street as the "street leading over said Neck." It became Gate Street and then Gates Street. James Garvin, who was state architectural historian after his work as curator at the Portsmouth Athenaeum and the Strawbery Banke Museum, suggested that it could refer to actual gates in a stockade that most likely encompassed the original thousand-acre Great House plantation of the first settlers in Portsmouth. The settlement was known originally as Strawbery Banke.

When the Sewalls moved to Gates Street there were not as many houses as there are today. Many more houses were built in the next twenty or thirty years, until most of the lots big enough for a house were filled. Some of the houses were built with one end to the street and the entrance in a passageway and these remain today, close up against the house next door. The street just south of Gates was known as Maudlin Lane, now Howard Street. In a 1793 deed it was called "Muddling Street," which may have been an apt description of the street at the time, as very few streets were paved. There were only one or two houses there along with the original Fowles Printing Office nearly opposite the Wentworth Mansion. Many of the houses were owned and occupied by mariners and people in the boat-building industry along the whole length of the "highway" from Pleasant Street to the river. At the Pleasant Street end was Stacey Hall's livery and stables. At the river end there were wharves. So, the Sewalls were living on Gates Street during that memorable occasion when George Washington came to visit Portsmouth at the end of October in 1789.

Huzza, huzza, huzza, huzza, for Washington and Gates Street?

George Washington wrote in his diary that while he was in Portsmouth he walked through most parts of the town. People who live on Gates Street today like to think that on his way back to Brewster's Tavern from his visit with Tobias Lear's mother on Hunking Street, he walked down part of today's Gates Street right past the home where the Sewalls were living.

When Washington and his party left the Lear's home after tea with Tobias' mother, they might have walked up Hunking Street and crossed over Water, now Marcy Street, and stopped to look at the Old South Meeting House that had been built in 1731 for the South Parish. This was the church of Dr. Samuel Haven who sat up during the night to make bullets with his family during the war.

From there he would have seen what is now known as the Captain Daniel Fernald House just ahead of him. It was built in 1730s and Fernald and his wife, Beulah Nichols, moved into the house in 1788. It had been her birthplace. Captain Fernald sailed merchant ships during the Revolutionary War.

Then Washington's party would have turned right down Peirce's Lane, now known as Manning Street. The lane was named after Joshua Peirce Sr. and his house, built about 1730, faced up toward the meeting house. Now its address is on Gates Street. Peirce bought the land for this house from John Pickering in 1720. The Peirce family still lived here at this time as it wasn't until 1832 that Andrew Peirce finally sold the house and land to Leonard Cotton.

At the bottom of Peirce's Lane is Gates Street. At this point Washington and his party turned left along the "highway." On the corner is the property of John Marshall, a boatbuilder. He had purchased it from George Atkinson and his wife in 1785. Atkinson was married to one of Jonathan's Salem relatives, Susannah Sparhawk. The property became known as the Marshall Estate and included land along the south side of Gates Street at the corner of Peirce's Lane. John's son Nathaniel was a small boy of five when Washington passed by. When Nathaniel died in 1851, he stated in his will that all his real estate should be sold, and the proceeds divided among his children. His two houses, two warehouses, and the wharves were put up for public auction in 1852.

The house next door was also owned by a boatbuilder, Reuben Snell. He bought the land from Daniel Peirce in 1758 and built his house there. Reuben and his wife, Lucy Marshall Snell, lived in the house with their four children: Sarah, age seventeen; John, fifteen; Lucy, nine; and Nabby, who was five.

Charles Bellamy Grace, a cooper, owned a house opposite the Snell's. A cooper made the barrels for everything that was being shipped. There was a shop adjoining the house. Grace served as an artillery man in New Hampshire's regiment in the Revolutionary War led by Captain Peirse Long.

The oldest house on the north side of the street, built in 1751, was owned by James McIntire, a mariner. He had also served in the Revolutionary War. It must have been wonderful for these men to see their commander in chief walking past their homes. Phillip Yeaton, another mariner, lived next door to McIntire with his wife and baby daughter.

RATIFICATION, CELEBRATION, HOME, AND THEATER

To greet Washington on the opposite side of the street was Jonathan Mitchel Sewall, the poet and lawyer, with his wife Sarah and their little daughter, Caroline. The two boys, Stephen and his brother John, aged fourteen and nine, were most likely running along the street as Washington made his way. Would the others have waited patiently to greet Washington as he passed their house?

Benjamin Lowd, a cordwainer or shoemaker, lived at the corner of Gates and Washington streets. A cordwainer made new shoes from leather and so was different from a cobbler, who repaired shoes. He had recently sold the property to his son Benjamin, a barber, with the stipulation that he "furnishes me with a comfortable room to dwell in till my decease in his dwelling house."

Washington's party could have turned right here and passed Jonathan Shillaber and his wife's large house with its gambrel style roof which had been built around 1767. Jonathan was a potter, and he and his brother Joseph had moved to Portsmouth from Salem, Massachusetts in 1766. Joseph served with John Paul Jones in the war.

Washington and his party may then have walked back to Brewster's Tavern along Washington Street, which must have been named for him. Did he really walk this way? We will never know for sure.

Difficult Work and a Joyous Event

On May 8, 1790, Jonathan represented the prisoner Dorothy Goss at the Superior Court held in Portsmouth. She had been charged with willfully murdering her infant child. The trial lasted from 9 in the morning until nearly 5 that afternoon. The jury withdrew and returned an hour later with a verdict of not guilty. She was immediately discharged (*Salem Gazette,* May 18, 1790).

The Sewalls celebrated a joyous event only seven weeks later on June 26, when Susan Atkinson Sewall was born to Jonathan and Sarah. Presumably, Susan was given the name Atkinson in memory of Jonathan's family connections to the

Atkinsons of Portsmouth. Like the Storers, George King Atkinson and Susanna Sparhawk Atkinson did not have any children of their own.

The Bow Street Theatre

The next time Jonathan became involved with a theater season was when the Bow Street Theatre finally opened in a converted warehouse at the end of 1791. The building had a pit and a gallery and could seat four hundred (Suffern 1972).

PORTSMOUTH, (Wednesday) Dec. 14.

The ladies are refpectfully informed, that the gentlemen, out of complaifance to them, intend to appear at the Theatre uncovered, all they hope in return, is, that the head drefs of the Fair may be comprifed within moderate bounds, and that hoops may be difpenfed with.

Advance notice for the Bow Street Theatre. *New Hampshire Spy*, December 14, 1791. GenealogyBank 2020.

There had been rumblings about the need for an actual playhouse for a number of years. The *New Hampshire Spy* printed an advance notice on December 14 with instructions for the ladies as seen here. On December 17, under the title *New Theatre (Bow-Street)*, they announced that Jonathan's prologue would precede the comedy of the "West-Indian" to be staged on the twentieth along with "several select pieces of music…performed by a number of Gentlemen." An interesting n.b. to the notice is "It is requested that all carriages in going to the Theatre, be ordered to proceed by the way of Market Street and return by the way of Chapel Street, in order to prevent difficulties which may arise from their meeting in the night." An early one-way system in Portsmouth is advocated due to traffic congestion.

The following week the newspaper printed Jonathan's "Introductory Prologue on opening the Theatre in this town—written by J. M. Sewall, Esq.":

> Oft shall the plaintive scene attract your eyes,
> And call forth all your fears and all your sighs
> Then old Flaherty, from Hibernia's shore,
> With blunders set the audience in a roar,

RATIFICATION, CELEBRATION, HOME, AND THEATER

While Music, at each pause, exalts, inspires,
Or ravishes with all Apollo's fires.
These various scenes shall still some good impart,
Or cheer the spirit, or amend the heart,
With pleasure, or improvement, still be join'd,
Promote the body's health, or better health of mind...

At 5 o'clock in the afternoon of the twenty-first there was a charity event to buy school supplies for the poor children that was held at Mr. Buckminster's North Meeting House. Many members of the state legislature were in attendance, along with "a very large number of the respectable inhabitants of this town." There was an oration and part of Pope's "Messiah" delivered by Mr. A. Bishop along with "pieces of instrumental and vocal music performed at the intervals by J. M. Sewall, Esq. and other patrons and lovers of that pleasing art." All the details of the evening are praised here in an article which was published in the *New Hampshire Spy* on the twenty-fourth and then repeated verbatim in a Boston newspaper the *Argus* on the thirtieth.

> PORTSMOUTH, (SATURDAY) Dec. 24.
> On Wednesday evening last, many members of the Hon. Legislature of this state, and a very large number of the respectable inhabitants of this town, were most agreeably entertained in the north meetinghouse, by an oration, address on charity — and part of Pope's Messiah, delivered by Mr. A. BISHOP——and pieces of instrumental and vocal music performed at the intervals by J. M. SEWALL, Esq. and other patrons and lovers of that pleasing art.
> The perfect order and solemn silence that reigned within and without the house, the eager attention with which the audience listened to the Orator, were the best testimonials of their approbation and proof of his ability to teach an art, in which he can give an example. But joined to this, the judicious admired the great propriety of the pronunciation, gesture and attitude; while the public, and the poor in particular, expressed their highest gratitude to the stranger and musicians for the favour of the entertainment, and to the company for the acceptable bounty collected for the poor children.

Instrumental and vocal music performed by J. M. Sewall. *New Hampshire Spy*, December 24, 1791. GenealogyBank 2020.

A prologue to the evening's entertainment at the Bow Street Theatre on July 31, 1792 was proclaimed by the director Mr. Watts. According to the article the following day in the

New Hampshire Spy, Mr. Watts "if he outdid himself in any thing it was in this." The prologue had been written by Jonathan M. Sewall, Esq. It does a wonderful job of describing the theater and the work of Mr. Watts and Mr. Civil who are the managers:

> Methinks I see him with his magic wand,
> Like some ole necromancer circled stand:
> He strikes the warehouse,
> and the fabric lo!
> Turns to a theatre beneath the blow,
> Where hogsheads, bales,
> were once promiscuous see,
> Here frowns a Monarch
> and there walks a Queen:
> That wood, that mountain,
> and that beauteous valley,
> Was where the worthy owner
> once kept tally:
> Where porter-men
> with muddy hoofs once flocked,
> Great Chrononhotonthologos has stalked;
> And where yon beauteous forms
> attract your love,
> Dry goods, teer, over teer,
> were piled above;
> Then Oh! This conjuror favour
> with your nod,
> If you refute—that self same potent rod
> That from a warehouse—
> reared this magick scene,
> Shall turn all to a paltry store again.

If Mr. Watts managed to say Chrononhotonthologos, he would have done a marvelous job! The *Tragedy of Chrononhotonthologos* was a satirical play by the English poet and songwriter Henry Carey from 1743. The prologue was printed in full in the *New Hampshire Spy* and in *The Diary or Loudon's Register* on August 15 in New York, as seen here.

> PROLOGUE.
>
> *Written by* JONATHAN M. SEWALL, *Esq.*
>
> THIS infant stage, by pious zealots curs'd,
> Rear'd by your favor, by your indulgence nurs'd,
> Still claims your patronage—nor hopes in vain,
> The same kind hands that rear'd it, to sustain.
> Ah! did you know the care, vexation, strife,
> That wait a Manager's and Actor's life;
> What straits, what shifts, what toil, to merit praise;
> Our sleepless nights, and long laborious days—
> Your added smiles would make us large amends,
> Our friends grow kinder, and our foes turn friends.
> For *me*, alas! a stranger in your State—
> Drawn part by inclination, part by fate;
> I beg your candor *still*, your smiles display,
> They'll wait a weary wand'rer on his way;
> He claims no higher merit or desert,
> Than some small genius, and an honest heart.
>
> Next for the Managers (you know the men)
> One guides the music, and one forms the scene:
> Here is their station—here in frugal way
> They paint, rehearse, eat, sleep, and play and pray.
> With nicest touches of their several arts,
> How have they labor'd to attract your hearts!
> When the play paus'd, the one with pleasing sounds
> Has cheer'd, or sooth'd, your souls, and heal'd its wounds;
> Like giant Handel, with his youthful band,
> Taught by his skill, and guided by his hand.
>
> The other Manager, the courteous CIVIL—
> Say, is he a magician, or the devil?
> Methinks I see him with his magic wand,
> Like some old necromancer stand:
> He strikes the warehouse, and the fabric, lo!
> Turns to a theatre beneath the blow.
> Where hogsheads, bales, were once promiscuous seen,
> Here frowns a monarch, and there walks a queen;
> That wood, that mountain, & that beauteous valley,
> Was where the worthy owner once kept tally;
> Where porter men with muddy hoofs once flock'd
> Great Chrononhotonthologos has stalk'd;
> And where you beauteous forms attract your love,
> Dry goods, teer over teer, were pil'd above.
> Then, oh! this conj'rer favor with your nod;
> If you refuse—that self-same potent rod,
> That from a warehouse rear'd this magic scene,
> Shall turn all to a paltry store again.

Bow Street Theatre Prologue. *The Diary or Loudon's Register* (New York), August 15, 1792. *GenealogyBank* 2020.

CHAPTER 10.

Celebrations and Demonstrations

Primus, Stephen, and the Portsmouth Newspapers

Primus came from Boston in 1756 with his owner, Daniel Fowle, and they published the first newspaper in New Hampshire. Fowle continued publishing it until 1785 when he transferred the business to John Melcher and George Jerry Osborne, two of his apprentices (Miller 1872). John Melcher continued with the *Gazette*, and the *New Hampshire Spy* was established by George Jerry Osborne on October 24, 1786.

John Melcher inherited Primus with the other business property, and he was enslaved by him until his death in 1791. He may have been the first slave to have had a notice of his death published in the newspaper in Portsmouth. The death notice for Jonathan Shillabar, the potter who lived around the corner from the Sewalls on Washington Street was included too, but Primus's notice was special. It was printed in italics and details of his funeral were given in the May 19 issue of the *New Hampshire Gazette*. The paper was published only once a week. On Wednesday, one week later, on May 26, the epitaph that Jonathan wrote for Primus was printed in the newspaper.

> In this town—Mr. Jonathan Shillabar.—Capt. Zachariah Fofs.—Mrs. ——— Flagg,—Mr. Richard Jackfon.—Mr. ——— Bartlett.—and
> *PRIMUS, a negro man, late the Property of Daniel Fowle, Efq. deceafed—his funeral will be on to-morrow, at fix o'clock, P. M. from the dwelling houfe of the Printer hereof, where his acquaintance may attend and pay the funeral obfequies.*

Funeral arrangements for Primus. *NH Gazette*, May 19, 1791. *GenealogyBank* 2021.

Epitaph on the Death of PRIMUS

Under these clods, old *Primus* lies
At rest and free from noise,
No longer seen by mortal eyes
Or griev'd by roguish boys;
The cheerful *dram* he lov'd 'tis true
Which hastened on his end.
But *some* in *paved*-street well knew
He was a *hearty* friend,
And did possess a grateful mind
Though oft borne down with pain,
Yet where he found a neighbour kind
He surely went again;
Too often did the mirth of some
His innocence betray,
By giving larger draughts of rum
Than he could *swill* away,
But now he's dead, we sure may say
Of him, as of all men,
That while in silent graves they lay
They'll not be *plagu'd* 'agen.

The epitaph reads as though it was given at the graveside as it begins "Under these clods." It surely gives the impression that Jonathan knew Primus well even to the painfulness of his aging shoulders and knees. With Jonathan's own propensity for drink, he must have shared quite a few "cheerful" drams with Primus. Primus may well have been the first enslaved person that Jonathan met in Portsmouth as they probably lived across the street from each other.

The printing office where the *New Hampshire Gazette* was published was originally located opposite the Wentworth Mansion on Pleasant Street. The office had moved around 1764 to what is now Market Street. In the June 12, 1767 edition of the newspaper, there was the first indication of the address "near the State House, in the Street leading to the Ferry." According to the descriptions in *Brewster's Rambles* the Fowles lived and worked on the opposite side of the street from John Pickering's home and office. When Jonathan first came to Portsmouth to study with John Pickering in the early 1770s, he would have lived with the Pickerings across the street from Primus and the Fowles.

It has been said that Primus could not read. If he were the only person working with Fowle it seems unlikely that he was unable to help with the typesetting. Shown here is the actual printing press that he used. His main task would have been setting the cases of print onto the press, setting the paper, and then inking the letters before the case went into the press. Then the lever was turned to pull the paper and the case of type into it and to press it down to make the print. When this was done, the lever was pulled back to take the case out and then, because the ink was oil based, the printed sheets had to be hung up to dry overnight. The type needed to be cleaned and returned to the letter cases. Upper-case letters were arranged at the top of the case and lower-case at the bottom, hence the term "case" when describing letters.

Daniel Fowle's printing press. Historical marker, Pleasant St., Portsmouth, NH.

What must it have been like for Primus to print ads for the sale of "Indian, Negro, or Mulatto" people as slaves and information about returning escapees to their enslavers every week?

Ads for slave sales and runaways. *NH Gazette*, various. *GenealogyBank*, 2020. Author's compilation.

Shown here are a selection of ads placed in the *New Hampshire Gazette* year after year. They often state: "Enquire at the Printer."

Jonathan's son Stephen would have been sixteen in 1791. Later he became a printer and for a short time published his own newspaper in Kennebunk, Maine, and then one in Portsmouth at the time of his father's death. It is most likely that at the age of about fourteen he became an apprentice.

The printing trade was a very good one to be in and a young boy could progress from his seven-year apprenticeship to become a journeyman and then a master printer himself. As a journeyman he would be able to get a job in almost any city. But at that time these steps would only be possible for a young white boy. Primus's "apprenticeship" lasted for all of his long life. A printer would not only print the newspaper, but broadsides, pamphlets, books, and many types of forms especially for the state. "Printing was nearly as elite a trade as silver-smithing" which was "at the top of the craft hierarchy" (Rorabaugh 1986).

By the time Stephen entered the printing trade both newspapers were being printed in Portsmouth. The reports in each paper of Washington's visit to Portsmouth in 1789 are almost word for word, so they must have been written by the same person. There are a few additional lines of poetry included in the coverage in the *Spy*.

1793 Civic Celebration

Another civic celebration took place at the Assembly Room on January 24, 1793. The day was "consecrated to the commemoration of the Revolution and late glorious successes of France." People from Portsmouth and the surrounding towns gathered in various parts of the town, all wearing the French cockade of red, white, and blue circular rosettes on their hats. One group converged on the Assembly Room at two o'clock. The entertainment included a number of songs, several composed for the occasion, that were sung and there was also instrumental music. During the music "a beautiful procession of Boys—wearing caps inscribed with the words 'Liberty and Equality' entered the room." After dinner many toasts were given "attended by a discharge of the Artillery."

Two of the songs composed for the occasion were printed as a broadside by John Melcher. One of them "Though printed anonymously, the song text appears in its general style as the work of Sewall's pen, especially in its imitation of his 'War and Washington'" (Spicer 2001, p. 41). It even notes that it is to be sung to the tune of "War and Washington." A copy of the broadside is held by the New Hampshire Historical Society. It has ten verses including this:

> God save the new Republic!
> and martial Dumourier!
> The national assembly,
> and each bold son of war,
> May wisdom all their councils guide,
> and glory's beam surround,
> The great example and the dread
> of all the nations round.

CELEBRATIONS AND DEMONSTRATIONS

The lengthy descriptions of the events in the *Gazette* and *Spy* are mostly identical again and include the toasts that were made at two celebrations. One of the other festivities was held at the home of "Citizen Melcher" on Gates Street. The group met at the Liberty Bridge "(the long favored spot that so often has witnessed the joy of our patriots on similar occasions) to congratulate each other on the birth of nations and to partake of a Civic Entertainment...Joy inspired every heart and generous libations were poured forth in honor of our Gallic brethren."

Universalist Church Petition

On June 1, 1793 Jonathan presented a petition to the New Hampshire Senate & House of Representatives in the General Court convened at Concord on behalf of the proprietors and owners of the land and building known as the Universalist-Meeting-House. His signature is first and then followed by twenty other notable men of Portsmouth. They ask to be incorporated as the Universalist Society. The main purpose of this is so that they

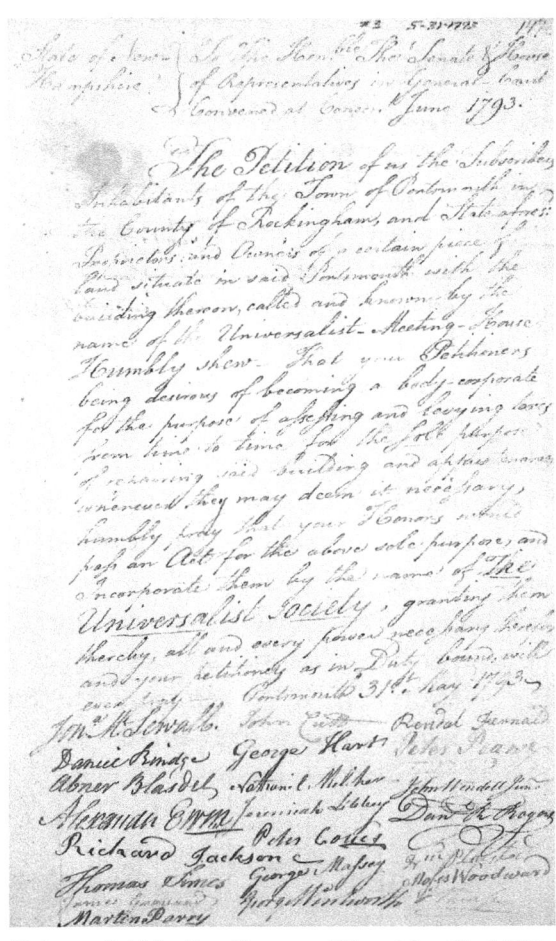

Universalist Meeting House petition. May 31, 1793. Courtesy of the New Hampshire Division of Archives and Records Management.

can assess and levy taxes for repairing the building. From the time of Noah Parker's death in 1787 they had been without a permanent pastor.

A few months after the death of Noah Parker a parish meeting had been held on October 9. It was "agreed to Invite our Brother Jonathan M. Sewall to speak on said days (Sundays), and that Mr. Peter Pearce, Mr. Alexander Ewen and Jeremiah Libbey, Esq., be a committee to invite Mr. Sewall for that purpose." But he did not accept (*Portsmouth Journal of Literature and Politics,* Oct. 25, 1873).

Piscataqua River Bridge

In June of 1794 the Sewalls sold the back part of the property that they had purchased on Gates Street less than three years earlier. It sold for £60 when they had only paid £45 for the entire property. In November of that year, it appears that they raised a sort of mortgage or loan on the 200-acre farm that Sarah had inherited from her father in Allenstown. The tenant, William Holt, gave them his note for £60 on the value of £90 to be paid off with interest within two years. It is interesting to speculate about why at this time they would need what for them would have been a considerable amount of money.

Perhaps the answer lies in the building of the Piscataqua River Bridge across the Great Bay between Newington at a point just outside of Portsmouth to Durham. It was completed in November 1794. Previously, traveling to Durham or further west to Concord and the interior parts of the state required crossing the river or some of its tributaries by boat.

Shown here is a drawing of the bridge from an article in *Structure* magazine by Frank Griggs Jr. (June 2013). It ran from

Piscataqua River Bridge (Griggs 2013). Reprinted with permission, *Structure*, August 2013.

Fox Point, Newington, to Rock Island with an arch on to Goat Island and from there to Meader's Neck at Durham. The proprietors of the bridge also constructed a tavern and stables on Goat Island to accommodate travelers.

Jonathan certainly experienced the difficulties of traveling to the interior of the state when he was registrar of probate for Grafton County in the early 1770s.

> **PISCATAQUA BRIDGE.**
>
> **PURSUANT** to a vote of the Directors of PISCATAQUA BRIDGE, the Proprietors are hereby notified, that the sum of *Fifteen Dollars* is assessed upon each share, agreeable to the articles of subscription—and that the same be paid to the subscriber at Portsmouth, on or before the 18th day of January next, of which all concerned will please to take notice.
>
> THOMAS MARTIN, Treasurer.
> Portsmouth, Dec. 7, 1793.

Piscataqua Bridge notice. *NH Gazette*, December 14, 1793. GenealogyBank 2021.

After 1775, with the outbreak of the Revolution, the state capitol was no longer in Portsmouth. The state's General Assembly met in Concord, Hopkinton, Dover, Amherst, Charlestown, Hanover, and at Exeter before it was moved permanently to Concord in 1808. This bridge would have been an incredible improvement for anyone who had to travel around the state.

Buying shares in the bridge must have seemed like an exceptionally good investment before it was built. The bridge cost over $65,000. It was paid for mainly by subscribers who bought one or more of the 500 shares on offer at about $50 each, believing that they would be receiving dividends for a long time to come. As early as December 1793 subscribers were assessed $15 for each share they had purchased (*NH Gazette*, each issue in December). During the building of the bridge in 1794 a total of about $85 was assessed for each share to cover the costs of materials and labor (Frink 2010, pp. 30–37).

The Piscataqua River Bridge contributed greatly to the prosperity of Portsmouth, but unfortunately for the subscribers, it was far from a financial success. Despite the collection of tolls, the cost of repairs and the other expenses incurred were enormous. Some stockholders lost their investment and never received the large amount in dividends they had expected.

1795 Civic Celebration

Another civic feast took place in Portsmouth on April 7, 1795. This time they were celebrating the French successes in Holland. "On Friday was celebrated here with true republican joy and festivity—the late brilliant and unexampled successes of our magnanimous Allies the French, in the compleat [sic] conquest of Holland, and the emancipation of that oppressed nation from the chains of despotism." The day began with the ringing of bells and a federal discharge of Captain Chadwick's artillery.

At two o'clock "a large number of respectable citizens" made their way to the Assembly Room for an "elegant entertainment." After dinner, as usual they drank many toasts: to the United States, to the President of the United States, to the mighty Republic of France, to the patriots of Holland, and finally the fifteenth toast was to "Peace, liberty and happiness to all mankind."

During the toasts patriotic songs were sung by "several French and other gentlemen of the company." And, of course, there was a song especially composed for the occasion by "Jonathan M. Sewall, Esq." This song had eight verses, with a different chorus for each verse.

> Columbia's sons in songs proclaim,
> Our brave Allies in union join'd;
> The noblest wreaths your skill can frame
> On Holland's brows, and Gallia's bind.
>
> Chorus
> The foes of Liberty restor'd,
> By reason conquer'd, sheath the sword.

And then towards the end of the song:

> Haste Glorious era when the world
> Shall live like brethren, equal, free,
> Thy standard union be unfurl'd,
> Nor Order jar with Liberty.

> Chorus
> Your great example all obey,
> France, Holland & America.

The description of the festivities was published in the *New Hampshire Gazette* in the April 7 edition. Jonathan's song alone was published the following day in the *Oracle of the Day* and a few weeks later in "The Poet's Corner" in *Greenleaf's New York Journal and Patriotic Register*, published in New York City. On the front page that day, there was a long description of a property described in French that was near the "florissante ville de Schenectady," including details of all the wonders that were to be seen there. The country seemed to be ever thankful for the help of the French.

The Jay Treaty and the Demonstrations

However, it was later this same year, in September, that some of the other citizens of Portsmouth were not celebrating with "joy and festivities" but rioting in the streets. They were demonstrating against the Jay Treaty, officially called the Treaty of Amity, Commerce and Navigation between Britain and the United States. Chief Justice John Jay had been sent to Great Britain to negotiate a treaty which was to settle some issues that were still unresolved between the two countries after America's independence. It was signed by Britain's King George III in London on November 19, 1794. But when it was presented to the US Senate, it only received a twenty-to-ten vote. Washington signed it in August 1795. Although it did accomplish the goal of maintaining peace, it was very unpopular with the American public (Office of the US Historian).

Protests over the treaty took place in many cities and continued into 1796. The riot in Portsmouth took place on Thursday, September 10, 1795. There was a town meeting called to discuss the treaty and to sign an address to the President. A handbill entitled the *Crisis* was posted around the town the day before. It informed people that the "Senate had bargained away their blood bought privileges, requesting them to shut up their shops, and assemble at the sound of the bells."

> A large number of signers to an address was never expected, the commerce of the town is yet on a small scale, the merchants are few. Some well wishers to the address have been intimidated by threats; thirty-nine had signed it when the late riot took place. (*NH Gazette,* September 15, 1795)

In the *Oracle of the Day* of the same day, the author of an article writes that the signers never thought anyone could:

> ...take umbrage at their expressing sentiments in this way, since they were expressions of regard and confidence in the Government—that the freedom of publishing our sentiments without molestation is an essential article of civil liberty, cannot be disputed by any, and to suppose that in a free Government like the American, this liberty should have been violated by a licentious Mob, would scarce be credited. (*Oracle of the Day*, September 15, 1795)

In the afternoon a public crier was sent around the town ringing his bell and inviting everyone to attend "the execution of those two bribed traitors," Chief Justice Jay and Samuel Livermore, who was a US senator from New Hampshire. The protestors had created effigies in the afternoon and in the evening a procession was formed. A cart with the two effigies led the procession and was accompanied with a drum and flags that paraded through Pleasant Street, Court Street, and Daniel Street to Jonathan Warner's wharf where the effigies were burned. The mob increased and they continued until nine or ten in the evening to parade through the town with a drum and fife beating a solemn mournful tune. As they passed the houses of the men who had signed the address they shouted in "abusive insulting Language." Although the mob dispersed, stones were thrown into the houses of Dr. Hall Jackson, Mr. Jacob Sheafe, and Mr. Chase.

Whether the Sewall's house was visited by the mob is not known. He was probably one of the signers of this original address and in April 1796 another address was prepared. The signers of the address state that "They are apprehensive from the refusal of the House of Representatives to pass the laws necessary to complete the execution of the Treaty." They are concerned that "commerce will be distressed, agriculture languish, manufactures decline, industry stagnate, and enterprise be without object." They "pray that the House of Representatives would endeavour to avert these evils" by passing the laws that would allow the treaty to be ratified. It is dated April 27, 1796 and signed by twenty people including Jona. M. Sewall (Jay Treaty Supporters 1796).

Signatures on second Jay Treaty address. 1796. Courtesy of the Portsmouth Athenaeum.

The House of Representatives tried to force Washington to submit documents that related to the treaty. Washington refused and insisted that the House possessed no constitutional authority to determine treaties. In May 1796 Washington expressed the hope that his ratification of the Jay Treaty would provide America with peace and the time to become a prosperous and powerful nation (Ebel 1988).

Perhaps not surprisingly, Jonathan also wrote a long poem on "President Washington's dignified refusal of the request made by the House of Representatives for the papers relative to the British Treaty of 1795." Interspersed among verses extoling Washington are these verses berating the rioters:

> Ye miscreants! who now the whole state would unhinge,
> Scarce a year has revolv'd since with bow, fawn, and cringe,
> Ye servilely worship'd whom now ye revile,
> In impudence Arnolds! Iscariots in guile!
> Who courts the mob's grace is unwise in extreme,
> 'Tis lighter than vapour, more vain than a dream.
> Far nobler incentives have Washington sway'd,
> A conscience approving, a Crown that Can't Fade!

and later:

> Under his able conduct, we now rest in peace,
> Manufactures, and Trade, Arts, and Science, increase.
> Crops luxuriant our fields and our pastures enrobe,
> Our Commerce is bounded alone by the globe;
> While beneath our own fig-tree, and vine, we obtain
> And enjoy all the fruit of our labor and pain.
>
> What madness then Citizens, prompts you to range,
> Or to risque [sic] for such bliss, so uncertain a change?
> The treaty with Britain can be but pretence [sic]:
> On its side rests the weight of skill, numbers, and sense.
> Besides, be the Treaty or censur'd or prais'd,
> We made it Ourselves when the Fabric we rais'd:
> How dare then our Servants, for faction, or gain,
> Infringe that wise system they've sworn to maintain!

At least one of the mob, twenty-five-year-old Thales Yeaton, who lived on Jefferson Street in a house that is now part of the Strawbery Banke Museum, was summoned to court in Exeter. But the charges were dropped and "he returned home to a rousing welcome" (Strawbery Banke Museum website).

CHAPTER 11.

Washington, Lawyers, Eminent Men

Washington's Farewell Address

George Washington had nearly universal approval for much of his two terms in office. However, around the time of the Jay Treaty, the country was becoming divided between those who favored Britain and a federal style government and those who favored France's more localized government control. The Federalists began to support Britain and the Jeffersonian Republicans supported France. Washington saw some of the men he had worked so closely with during the early years of the country turn against him. Perhaps he had had enough of politics and just wanted to retire to his home in Virginia. In 1792 he had asked James Madison to compose a valedictory address at the end of his first term. Then in 1796 he asked Alexander Hamilton to edit Madison's draft. Washington amended this version, and he also asked Secretary of State Timothy Pickering for his opinions as well.

Washington's decision not to be considered as a candidate was printed in this notice in the *New Hampshire Gazette* on September 24, 1796.

The Address of Gen. Washington to the People of America on His Declining the Presidency of the United States was first published in the *American Daily Advertiser* in

> The Editor of the Philadelphia *Aurora*, asserts, unqualifiedly. That his Excellency GEORGE WASHINGTON, will decline being considered a candidate at the next election of President.

George Washngton will not be a candidate. *NH Gazette*, September 24, 1796. GenealogyBank 2021.

Philadelphia on September 19, 1796. It was his "Farewell Address" to the people that appeared just ten weeks before the presidential electors were to cast their votes in the 1796 election.

When Jonathan first read the address is not known, but he declares, in the preface of his versification of it that "His motives were, a desire to serve his country, and an ambition to testify his profound veneration for its illustrious defender." He went on to write that people might think that the subject was not proper for poetry and he agreed with them, adding, however: "But as verse commonly makes a deeper impression, and is more easily retained in the memory, than prose (however inferior the former may be) he flattered himself that this essay might be attended at least with that peculiar advantage....so he hoped that cloathing [sic] the same thoughts in a new, though homelier garb, by exciting curiosity and awakening attention, might succeed, in some instances, where the original failed." He continues lauding George Washington, explaining that composing it was a lot more difficult to do than he had realized, and asking that he be entitled to "some small applause for his Patriotism" if not for his poetry.

A Versification of President Washington's Excellent Farewell-Address to the Citizens of the United States by a Gentleman

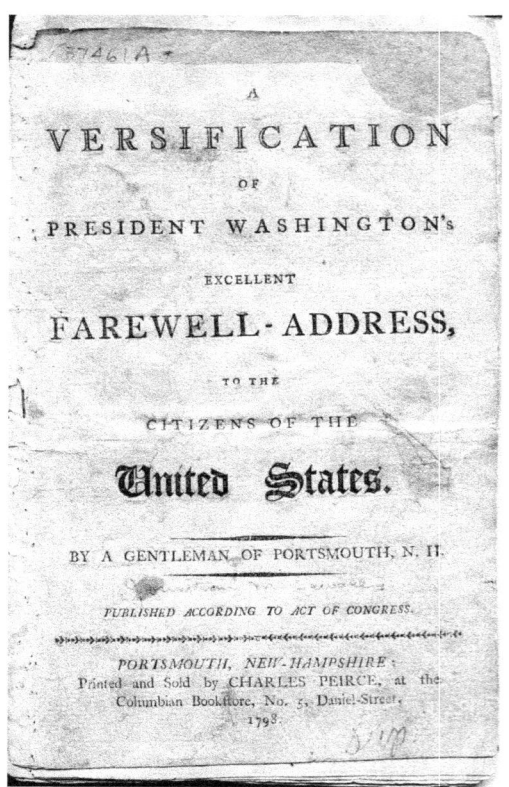

A Versification of President Washington's excellent Farewell Address. (Sewall 1798). Courtesy of the Portsmouth Athenaeum.

of Portsmouth, N. H. Published according to Act of Congress was published by Charles Peirce of Portsmouth in 1798. "The Author" dedicates it to Col. Timothy Pickering, secretary of state to the United States.

Timothy Pickering was a contemporary of Jonathan's from Salem, Massachusetts. Jonathan mentions their "private friendship" in this dedication. Timothy graduated from Harvard College in 1763, and then he worked as a clerk for John Higginson, the Essex County register

Dedication of the *Versification* to Col. Timothy Pickering (Sewall 1798). Courtesy of the Portsmouth Athenaeum.

of deeds in Salem, another of the Higginsons to whom Jonathan was related. It was around the time Pickering worked for Higginson that Jonathan came back from Boston and lived in Salem to be apprenticed to his relatives there. On Higginson's death in 1774, Timothy Pickering became the register of deeds, an office that Jonathan's father had held at his death in 1748. That Jonathan and Timothy knew each other from their youth seems impossible to disprove.

By the time of the Jay Treaty, Timothy was Washington's secretary of state, and it was he who managed to get the Congress to pass the necessary appropriations to implement the treaty. Timothy and Washington became the main villains as far as the radicals were concerned. In his defense, Timothy had asserted that a mob could never be right.

Did Jonathan send his poem "The Inflexible Patriot" that he wrote in support of Washington and decrying the mob in Portsmouth to his old friend? Perhaps when Washington published his "Farewell Address" which Timothy also had a hand in, he sent it to his friend Jonathan and asked if wanted to try to put it into verse as well.

Charles Brewster wrote about Jonathan's *Versification* in his *Rambles about Portsmouth* (Brewster [1859] 1869, Ramble 125): "The poem, if such it may be called, occupies forty-four octavo pages, and is almost a literal presentation of the original in rhyme."

At the beginning of his address Washington offers "to your solemn contemplation, and to recommend to your frequent review, some sentiments..." So, perhaps Jonathan was justified in thinking he should attempt its presentation in verse as he believed that people found it easier to remember something written as poetry. He must have felt that they would be able to memorize sections of it and remember the president's thoughts.

Washington's phrase "The very idea of the power and the right of the people to establish government presupposes the duty of every individual to obey the established government." Jonathan interpreted it as:

> Th' idea of the people's pow'r and right
> T' establish government, implies at sight,
> That each is bound by duty's sov'reign sway,
> The government establish'd, to obey. (Sewall 1801, p. 27)

A longer example is Washington's:

> Observe good faith and justice towards all nations; cultivate peace and harmony with all. Religion and morality enjoin this conduct; and can it be, that good policy does not equally enjoin it? It will be worthy of a free, enlightened, and at no distant period, a great nation, to give to mankind the magnanimous and too novel example of a people always guided by an exalted justice and benevolence. Who can doubt that, in the course of time and things, the fruits of such a plan

would richly repay any temporary advantages which might be lost by a steady adherence to it? Can it be that Providence has not connected the permanent felicity of a nation with its virtue? The experiment, at least, is recommended by every sentiment which ennobles human nature. Alas! is it rendered impossible by its vices?

Jonathan renders it as:

> Ne'er from good faith, and strictest justice swerve
> But tow'rds all Nations rigidly observe.
> Cherish mild peace, and harmony with all;
> Int'rest and duty, for this conduct call.
> Morality, Religion, this enjoins,
> With these, the wisest policy combines.
> 'Twill be a noble, and a brave essay—
> —A *wise*, a *free*, and (at no distant day)
> A *great*, and *pow'rful* NATION! calm, sedate,
> Displaying to th' admiring world, the great
> Magnanimous example (ne'er display'd)
> Of a whole people, uniformly sway'd
> By purest dictates of the moral-sense,
> Exalted Justice! and Benevolence!
> What mind can doubt, that in the course of time
> And progress of events, the fruits sublime
> Of such a plan, would amply pay again,
> Each temporary loss you might sustain
> By its observance?—Who shall dare surmise
> That Providence, all-bountiful and wise!
> The lasting bliss of nations, or mankind,
> Has not with virtue intimately twin'd?
> "Tis worth the trial! recommended too,
> By ev'ry motive, sentiment, and view,
> That governs *human-nature*, or exalts!
> —Can it be render'd frustrate, by its *faults*?
> (Ibid., pp. 40–41)

Each year on or near his birthday on February 22, Congress reads George Washington's "Farewell Address." The tradition began in 1862 and became an annual event in 1893. It was read on Tuesday, February 22, 2022, by Senator Patrick J. Leahy of Vermont. The address consists of 7,641 words. Jonathan's version is probably considerably longer, as in the above example Washington uses 140 words to Jonathan's 173.

New Hampshire Lawyers

By this time Jonathan had become known as one of the "able and distinguished men of his profession." The New England Historic Genealogical Society published a biographical sketch about William Plumer Sr. in their *Register and Antiquarian Journal* (NEHGS 1871). Plumer was another one of the early New Hampshire lawyers. The profession is described in some detail:

> At that time (c.1787) a New Hampshire lawyer was required to fill the offices of attorney, counsellor, conveyancer and advocate, and these several duties, with much other incidental labor, both in and out of court, rendered the work of the profession far more arduous than it is at present. In addition to this, it was the custom for the bar to follow the court in its circuit of the State. In order to fulfil these duties satisfactorily to his clients and to the court, there was required of the lawyer versatility of talents, capacity for labor, and good business habits...

It continues:

> ...the lawyer must bring to his work a mind trained and enriched by study; a body that never tires; a zeal that never languishes; and over all this, as a sentinel, that senses right and wrong, which neither flattery, nor bribes, nor selfish ambition can corrupt or expel. The current of his professional life intermingles with the familiar concerns of his friends and neighbors.

> He is their trusted counsellor; their shield against oppression; the sworn defender of their lives, property and honor. His bosom receives and holds with inviolable faith their choicest secrets; his hand shapes and fortifies the channels of their benefactions and executes their dying bequests. But the theatre on which he prosecutes his labors, wins his victories and suffers his defeats, is generally far removed from public observation.

The description continues that in 1787 there were:

> few well-read lawyers, and yet there were many able and distinguished men in the profession. Among these were John Pickering, John Sullivan, John Prentice, Joshua Atherton, William K. Atkinson, Jonathan M. Sewall, William Parker, Oliver Peabody, and Daniel Humphries...The united efforts of these men raised the law from the state of uncertainty which had characterized its administration and practice and aided in giving to the State a body of judicial decisions which command the respect of the profession at large...

Profiles of Eminent Men and Epitaphs

Certainly, in the case of Jonathan M. Sewall among these men, he appears to have been extremely well-read. His "Profiles of Eminent Men," composed when he was ill "to divert his attention from himself," includes Bacon, Locke, Newton, Homer, Virgil, Pindar, Horace, Juvenal, Ovid, Vida, Ariosto, Tasso, Chaucer, Spenser, Shakespeare, Milton, Waller, Cowley, Denham, Roscommon, Dryden, Pope, Addison, Johnson, Price, Swift, Young, Gay, Thomson, Watts, Collins, Churchill, Gray, Shenstone, Cervantes, Fielding, Le Sage, Richardson, Ossian, Fingal, and Handel. He used the letters of their name to begin each line of his poem and hoped that in "some instances a likeness will be discovered by others between the picture and the original." How else would he have determined their likeness without having studied them or their works? Here is his profile of "Shakespeare" with a copy of the page from that section of his own book *Miscellaneous Poems*:

> **S**weet Bard of fancy! nature's darling child!
> **H**is native wood-notes how he warbles wild!
> **A**w'd by his nod, elves, witches, ghosts, obey,
> **K**neel to his pow'r, and own his magic sway.
> **E**xcursive o'er creation's bounds he flies,
> **S**trikes his all-potent wand, and bids new worlds arise.
> **P**leas'd with th' ideal scenes, we range alone,
> **E**xplore each part, and think 'tis nature's own.
> **A**dieu blest bard! thy works shall never die!
> **R**ehears'd on earth, re-acted in the sky,
> **E**nhancing human bliss thro' all eternity!

Perhaps these attempts to capture the likenesses of a person in verse were the exercises that led to his composing epitaphs for many people in the Portsmouth area. The one for Primus in the *New Hampshire Gazette* was one of the first of his to be published. Included in his *Miscellaneous Poems* (1801) are a number that were written mostly during the 1790s. In a cemetery walk in Portsmouth, Glenn A. Knoblock, author of *Portsmouth Cemeteries*, thought there could be many of Jonathan's compositions in the local cemeteries that haven't been attributed to him. Included in Jonathan's book are "To Mrs. L. on the sudden death of her Infant, Epitaph on Mrs. J. G. of Portsmouth, who died

"Shakespeare" from Profiles of Eminent Men in *Miscellaneous Poems*. (Sewall 1801). Author's copy.

October 1790, Epitaph on John Hale, Esq. who died July 13th, 1796, To Mrs. E. W. on the Death of her Son, who died abroad, and Epitaph on Mr. Joseph Sherburne Hill who died May 14th 1798." Knoblock's book also includes Jonathan's epitaph on the gravestone in the North Cemetery of Abraham Isaac, who died in 1803. He states that "The fact that Isaac's epitaph was written by local poet Jonathan Mitchell Sewall speaks volumes about his character. 'A son of faithful Abra'm sleeps in peace... Through various toils his active spirit ran. A faithful steward and an honest man.'"

In addition to these epitaphs for friends, he also wrote about the death of various animals: a dog, his own horse, and one entitled "On the Death of an Ox who died suddenly in Portsmouth Street July 1798."

> Adieu, faithful slave! fate has rescu'd thy life
> From the harrow, plough, team, and dire butcher's fell knife.
> No longer a servant, thy free spirit strays,
> O'er pastures elysian forever to graze.
> Tho' a stranger the bard to thy *personal* worth,
> The renown of thy species has fill'd the wide earth.

Continuing to praise the ox, he noted that in Egypt the ox had once been acknowledged as a God. He also managed to include a few digs at others:

> From the Ox what rich blessings our species derives!
> The defence of our limbs, and support of our lives.
> His labor procures us the corn and full sheafe,
> We're indebted to him for our pudding and beef,
> (Such life-giving food dress'd in true British stile,
> Gave Nelson the day on the streams of the Nile.)
> And ne'er while Columbians can banquet on those,
> Will they heed the proud vaunts of their frog-eating foes,
> Be dismay'd by their threats, or cajol'd by their lies
> Till the croaking race swell to the Ox's vast size,
> Till our pastures prove barren, our meadows a bog,

Or the noble beast shrink to the size of a frog.

When the eminent local physician Hall Jackson died in 1797, Jonathan wrote the epitaph that appears on his tombstone in the North Cemetery.

> To heal disease, to calm the widow's sigh,
> And wipe the tear from poverty's swol'n eye
> Was thine! but ah! that skill on other's shown,
> Tho' life to them, could not preserve thy own.
> Yet still thou liv'st in many a grateful breast,
> And deeds like thine, enthrone thee with the blest.

In contrast to these noble thoughts, Jonathan's book of poems includes an "Epitaph to a QUACK who died of an Asthma." Phthisic is a wasting disease of the lungs such as asthma or tuberculosis, and physic in this sense is the medicine:

> Here lies death's caterer, breathless with the phthisic,
> Who liv'd by what kill'd all his patients—PHYSIC.

Portsmouth Celebrations 1798–1799

Portsmouth appears to have excelled in its celebrations, and Jonathan was always ready to contribute a song or an ode for the occasion. In October 1798 the citizens of Portsmouth gathered again for a grand celebration for the birthday of their new president, John Adams. There were the usual military salutes from ships in the harbor as well as from "two brass field pieces centrally disposed in Capt. Whidden's [Assembly House] garden." There was much parading through the streets and then they escorted New Hampshire Governor Gilman into the town, where another dinner was held at "Mr. Whidden's." Gilman, the clergy, and a great number of militia in complete uniform, proceeded to the dinner after which "a number of federal and patriotic Toasts were given out, and the following original and most excellent songs sung with high approbation" (*Oracle of the Day*, Oct. 20, 1798).

In this song Jonathan denounces France. How things had changed from five years earlier when the "Citizens" of Portsmouth were all celebrating with the French cockade in their hats.

> Then Jove, in the name of the gods, thus decree'd.
> The petition prevails—my sons are victorious;
> 'Gainst treason, and Gallia, they still shall succeed,
> And rise on her ruins, triumphant and glorious.
> Their thunder shall roar
> Round each ocean and shore,
> Till haughty France humbled, too late shall deplore.

The following February, Portsmouth observed "Lt. Gen. Washington's" birthday. Once more there were cannons and "a joyful peal of bells." Between two and three in the afternoon the Assembly Room filled with the town's gentlemen, including the judges of the Superior Court and the clergy. There was an "excellent entertainment," toasts were drunk "accompanied by echoing cannon...the felicities of the occasion greatly augmented, by an incomparable Song, the handy work of that celebrated genius J. M. Sewall, Esq. who amid the avocations of the bar and a press of clients, devoted a few pleasing moments to celebrate the praises of a Washington" (*NH Gazette*, Feb. 27, 1799; *Oracle of the Day*, Feb. 23, 1799; also reported in the *New York Daily Advertiser*, Mar. 12, 1799).

The Oracle of the Day includes a biographical sketch of Washington that comments about his decision to retire. "This determination though founded in wisdom and sanctioned by prudence, was heard with pain from one extremity of the continent to another, and if Adams had not have existed to supply the place of his august Predecessor, the general regrets would have forced continuance in office." It then goes on to comment on his "Farewell Address," saying it "ought to be transcribed in letters of gold, and ever expanded to the instant view of all Legislative bodies." The "incomparable song" begins:

> From Helicon's embow'ring shades,
> Descend each muse, on rapture's wings;
> Apollo, join th' inspiring maids,
> And sweep the loud-rewarding strings!
> While answ'ring echoes hail the morn
> When Thou, Great Washington! was born!

Then on Thursday the Fourth of July, the "excellent" light infantry "paraded at an early hour, and marched through all the principal streets in town, and kept up a regular, constant and masterly fire, which received the approbation of a crowd of spectators." At the dinner at Captain Whidden's Assembly Room they ate and drank toasts and heard "some very capital Songs sung." "Two original compositions by J.M. Sewall, Esq. were received with high plaudits." There were also parties at the Portsmouth Pier, the bridge, and on the river. *The Oracle of the Day* printed both of Jonathan's songs, which were "sung with peculiar animation in town, at the bridge and in all parties."

> Heav'n and the fates this day decreed
> Our happy country should be freed!
> Columbians rise! loud cannons roar!

This is the beginning of the song or "Ode to Independence" as Jonathan names it in his own book of poems, but it goes on to condemn the French in every verse and ends with this chorus:

> Columbia rise! be firm, be free!
> The friends of France are foes to Thee.
> Detest the tools of Talleyrand,
> And spurn each Traitor from the land!

The second festival song is written from the viewpoint of the "gods" and begins:

> Late Jove and blue Neptune in conference met,
> On Ida's high summit reclin'd;
> The theme was Columbia! her fame and her fate
> Engross'd each Celestial's high mind.
> First Neptune began—"Scarce three ages have past,

> Since the land we adopt for our own,
> Haunt of savage, and brute, was a rude howling waste
> Undiscover'd, unpeopled, unknown.

It goes on to explain how the country grew and ends with:

> Sage ADAMS for wisdom, with PALLAS may vie,
> And WASHINGTON equals a JOVE!

Even in this song, as well as almost everything Jonathan wrote during these years, he cries out about the brutality of the French that has taken place. During this same year he also wrote a rather damning "Parody on Marseilles-Hymn." The words to the hymn were written in 1792 when the French had declared war on Austria. The original title (translated into English) was "War Song for the Army of the Rhine." It had been adopted as the National Anthem for the French Republic in 1795 only a few years before Jonathan wrote his parody. The first line "Allons enfants de la Patrie, Le jour de gloire est arrivé!" becomes "Columbia's sons, arouse to glory!"

John Adams' birthday was on October 30 and there were great celebrations in Boston and Salem as well as Portsmouth. The same description of the day in Portsmouth was carried in the *New Hampshire Gazette* (Nov. 2), *Oracle of the Day* (Nov. 6), and the *Salem Gazette* (Nov. 8). There were bells pealing joyously, military parading, firing, and saluting, and then at 3 p.m. there was again a "very elegant entertainment" at the Assembly Room. "Many excellent Songs heightened the joys of the hour, and among them we recognize with pleasure a spirited performance, by the American Apollo, J. M. Sewall, Esq." The final verse:

> Not a Nation on earth, would we fear with such aid,
> (Heav'n save us alone from *internal* commotion!)
> Not *Britain, France, Europe*—COLUMBIA would dread,
> Their *Forces* by *Land*—their proud *Fleets* on the *Ocean*,
> Our Heroes prepar'd,
> Would their progress retard,
> Sage Adams to guide, and Great Washington guard.

Death of Washington

At the very end of the year, on December 14, George Washington died peacefully at home in Mt. Vernon, Virginia. The *Federal Observer* newspaper in Portsmouth was only published from March 1799 until June 1800, almost as though it was founded especially in anticipation of this event. It reported his death on December 27. It announced the planned procession, and that Jonathan would deliver the eulogy at St. John's Church. The first issue in January 1800 has each column of the paper surrounded with thick black lines. It carries the most complete coverage of all the events surrounding Washington's death, including a diagram of the funeral cortege. The *Federal Observer*'s newspapermen searched "the darkened columns of every paper which reaches us, and carefully select each paragraph which involves the interesting subject." It carried reports from Washington, DC, with the messages from the House of Representatives including John Adams' reply, the Senate, and the War Department. Tobias Lear's letter from Mt. Vernon announcing the death was included along with the happenings in Alexandria, Philadelphia, New York, Salem, and Boston as well as in Portsmouth.

In the *Republican Ledger and Portsmouth Price Current* on January 1 all the words to the dirges that were sung in the church are printed and then the eulogy is described:

Eulogy on the Late General Washington (Sewall 1799). Courtesy of the Portsmouth Athenaeum.

> The audience were then entertained by, perhaps, one of the most sublime and pathetic orations ever delivered in this town, by Jonathan Mitchel Sewall, Esq. Minute guns were fired during the procession. The citizens wore a black crape round the left arm. The church was hung in black, and every thing bespoke the sincerity of the grief depicted in every countenance; and the poignancy of their sorrow which the death of Washington has created.

The "American Apollo" may have given his greatest performance that day.

The eulogy was published "At the Request of the Inhabitants" on January 17, 1800 by William Treadwell, who was the publisher of the *Federal Observer* during its brief life. Only six hundred copies were printed but they hoped that "the inhabitants of this town will evince their liberality by purchasing not only for themselves, but for their friends in the country."

CHAPTER 12.

His Book, His Family, His Friends

The Fourth of July in 1800 was celebrated in the usual manner except that this time about seventy gentlemen had dinner and drinks at the Piscataqua Bridge Tavern. This was the tavern on Goat Island in the middle of the river between the Newington and Durham ends of the bridge that was built in 1794. Patriotic songs were sung "among them an admired original, composed for the occasion, by Jonathan M. Sewall, Esq." (*US Oracle of the Day*, July 5, 1800). The tune was "Rule Britannia." Wasn't it time to use some new tunes?

> Sage Adams guides the helm of State,
> Our Senators are wise and true;
> More skill in counsel and debate
> Greece, Rome, or Albion never knew.
> Still Independence they'll maintain,
> Tho' Europe bleed at ev'ry vein!

And then:

> Party and Faction, taught at last,
> Shall guard the government they chose,
> In tears deplore their errors past,
> And hurl their wrath on foreign foes.
> Blest Independence, warm all hearts,
> In spite of Diplomatic arts!

There was another group of some eighty men who met at the Assembly Room that year where they "drank a number of

Republican toasts; sang Republican songs; and enjoyed themselves in a Republican style" (*US Oracle of the Day*, July 5, 1800).

Miscellaneous Poems

For many years, Jonathan had wanted to publish a book of his poems and attempted to raise the money for publishing it in various ways. As early as 1786 his brother-in-law wrote in his diary, "The subscription for Mitchell's poems goes on rapidly" (Oliver 1890, p. 233). The proposal was advertised in the *New Hampshire Gazette* that year. The cost was nine shillings, and the subscribers were to pay two shillings on application. The five hundred subscribers obviously were not found.

In June 1801, Jonathan petitioned the state for permission to raise $2000 by lottery to enable him to have his poems printed. The wording of the petition was rather despairing. It began "To the Honorable, The General Court, of the State of Newhampshire, Convened at Hopkinton, June 1801. Respectfully Sheweth Jonathan Mitchel Sewall, of Portsmouth, Attorney at Law, that a great part of his time, and the best powers of his genius, have been faithfully devoted to the service of his Country, in supporting the cause of Freedom, Independence and Government, by the energies of his pen." He stated that his family was growing up and was now "principally composed of females, of daughters, [who] demand an impression of his varied literary labors. Necessity impels to this, as the indisposition of a husband, a father, equally precludes future mental exertion, and bodily labor. The

> PROPOSALS for printing by Subscription, the poetical Works of JONATHAN M. SEWALL, Esq. containing a version of many of the POEMS of OSSIAN, and a number of other POEMS on a variety of subjects and occasions. To be printed in one large Octavo Volume, to contain about 400 pages on good Paper, with a fair new Type. To be neatly Bound and Lettered, and put to the Press as soon as 500 Books are subscribed for. To be delivered to the Subscribers at *nine shillings* each *Book*. *Two shillings* to be paid on subscribing.
>
> Subscriptions taken in for the above at the Printing-Office in Paved street, Portsmouth.

Proposals for printing by subscription. *NH Gazette*, March 11, 1786. GenealogyBank 2021.

wants, the daily wants, of a family, cannot be supported, without means; and sickness, denies the possibility of these." After all his work for other people for which he took little or no money, it appeared that he was not well and was not able to "furnish the means of subsistence to a distressed family of females..."

The original petition is found in the New Hampshire State Archives. However, whether or not it was presented is not known. Perhaps those who saw it decided to help. In July and August of 1801, again a proposal for subscription, rather than lottery tickets, was advertised in the *United States Oracle of the Day* every week during July through the first of August. This time it stated that the book was already in the press, and it was to be published the last week in August. But at the beginning of September they printed another request for gentlemen holding subscription papers to return them to Treadwell's in Portsmouth or to E. & S. Larkin in Boston.

Petition to the General Court for a lottery to raise the money for printing. Jonathan M. Sewall. June 1801. Courtesy of the New Hampshire Division of Archives and Records Management.

Finally on October 10 "in conformity to the act of the Congress of the United States intituled 'an Act for the encouragement of learning by securing the copies of maps, charts and books to the Authors and Proprietors of such copies during the times therein mentioned.'" That same day the announcement was made that "Subscribers are requested to send for their Books on Tuesday next."

Beginning in November 1801 the book was advertised in various newspapers across New England. Boston's *Columbian Centinel*, Jenk's *Portland Gazette*, and Keene's *New Hampshire Sentinel* published the same article and included the entire preface to the book. "We should fail in our duty were we to neglect recommending the volume to every American Patriot, and Real Federalist."

A short piece about the book in Boston's *Massachusetts Mercury* in December 1801 mentioned that it was for sale at several bookstores in the town: "The little encouragement afforded American genius has been the subject of much complaint..." and they hoped this meant better times for authors. "The well-known talents of Mr. S. insures indemnity in instruction and amusement to every purchaser."

In 1802 Angier March, a bookseller in Newburyport, Massachusetts, advertised the book and wrote: "The friends of genius and polite literature will, it is expected, avail themselves of this opportunity, not only to add to their libraries a valuable production, but also to evince their regard for one so eminently

Notice re: deposit of *Miscellaneous Poems* with the District of New-Hampshire. *US Oracle*, October 10, 1801. GenealogyBank 2021.

distinguished by his talent, his benevolence and his misfortunes" (*Newburyport Herald*, June 4, 1802). This may imply that the sad state in which Jonathan found himself when he wrote his petition to the state was known by many or even that the Newburyport bookseller was a friend of his family. March's bookshop was only twenty miles from Salem and many Sewall friends and relatives lived in the vicinity.

There was a review of the book "by Mitchell Sewall, Esq. of N.H." published by the literary correspondent of the *Philadelphia Repository and Weekly Register* on November 6, 1802, "The author discovers taste, ingenuity, a fine imagination..." He goes on to decry the lack of interest of books published by Americans. "It would seem that every American work must cross the Atlantic, and receive the approbation of British Reviewers ere we can appreciate its value... These Poems so deservedly noticed by our literary correspondent, have already obtained considerable celebrity to the eastward, tho' only published last year." Then most of the preface to the section "Profiles of Eminent Men" was quoted and the first few profiles were printed. During the next five weeks some of the profiles were included in the newspaper each week

---

> **"SEWALL's POEMS."**
>
> A small volume, bearing this title, has lately been published at *Portsmouth*. It contains about 300 pages of the miscellaneous poetical productions of J. M. SEWALL, Esq. The Man of Science, and the Poet need not be stimulated to encourage productions of so much intrinsic merit, and to those who recollect the enthusiasm with which the American soldiery were inspired by the songs of this gentleman in the earlier stages of our revolution, particularly the one intitled "*War and Washington*;"—and to those who have heard and read his late numerous productions, calculated to excite the public attention to the inroads of Jacobinism in our country ;—nothing need be said to engage the patronage of an enlightened and grateful public to the works. We should fail in our duty were we to neglect recommending the volume to every American Patriot, and Real Federalist :—To which end, we transcribe the preface to the work.
>
> **PREFACE.**
>
> "IT is with great diffidence that the author submits the following poems to the public eye. The world is already so amply stocked with bad poetry, that a writer should be cautious how he increases the heap ; and a real patriot ought to be tenderly jealous, even of the literary reputation of his country.
>
> "Many of the original pieces here presented to the public were written at an early period of life—not a few were only momentary effusions, and none of them were composed with much premeditation. But as nothing he can now offer will make them better, he desists from any farther apology, and quietly resigns them to their fate.
>
> "The specimens from *Ossian*, are taken from a work more leisurely composed, and therefore, if bad, have less to plead in their excuse. Macpherson's prose-translation of these poems fell into the author's hands as early as the year 1770, when they were but little known in this country, they pleased him, and he then attempted to turn a few passages into heroic verse. The work was amusing, and he has from time to time continued it. The greater part of these poems are now completed ; and on the favorable reception of the specimens will depend the future publication of the whole version.
>
> "Should he meet with the encouragement which every author wishes, he purposes to give his version to the public in two Octavo volumes with explanatory notes which he has already prepared, and also to offer some arguments in addition to those urged by Mr. MACPHERSON, Dr. BLAIR, and others, in favor of the authenticity of *Ossian's* poems, against the opinion of Doctor JOHNSON and his party."

Columbian Centinel Nov. 14, 1801 (Boston)

Review of "Sewall's Poems." *Columbian Centinel*, November 14, 1801. *GenealogyBank* 2021.

until they were all reproduced. This same review was in the Dover *Sun* and Amherst's *The Farmer's Cabinet* within a few months. As the writer of the article attributes the book to Mitchell Sewall, the correspondent may have been a friend as well.

In 2021 Amazon was advertising a leather-bound copy of the book "printed on high quality Paper, re-sized as per Current standards, professionally processed without changing its contents" for about $75. Occasionally copies of the original are advertised at considerably more than that, some of which are not surprisingly in very poor condition after more than two hundred years.

A song that is included in the book has been republished many times without being attributed to Jonathan. It is entitled "Anniversary Song" and was obviously written sometime before Washington's death. The song begins:

> When our great Sires this land explor'd,
> A shelter from tyrannic wrong;
> Led on by heav'ns almighty Lord,
> They sung[sic], and acted well the song.
> Rise united! dare be freed!
> Our sons shall vindicate the deed.

The words appear in many anthologies of patriotic songs, again to the tune of "Rule Britannia." One of the interesting uses of the song is in a book written in a series called "Classics for Home and School" with the wonderful title *The Boston Tea Party and Other Stories of the Revolution relating many Daring Deeds of the Old Heroes*. It was revised and adapted from Henry C. Watson, the author of *Noble Deeds of Our Fathers as Told by Old Soldiers of the Revolution Gathered around the Old Bell of Independence* and published in Boston in 1889, the year after the *Noble Deeds*. Both of these books were part of a series for schools. Many of the stories were written like novels with dialogue and this song appeared as one that a young man got up to sing that was "written for the occasion, but which his modesty had hitherto held back." Only a few words were changed from the original. "As Jove's high plant inglorious stands" became

"As the proud oak inglorious stands." By the late-nineteenth century, children were reading stories like this instead of ones about ancient Rome and its gods.

Jonathan's poem appeared in a story about General Putnam's escape, which took place in 1779 many years before the song was written. Only the first five verses are used as he goes on to speak of Adams. The final verse was:

> So when Elijah, call'd to heav'n,
> Up in the flaming chariot rode;
> Elisha took the mantle giv'n,
> And rose a prophet, or a god.
> Then shout great Adams! Freedom's son!
> Immortal heir of Washington.

Family and Friends

In his petition Jonathan spoke of his "family of females." They were his wife Sarah, then fifty-two-years old, and their two daughters; Caroline, age sixteen; and Susan, age eleven. The boys were established in their professions and must have been living away from home. Stephen, then twenty-six, had become a printer in his own right. The Portsmouth Athenaeum has original copies of various pamphlets he published. One of these was a discourse delivered at the ordination of Brother Thomas Barnes of the Universal Societies. On January 13, 1803 the first issue of *The Annals of the Times* appeared in Kennebunk, where their cousin David Sewall and his wife Mary Langdon who was from Portsmouth lived. It was a weekly paper published every Thursday from "S. Sewall's office" there. Stephen also sold books and his father's book of *Miscellaneous Poems* was usually listed among them. Occasionally a poem by his father was included. Many of the advertisements and articles are about Portsmouth, especially notices due to the Portsmouth fire in December 1802. On the Fourth of July in 1803 in Kennebunk "the performances were closed by an ode by S. Sewall set to music by Dr. Emerson" (*The Annals of the Times,* July 7, 1803).

As early as 1799 their son John, at twenty-one, had become a member of Governor Gilman's Blues the "Select Military Company" established that year (*Governor Gilman's Blues Militia Record Book 1799–1813*). On July 16, 1802, he opened a store in Market Street where he sold "English Goods suitable for the season" (*US Oracle*, July 24, 1802). A long list of these goods was published in the *Republican Ledger* on August 31 (shown here). By December of that year his shop was at 2 Bow Street, and it was one of those that burned in the December 26 fire. "Nearly three quarters of the European and India goods in the town had been deposited in the stores and shops which were consumed." However, with the help of friends much was preserved (*The True American and Commercial Daily Advertiser* [Philadelphia], Jan. 5, 1803). In April 1803, having lost his shop in the Great Parade Fire, he moved into a store on Buck Street (now State Street) "lately improved by Abraham Isaac." Isaac died in February 1803 and had been an auctioneer as well as a shopkeeper. John Sewall soon became an auctioneer, too.

The New Hampshire Fire & Marine Insurance Company was incorporated in 1803. John became its secretary and continued to be so for about ten years. He, Daniel Treadwell, and Samuel Elliot had been appointed as a committee to receive donations

John B. Sewall opens shop in Market Street. *Republican Ledger*, August 31, 1802. GenealogyBank 2021.

for the sufferers of the fire. They wrote to John Langdon and others to express their thanks for the response in the *Oracle Post* of May 15, 1804. On May 2 there had been an auction to sell "all his stock in trade" from his shop on Buck Street. A "new Brickstore on Spring-hill" was available at his previous address of 2 Bow Street at the bend of Market and Bow Streets by December 1805. He advertised himself there as an auctioneer and continued to sell English and India goods.

Abraham Isaac died in February 1803. He and his wife were the only Jewish couple in Portsmouth at that time. He was buried in North Cemetery and "the Grand Lodge of Newhampshire, and the Lodge of St. Johns, The Most Worshipful Thomas Thompson, Esq. Grand-Master of Masons performed the funeral obsequies" (*US Oracle,* Feb. 19,1803). His epitaph was written by Jonathan:

> Entomb'd beneath, where earth-born troubles cease,
> A son of faithful Abraham sleeps in peace.
> In life's first bloom, he left his native air,
> A Sojourner as all his fathers were.
> Thro' various toils his active spirit ran,
> A faithful steward, and an honest man,
> His soul, we trust now freed from mortal woe,
> Finds in the Patriarch's bosom sweet repose.

The Isaacs must have been good friends. Not only did Jonathan write his epitaph, but John was one of the appraisers of the inventory of the Isaac's shop with its extensive list of goods, from fabrics to pots and pans and everything in between. Unfortunately, nearly everything was sold to cover Isaac's debts.

Fourth of July 1801–1804

The Fourth of July in 1801, according to the *New Hampshire Gazette* (July 7, 1801), "was remarkably serene, and joy seemed to glow in every countenance." There were various gatherings and "the greatest harmony was observed through the whole..." However, the following year things became rather unpleasant.

Jonathan wrote a stinging rebuke of the Republicans that he entitled "Washington Hall." It was sung by the Federalists at the Piscataqua Bridge meeting on Goat Island and was published in various newspapers including the *United States Oracle* on the tenth, the *Columbian Centinel* (Boston) on the fourteenth, the *Republican or Anti-Democrat* (Baltimore) on the nineteenth, and the *New Hampshire Sentinel* (Keene) the twenty-fourth. The *United States Oracle* reported the celebration at the bridge by a "number of Gentlemen, true Federalists of Portsmouth, and some very respectable Gentlemen from the country…much the largest ever known to assemble there upon a similar occasion." Included are the words to his song and one from the Republican meeting with a note that the editors claim impartiality because they have published both songs, "and surely neither party can complain that the poison is not accompanied with its antidote."

Some of the seven verses of "Washington Hall" include:

> The diff'rence how vast! in Sense, Genius and Worth,
> 'Twixt *Vernon's great Chief,* and his present Successor!
> Day's Regent! compar'd to a *glow-worm of earth!*
> What a contrast! a foil! to his great Predecessor!
> While majestic He sway'd,
> No dire factions dismay'd,
> All nations rever'd, and *Columbia* obey'd.
> Away, then, from Faction at Liberty's call!
> And court the bright Goddess in *Washington-Hall!*

> If e'er we forget Thee! Thou Great, Just and Good!
> Or astray from thy precepts are basely found running,
> May our tongues to the roof of our mouths be fast glu'd!
> And our right-hand forget, to all ages, its cunning!
> Thy worth, valor, fame,
> All our souls shall inflame,
> And eternity ring with Great Washington's name,
> Away, then, to Freedom! at Gratitude's call!
> Away, then to Freedom! Leave Jefferson's stall!
> And court the bright Goddess in *Washington-Hall!*

Some of the newspapers also included the song "Jefferson Hall" "from the pen of John Wentworth, Esq." (This John Wentworth was the son of Thomas Wentworth, a brother of the John Wentworth who was the last colonial governor.) The Republicans met at the hall above the market in the Parade. It had been named Jefferson Hall for the president. The *New Hampshire Gazette* (July 6, 1802) tells of the "large and respectable company of citizens as ever graced any board on any former occasion in this place." Included are the words to "Jefferson Hall," the song by John Wentworth. It is certainly much more relaxed than Jonathan's song and ends with this verse.

> Let *Envy*, let *Malice*, let *Faction* retire;
> *Republican* virtues our bosoms inspire:
> Would you know how they flourish in us one and all,
> *You have only to join us in* Jefferson Hall.

In the *New Hampshire Gazette* the following week (July 13, 1802), John Wentworth wrote a long rambling letter to the editors complaining about the insinuations made of him in the *United States Oracle* and made some very cutting comments about the "Poet of the Day" whom he does not name:

> ...that the *Poet of the Day,*...could *bring himself* to calumniate and abuse his *very* benefactor, whom he represents to be a *beast* in Jefferson's stall, with those *beasts* of Republicans, his Fellow-Citizens and Fellow-Townsmen—This benefactor, the poison Songster, whose heart has been as open as charity to the distress of the poor Poet: to refer again to the principle of a *Gentleman* I know not, or does any person who had the honor to attend Jefferson-Hall, on a day that every American has been used since the Spirit of 76 *arose.*

Later he went on to say:

>...am I a vile, jacobin, traitor, confounder, constitution destroyer, as the tories and poet would make me,
> and never to enter those gates that are to fly open to receive the poet of the day drunk or sober—to greet Washington in Washington Hall!

There Wentworth said it, "drunk or sober." His letter covered two and one-half columns in a newspaper that only had four pages of four columns. He said he would explain more when he returned from the country, only nothing more can be found. He had obviously done something to benefit the Sewalls, perhaps just bringing Jonathan home one evening when he had too much to drink? John Wentworth wrote the letter to the editors of the *New Hampshire Gazette*, Nathaniel and Washington Peirce, on Saturday evening July 10, 1802, from Little Harbor, his wife's family home.

It was on December 26 that year that the Great Parade Fire, the first of the three devastating Christmas fires, took place in Portsmouth. It totally gutted the Jefferson Hall that Jonathan had raged about in his song, along with about 120 homes, barns, and shops. This included the home of John and Abigail Pickering on Market Street where Jonathan studied when he first came to Portsmouth, as well as his son John's shop at the corner of Bow Street. How many of the "fashionable straw bonnets and fine beaver hatts" were lost?

The following July, the *New Hampshire Gazette* and *Republican Ledger* published an article about the Republican gathering which was in the Assembly Room that year. John Wentworth composed another "Patriotic Song" which was sung. The other group was mentioned in a few lines at the end of the *Republican Ledger* article: "We understand also, a company of federalists *retired* to Piscataqua Bridge, where they had an entertainment, and enjoyed themselves, *in their way*" (July 5, 1803). The *United States Oracle* had only a small notice that told of the great number of Federal Republicans who dined at the Piscataqua Bridge where "The day was passed with that pure hilarity, which animates only the bosoms of true Washingtonian Republicans" (July 9, 1803).

There was no mention of the usual poet, but that was the year when his son Stephen composed the ode for the celebrations in Kennebunk, so perhaps the family gathered there instead.

By the following year both the now *Portsmouth Oracle* and Jonathan seem to have recovered their voices. There was a long article about "A large party of respectable citizens repaired to *Piscataqua Bridge* where they partook in *Washington Hall* of an elegant dinner... The enjoyments of the day were greatly heightened by an *excellent* Song from the pen of the celebrated author of "War and Washington,"—it combined the *first* classic elegance with the pure spirit of Washingtonian principles" (July 7, 1804). The tavern on the bridge had named its meeting place Washington Hall. The tune was "Hail Columbia," a new song written in 1798. There were seven long verses with many allusions to the classics including the Bible. The chorus went like this:

> Though desp'rate pilots rule the helm,
> Storms rend the bark, and surges whelm,
> Heav'n shall control the raging blast
> And guide her to the post at last.

Judge John Pickering

Earlier that year there had been distressing news. John Pickering was impeached from his seat on the US District Court for New Hampshire and was very ill. Pickering served in the New Hampshire State Legislature from 1783 to 1787, was appointed to the New Hampshire Superior Court in 1790, and had become its chief justice. By 1794 "The hypochondria of Judge Pickering" was well known (Plumer 1857, p. 273). But on Feb. 10, 1795, George Washington had nominated him to the post. He was confirmed by the US Senate.

By 1800 Pickering was not well at all and often did not show up for his court sessions. According to William Whipple at a trial on November 11, 1802, it was obvious that Pickering was intoxicated. Judge Pickering actually confirmed that was true and said, "Adjourned. I shall be sober tomorrow morning. Today I am damn drunk." At the time R. Cutts Shannon in a sworn oral testimony said: "I further testify that I have had frequent opportunities of seeing and conversing with Judge Pickering for more than three years past, during the whole time, he has appeared to me to be greatly deranged in his mind which I believe has been much increased, if not altogether occasioned by habits of intemperance."

President Thomas Jefferson sent evidence of this to the US House of Representatives in February 1803, and they voted to impeach Pickering on March 2 on charges of drunkenness and unlawful rulings. The US Senate tried the impeachment beginning January 4, 1804. Pickering's son, Joshua, went to Washington to testify and said that his father was insane at the time and was still mentally unstable. He asked that he could be given time to recover so that he would be able to defend himself, but the motion was turned down. The only newspaper where this petition was seen was in Stephen's newspaper, *The Annals of the Times* from Kennebunk (May 10, 1804). It filled over two columns on the front page.

Petition to the High Court on behalf of Judge Pickering. *The Annals of the Times*, May 10, 1804. GenealogyBank 2021.

Federalists argued that Democratic-Republicans were attempting to remove Pickering from office even though he had not committed high crimes or misdemeanors as set forth in the Constitution. Pickering was convicted on March 12, 1804, of all charges presented by the House by a vote of 19 to 7, which immediately removed him from office. Just over a year later he died on April 11, 1805, as did his wife Abigail in December that year.

William Plumer Jr. in an autobiography of his own father, who was a US senator for New Hampshire then, felt that because Pickering became ill, he was made to be a criminal which was a total distortion of justice.

In 2016, Fritz Wetherbee talked about John Pickering on *New Hampshire Chronicle* (Nov. 29). He thought Pickering was most likely suffering from Alzheimer's disease.

Jonathan's reputation for drinking and for nervous complaints was much the same as Pickering's. They must have had some wonderful times together working, laughing, complaining, and drinking during all those many years.

CHAPTER 13.

Parody, Celebration, and Death

A Letter to a Federalist and its Parody

New Hampshire and Massachusetts were the only two states which did not vote overwhelmingly to reelect Thomas Jefferson in 1804. The run up to the New Hampshire state election that was to be held on March 12, 1805, seems to have been fought out through the newspapers and pamphleteers. Thomas Elwyn, Esq., an Englishman who married John Langdon's daughter, was a lawyer, and he and Elizabeth lived in Portsmouth with their children. His father-in-law was running for governor of New Hampshire again, this time as a Democratic-Republican. The incumbent was Federalist John Gilman who had been the governor since 1794. Elwyn wrote a thirty-one-page pamphlet, *A Letter to a Federalist in reply to some of the popular objections to the motives and tendency of the measures of the present administration*, in which he attempted to convince Federalists that the Democratic-Republican Party stood for everything that they wanted. The press that supported his views wrote "The moderation of the sentiments, and the spirit of good manners, which runs through the whole of this persuasive Letter, is highly creditable to the writer" (*NH Gazette*, Feb. 25, 1805). An article in the March 23, 1805 *Farmer's Weekly Museum* of Walpole, New Hampshire, about the letter, after saying it was beneath the attention of a critic, described the author this way: "The writer must be either an egregious numbskull himself, or have a most contemptible opinion of his readers."

John Langdon won the election for governor, but on March 30 the *Portsmouth Oracle* and the *Columbian Centinel* (Boston) advertised a pamphlet entitled *A Parody on some of the most striking passages in a late pamphlet entitled "A letter to a Federalist" with large additions and improvements* by Vernon H. Quincey, published by the *Oracle Press* in Portsmouth. The thirty-one-page letter written by Thomas Elwyn had been turned into a forty-seven-page poem with copious footnotes. Everyone must have known that it was really written by Jonathan Mitchel Sewall. "Every Federalist, every man of taste and sentiment should possess a copy of this interesting Pamphlet" (*Portsmouth Oracle*). One of the quotations at the beginning is from Pope: "Ask you what provocation I have had? The strong antipathy of Good to Bad." However, the *New Hampshire Gazette* in a piece published April 16 wrote: "the author [of the Letter, Elwyn] was violently attacked by the whole class of his opponents, as the production of a man—without sense, argument or reflection and they have even provoked the pen of a once distinguished fellow citizen [Sewall] to lampoon by parody and buffoonery, this truly sentimental and friendly Letter, with unusual severity." And finally, "his [Sewall's] many friends who consider his henpick'd [sic] situation more to be pitied than envied." Did his "family of females" accompany him everywhere?

"Parody of A Letter to a Federalist," *Portsmouth Oracle*, March 30, 1805. *GenealogyBank* 2020.

Fourth of July 1805–1807

For the Fourth of July each year the bells in the town were rung, flags were hoisted on the ships in the harbor, cannons were sounded, the shops and stores were closed, and everyone celebrated. Often the military paraded at five until nine o'clock in the morning. After a drill they marched through the streets and fired rounds at various locations. There was usually a procession to a meeting-house, where there was music, the reading of the Declaration of Independence, and an oration followed by the entire procession including the people of the town marching through some of the principal streets.

Beginning in 1800, after these festivities, there were always groups of men who gathered for two or more separate events depending on their politics. "Two excellent Songs from the elegant and ingenious pen of J. M. Sewall, esq." were sung at the gathering in the Assembly Room in 1805 (*Portsmouth Oracle*, July 6, 1805). One of the songs was printed in the *Green Mountain Patriot* in Peacham, Vermont, "A Song for the Anniversary of Independence, July 4, 1805," and was introduced like this: "The union of genius and patriotism is rare and valuable, and deserves to be greeted with particular applause. For this reason the following very excellent Song merits a place in every paper in the Union, not only as a compliment to the author, but in justice to the nation."

However, it was the other song that appeared in all the newspapers. "The Hobbies Parodied" was introduced in the *Gazette of Maine* (Bucksport) in this way: "The following humorous and satirical Song was composed by J. M. Sewall, Esq. of Portsmouth, N. H. a gentleman whose poetick [sic] talents have often contributed largely to the amusement of his friends." The song has fourteen verses, each one speaking of the "hobbies" of various men or groups or states, including Washington, Jefferson, Adams, Jay, Franklin, Britain, Jacobins, Federalists, Connecticut, Massachusetts, and New England. An example for Benjamin Franklin:

> Franklin's hobby was lightning-rods, thunder, and fire,
> How he joy'd to bestride the electrical wire!
> When Oppression's bolt strove Freedom's fane to disjoint,
> He repell'd the Explosion and struck to the point.
> That was his hobby…

"The Hobbies Parodied" including most of its verses was found in the newspapers from nearly all of the states from Portland, Maine, to Charleston, South Carolina, including five in New York City, three in Boston, as well as those in many other cities and towns.

In 1806 the Democratic-Republicans met at Jefferson Hall again. This time their song parodied one of Jonathan's: "What a terrible bustle the Federalist made! ... What lies and what stories, were told by the Tories, Our Chief to defame and to tarnish his glories!" (*NH Gazette,* July 22, 1806).

Those who were now described as the "Federal Republicans" had their celebrations at the Assembly Room that year. "Two excellent songs composed by J. M. Sewall, Esq. added greatly to the enjoyment of the day" (*Portsmouth Oracle,* July 5, 1806), this time sung to "Hail Columbia." One of the songs was reproduced in full in the *Newport Mercury* on August 2 and begins with "Hail Independence! happy day," but by the seventh and final verse he wrote:

> Sons of Columbia! still oppose,
> And hold no commerce with her foes!
> Detest the sycophantic tribe,
> And scorn the hand that holds a bribe.
> Remember Washington, your fire;
> Add dauntless Adams, stern, yet mild,
> Unrivall'd both, yet both revil'd;
> Soon may such patriots rise elate,
> And Gilmans once more guide the state.
>
> Chorus:
> Short, tho' triumphant, falsehood's reign,
> While Truth eternal will remain,
> Heav'n shall dispel Columbia's woes
> And doom to infamy her foes!

In a biographical sketch in *The Poets of Essex County, Massachusetts* (1889), Sidney Perley wrote that Jonathan was ill for about eighteen months before his death in March 1808. Eighteen months would be from about October 1806.

Another devastating fire started on December 24, 1806, only three years after the one that had gutted John Barnard Sewall's old business. It began in the evening just across the street from his new brick store at the end of Bow Street. It was thought that the fire had established itself in Stephen Little's store near the intersection with Merchant's Row, the newly built brick buildings along the waterfront in what is now Ceres Street. It quickly spread up Bow Street through the buildings next to it that contained rum, brandy, and other merchandise that easily caught on fire. As the fire made its way along the street some burning shingles blew up into the steeple of St. John's Church at the top of the hill. The Portsmouth fire engines were not powerful enough to extinguish the flames. People ran into the building and saved many of the valuable items in the church, but the entire wooden building that had been there since 1732 was lost. The next day the parishioners of St. John's met at the North Meeting-house to observe Christmas. A brick-built St. John's Church was completed in 1807 and it stands there today.

On Independence Day in 1807 the Republicans, "among whom we are proud to mention our well beloved Governor" (John Langdon), celebrated at John Davenport's Ark Tavern on Daniel Street. The Federalists met at the Assembly Room again, others met at the Bridge and many people "regaled themselves on the water—some went to the Shoals, others to various Islands in and outside of the harbour" (*NH Gazette,* July 7, 1807). The *Portsmouth Oracle* reports about the celebration at the Assembly Room that "A great number of patriotic and festive songs added greatly to the happiness of the meeting...they do equal honor to the head and heart of the poet." They include this verse "which every American should join in full chorus":

> But Independence we'll maintain,
> Our Constitution and our Laws,
> Stand Pillars of bright Freedom's Fane,
> And smile at death in her proud cause!
> And shou'd her glorious dome be riv'n,
> On her last blaze ascend to Heav'n.

The *Intelligencer* was a new paper that produced its first issue in December 1806 just weeks before the Bow Street Fire. The publisher was Samuel Whidden and his office was at Spring-Hill, opposite Merchant's Row, and just around the corner from the source of the fire. On July 9, 1807, he published a piece about the Fourth of July festivities that included descriptions of all the parties that had been held: "In short the festivity was general, and every face expressed, (what no American ought ever to forget,) that we are FREE, SOVEREIGN and INDEPENDENT." But then on the next page he wrote with the heading "To gratify the desires of some of our customers to know who the great Poet Laureat to the Muses is, to whose poetic genius our paper would have been highly indebted.—The following ACROSTIC will lead to a discovery."

Poet Laureat to the Muses acrostic. *Intelligencer* (Portsmouth), July 9, 1807. *GenealogyBank* 2021.

Justice demands, to consecrate the fame
Of one, who bears th' immortal SEWALL name,
No sordid, selfish views debase his mind,
And ev'ry wish, is, love to all mankind,
The SACRED NINE, as proof of their esteem
Have CROWN"D him Poet Laureat to THEM,
And who can better claim this right than HE,
None, surely none, in point of poetry,

Mark the bright genius of this great man's pen,
It charms and animates the souls of men,
The Muses too, oft call on him to write
Chaste themes of love, of pleasure and delight
His compositions hear attentive, while
Each look betrays the approbating smile,
Lo their decree! TO ALL MEN BE IT KNOWN,
Let SEWALL henceforth wear, th' Aonian crown.

Such HIGH applause was never known before
Exalted thus! what bard could ask for more?
When this decree to Sewall first was read,
Amaz'd he stood, like one rose from the dead
Let me, said he, ask one more gift beside,
Let Sewall sometimes lay his crown aside.

The Sacred Nine are the ancient Greek goddesses of literature, science, and the arts. What a beautiful tribute. Jonathan was surely the first poet laureate of Portsmouth.

In February 1808 his *Miscellaneous Poems* book is listed among those in Sargeant's Circulating Library at No. 39 Wall Street in New York City (*Spectator*, Feb. 13, 1808). That same month Jonathan's son Stephen began publication of a weekly paper in Portsmouth entitled *The Literary Mirror*. Charles Brewster in *Ramble #96* comments "The most youthful and the last of these relics of ancient journalism, is *The Literary Mirror*, of various dates in 1808, published by Stephen Sewall, in Court St., opposite the Brick Market [behind the North Church], neat and tasteful in its typographical execution, and containing a judicious variety of original and selected matter. It was published, I think, but a single year, though deserving a longer lease of life."

Logo of Stephen Sewall's *The Literary Mirror. The Literary Mirror*, 1808–1809. Courtesy of the Portsmouth Athenaeum.

Jonathan Mitchel Sewall, the great and good—is no more.

The announcement of Jonathan's death was included along with others in the April 2 issue of *The Literary Mirror*: "In this town, on Tuesday evening last, in the 61st year of this age, JONA. M. SEWALL, Esq." The following Saturday, the entire final page of the paper was an Elegy to his father written by Stephen.

The funeral arrangements were announced in the *Portsmouth Oracle* on April 2, 1808: "His funeral will be at 4 o'clock this afternoon, and will proceed from his late dwelling house in Gates-street; where relatives and friends are requested to attend."

Jonathan was buried in the North Cemetery and his tombstone reads:

> **Sacred to the Memory of Jonathan Mitchel Sewall, Esq.**
> **Counsellor at Law who died March 29, 1808 Age 60**
> In vain shall worth or wisdom save
> The dying victim from the destin'd grave,
> Nor Charity, our helpless nature's pride,
> The friend to him who knows no friend beside,
> Nor genius, science, eloquence have pow'r,
> One moment to protract the appointed hour.
> Could these united have his life repriev'd,
> We should not weep for Sewall still had liv'd.

His age is incorrect on the tombstone, as he had just had his sixty-first birthday a few days before he died. Notice of his death appeared in many newspapers, not just in New Hampshire but it was also found in papers in Massachusetts, Connecticut, Rhode Island, and Vermont. The *Columbian Phenix* in Providence noted: "At Portsmouth, J. M. Sewall, Esq. the New-Hampshire Bard, aged 61." The long obituary that was originally published in *The Literary Mirror* on April 16 was reproduced in full in newspapers in Charleston, South Carolina; Salem, Massachusetts; Philadelphia; and even Doylestown, Pennsylvania; as well as in

ELEGY
ON THE DEATH OF
J. M. Sewall, Esq.

Farewel dear SIRE thy cheering face no more,
Shall we behold on this inclement shore!
Nor shall AFFLICTION with her *poignant* dart,
Again o'erwhelm and *wound* thy *feeling* heart!

Life's storms are o'er, its boist'rous winds are laid,
And *peace* and *rest* attend thy silent *shade*;
But our warm *heart*, shall be thy *noblest* shrine,
There shall thy *virtues* everlasting shine.

Lo GENIUS *weeps!* on sighing zephyrs borne,
O'er thy *sad grave* the heav'nly MUSES *mourn!*
And SPRING, in all the *loveliness* of *tears*,
To *grace* thy *grave*, with sweetest flowers appears.

And ah! the *tear*, still streams from MEM'RY's eye!
Still, fond AFFECTION, heaves the *sorrowing sigh!*
A thousand *tender thoughts* incessant rise,
Dissolve the soul, and overflow the eyes!

But like an angel's, thy lov'd voice I hear,
"Forbear! forbear! and *dry up each fond tear!*
"Unbind the CYPRESS, look beyond the tomb,
"And round your temples let the MYRTLE bloom;

"Dispel each grief, cast off the weeds of woe,
"And in your breast let JOY's bright flow'ret blow;
"*High in salvation and the climes of bliss,*
"I taste unutterable happiness!"

Then let us in his excellencies soar,
And be what men and angels must adore,
Practice his *precepts* as we *lov'd* his *name,*
And make our *lives* his monument of *fame.*

What kind compassion fill'd his gen'rous breast!
What tenderness! what pity! for th' oppress'd?
Such ever found in the *extreme* of *need,*
In him, a *guardian, father, friend,* indeed!

The widow's sorrowing heart, behold him cheer,
And gently wipe the weeping orphan's tear!

With what concern he heard their moving cries,
While all the angel glisten'd in his eyes!

With cold disdain he never turn'd away,
From a poor supplicant who had nought to pay;
But glori'd to maintain his right the more,
And warmer strove, because the wrong'd *was* poor.

Falshood, hypocrisy, and knavish art,
E'er met the deep abhorrence of his heart:
How 'gainst injustice all his soul awoke!
And flash'd in lightning, and in thunder broke!

Not earth's proud throne, a system's boundless sway
Could tempt his mind from rectitude to stray:
Stern in integrity, fix'd as a rock,
Which ocean's billows, and the tempests mock.

But what was earth in all its power and show
To his vast mind? what had it to bestow?
He higher look'd, and on *faith's* flaming wings,
Soar'd far beyond all sublunary things.

Above, he saw of *wealth* a glorious mine,
And as imperishable, as divine,
There lay his *treasure* purchas'd for the blest,
There dwelt his Saviour, *there* his hopes had rest.

Borne from this *vale of tears* with tempests riv'n!
He reaps the harvest, quaffs the joys of heav'n;
There, see, in full orb'd majesty divine,
His *Genius* all sublim'd transcendent shine!

Rapt to the highest heaven, his "*Muse of fire,*"
Awakes in boundless strains th' immortal *lyre!*
Strains sweeter than the music of the spheres,
Ah! strains that ravish ev'n Angels' ears!

Soon, soon, will *life's* sad pilgrimage be o'er,
And *death* will land us on th' eternal shore;
Then, in his godlike virtues let us rise,
And join his *sainted* SPIRIT in the skies!

PUBLISHED BY S. SEWALL.

"Elegy on the Death of J. M. Sewall, Esq." *The Literary Mirror*, April 9, 1808. Courtesy of the Portsmouth Athenaeum.

various places in New Hampshire. This biographical sketch was "presented by a Friend" to *The Literary Mirror*. It contains many of the details of his life that are also recorded in his biographical sketch in the *Early State Papers of New Hampshire.*

However, an even more personal obituary appeared in the Portsmouth *Intelligencer* on April 21 and began like this:

THE LIFE AND TIMES OF JONATHAN MITCHEL SEWALL

It is very important that the memory of memorable men should be imprinted on the minds of contemporaries, as well as to hand down to posterity such qualities as adorn our own natures in our own time, and to infix the quality of goodness and perfection as it...belongs to one of the most remarkable and considerable persons that we have lately known—JONATHAN MITCHELL SEWALL—delicate is the attempt, unassuming as to regards the superior and extraordinary accompaniments of his genius and mind...- The tribute to exalted merit exulting in its own strength of conscious faculty, unbounded philanthropy, distinguished greatness as a man; is a duty & unpardonable neglect not to offer the silent homage to your precious and never to be forgotten remains. ah! Mitchell Sewall. "You sleep upon the lap of death", and the herald of bliss has welcomed you to never ending happiness unfading laurels bloom over your blest immortal soul—like your own Ossian, you lived to beautify, & rejoice now in celestial beatitude. This singular prodigiously qualified man was very early initiated into the profession of the law of which he was never fond—the peculiar turn of his mind was philosophical—and his abilities profound and masterly were led to an imitation of the ancient poets; he excelled some of the greatest modern poets in force, thought, versification, and imagery...The peculiarities of his life were extraordinary; but, question his friend, his brother in his profession, his relative in life, the stranger, the poor, the widow, the orphan, the fatherless, the destined culprit, the helpless prisoner, the unfortunate beggar; and the answer is he "opened his mouth for the oppressed" and pleaded the cause of the poor, their unaffected and impassioned accents of gratitude were "Mitchell Sewall is a great good man."

It is in this obituary that we find the intriguing statement that he resembled Edmund Burke:

> In his person, manner, gesture and look it is a striking fact he had a resemblance to Edmund Burke—his colloquial talent was unbounded, his fertility of invention, his exuberance of fancy; his wit and jocoseness; his wisdom mixed with mirth; would to an utter stranger to him, evince a most astonishing person of singular genius.—In the clouded and unclouded scenes that passed before him, he was the same; latterly from filial duty and honorable sentiment he was made perfectly easy and comfortable, and as he said happy as to worldly concerns—an amiable family, tho' his family was the whole world—and all endeavored to render him happy—and it is not among the least of the consolations of those who respected him that all credit is due to his respectable lady, sons and daughters—I close these interesting lines—and hope tho' despair that in our age we may see many such good men as "Sewall ! ! !" but not to lament his irreparable loss as an amiable worthy man.

Nearly fifty years later, this tribute was contained as part of an oration by the Rev. Dr. Peabody at the "Centennial Celebration of the introduction of Printing into New-Hampshire, held at Portsmouth, Oct. 6, 1856" (*Celebration of the Centennial Anniversary*, 1857, p. 27):

> ...none can take precedence, in point of genius, versatility, and ability of Jonathan Mitchell Sewall... His success as an advocate was great and might have been pre-eminent had he not preferred the wild-wood paths pervaded by the murmurs of Helicon, to the straight walks and clipped hedges of Themis, and in conversational grace and power he had no superior.

And in this Portsmouth newspaper published by his son Stephen:

> Virtues like those of a Sewall will long embalm the memory of departed worth. And, while Genius, without sensibility, lives unbeloved, and Science without philanthropy dies unregretted; the fatherless, the widow, and the poor, gather round his grave; and even the prisoner and the appointed for death, exclaim: There sleeps our warmest, truest friend!
> (*The Literary Mirror,* April 16, 1808)

CHAPTER 14.

The House on Gates Street

An unpublished manuscript by Dorothy Vaughan from 1972 held at the Portsmouth Athenaeum includes a picture of the house at 64 Gates Street. She wrote: "The only claim to fame which this little house has is the fact that it was the home of a Portsmouth writer and poet, Jonathan Mitchell Sewall…"

During the 1950s, she and Natalie Fenwick wrote a series of articles for the *Portsmouth Herald*. The accompanying editor's note stated:

> Portsmouth has many old structures whose historical significance has been relegated to obscurity by time and indifference. Some of them stand unrecognized even by local residents, while there is no means provided for identifying them for out-of-town visitors who come here searching for traces of the city's colonial past. The accompanying article was one of a series prepared by Mrs. Marston S. Fenwick of 576 Sagamore Ave. and presented by *The Portsmouth Herald* with a view toward awakening interest in these living symbols of Historic Portsmouth.

It was a time when many old buildings were being raised to make way for more modern structures. Dr. Vaughan and Mrs. Fenwick together were trying to awaken the people of this city to the heritage which was being destroyed.

By the time that the article was printed in December 1958, the Sewall Family had been well established in the history of Portsmouth in this "modest little house at 64 Gates Street." When my sister and I bought the house in 2003, there was a historic horse and buggy tour through the Portsmouth streets. It was run by Ray Parker's Portsmouth Livery Company, and they always stopped out front and told people about Jonathan Mitchel Sewall who lived there.

An article in the *Portsmouth Times* as far back as 1910 included: "Jonathan M. Sewell [sic], one of the most noted lawyers of his day, a poet-writer of eminence resided in the house on the south side of Gates Street, the first house from Washington Street."

In 1902, C. S. Gurney published photographs of many houses in the city in *Portsmouth historic and picturesque* that included a photograph of the house. The caption is "On the south side of Gates Street, the first house from Washington Street is the dwelling occupied until 1808 by Lawyer Sewall..."

In 1876, 1884, and 1896, *The Portsmouth Guide Book* by Sarah H. Foster consists of a series of walks through Portsmouth describing

64 Gates Street house in 1902. (Gurney 1902).

the historic buildings. Walk Three includes: "In No. 5 [now 64] Gates street lived Jonathan M. Sewall, our Revolutionary poet, who died in 1808..."

Interestingly, in *Brewster's Rambles* #125 in 1869 we read: "Prominent among the poets of the Revolution, whose verses carried spirit into the camp, and stirred up the patriotic fires of those who performed the statesman's duties at home, was that philanthropic man, Jonathan Mitchell Sewall, Esq., whose home was in Portsmouth, and whose last place of abode was the house on Gates street nearly opposite that of Capt. Joseph Grace." Joseph Grace lived farther down the street at 99, not "nearly opposite" 64 Gates St.

When we purchased the house in 2003, we went to the Rockingham County Registry of Deeds and had copies of the Sewall deeds printed for us. Their original deed for the purchase of the house in 1791 is 129/176 Wentworth to Sewall and it reads: "Certain lot of land with a dwelling House thereon situate in Portsmouth... Said Premises are situated on the Southerly side of Gates Street and now in the Occupation of the said Jonathan Mitchel Sewall Esquire." The deed gives no indication as to who lived on any side of this property, a detail that is found in most deeds.

The other notable piece of information that I gained early on here on Gates Street was from one of our neighbors from two doors down the street. One day as we were standing talking in Gates Street, he said: "We like to think that George Washington schlept here." Once I found out more about Jonathan Mitchel Sewall, I realized that he not only idolized George Washington, but had written the words to the Revolutionary War song "War and Washington" as well as the three odes that were sung outside the State House when Washington visited in 1789. In 1799 he gave the eulogy in St. John's Church after the death of George Washington and wrote several other laudatory poems about the president throughout his years in office. And maybe George Washington walked down the street where we lived.

In my research for this book I decided it would be interesting to find out who lived on Gates Street when George Washington may have "schlept" here. I worked my way up from the corner of Gates and Manning because I thought when Washington and his entourage left Mrs. Lear's house they would have walked past the old Meeting House and down what was then known as Peirce's Lane (Manning Street) before turning into Gates Street. Deeds for some of the houses were easier to work through than others and some seemed to come to a dead end. There was a curious one at 90 Gates Street, Deed 366/315 Lowd to Deering in 1856, which describes that house as: "A certain piece or lot of land beginning at the southeast corner of land owned and occupied by Miss Susan Sewall, etc." This was obviously wrong as that house was three doors down the street from 64 Gates Street.

As I worked my way through Jonathan's life, I came to a time in 1794 when the family obviously needed to raise money because they sold off the back half of their property which ran through to Howard Street. Deed 136/401 Jona M. & Sarah Sewall to John Seaward, Mariner describes it as: "land bounded 60 feet on Maudlins Lane, 60 feet on land of Benjamin Mackey, dec., 60 feet on land of George Wentworth, 58 on land of Sarah Sewall." After I found that I kept looking out the back window of our house and trying to work out how that could be true, as behind the house was the garden of a house on Washington Street and beyond that part of the house at the corner of Washington and Howard Streets.

When I found Deed 137/268 from 1793 for 11 Howard Street, which was behind the house next door to me on Gates Street, I began to wonder about the Sewalls. This was the year before they sold the back half of their land. Elizabeth Pascal sold to her son George Wentworth "beginning on the southeast corner of a lot of land I sold some years since, to John Libbey, cordwainer, dec. and said lot sold Libby being partly on Washington St, and partly on Muddling Street 40 feet from southeast corner of Libbey's lot to lot of Jona. M. Sewall Esquire, thence

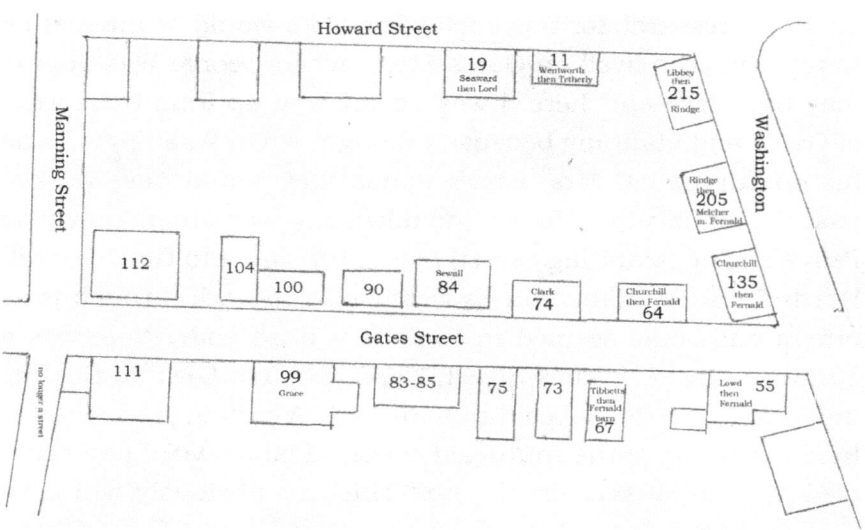

Gates and Howard Streets houses with current house numbers. Author's graphic.

northerly by said Sewall's lot 80 feet to lot of the heirs of Thos. Clark, Weaver, dec. thence westerly by Clark's, lot of Nathaniel Melchers 40 feet thence partly by Melcher's lot and by Libbey's lot 80 feet to Muddling St."

Who was Thomas Clark, weaver? He sounded very interesting to me as I used to weave myself. I could imagine a weaver living in this small house more easily than a lawyer and well-known local poet. The inventory of Thomas Clark's "estate" is available and includes £300 for "2 setts Weavers Looms Compleat [sic]." By this time I really wasn't sure that the Sewalls had lived here at all. But perhaps they had to move down the street before he died because it is written in his biography in the *Early State Papers of New Hampshire*: "On the 29th of March, 1808, he died in great poverty, but with great equanimity and fortitude, in the sixty first year of his age." Maybe they moved to save money?

When I found the deed for 74 Gates Street (the house that is there now is not of as great an age) which is next door to 64, I found that Mary Holmes, who appears to be the granddaughter of Thomas Clark, sold that property to A. Penhallow: Deed 393/137 in 1861: "Land Northerly by Gates St., easterly by land of Susan A. Sewall and others, Southerly by Land of George Tetherly and westerly by Land of the heirs of Amos Fernald, dec." Thomas Clark, weaver, didn't live here, either; he lived next door.

The 1832 probate of the estate of Amos Fernald includes: "2/6 of the undivided House and land bounded on Washington Street and Gate Street now occupied by Mr. Henry Cotton and One two story dwelling house on Gate St., adjoining the above, and standing on the above undivided land." That two-story dwelling is 64 Gates Street.

Part of my confusion lay in a deed from 1828, 221/170 Sarah Sewall to Amos Fernald, where he paid her $200 and she appeared to sell him "the house where I now live..." This fit in with the other deeds for 64 Gates Street which became another of Amos Fernald's properties. When I was attempting to find out if the Sewalls had become so poor in 1794 that they had to sell the back half of the property, they also appeared to sell a farm that Sarah's father had left to her in his will. The various deeds didn't make much sense until I discovered that one way to get a loan at that time was to give your house as collateral for the money loaned to you by another individual. So, this Sewall to Fernald deed was not a sale but a way to raise money and that was the same for the farm.

Many times, I attempted to find the illusive deed that sold 84 Gates Street to Oliver Ayers. The house was easy to trace back to the Ayers. In the 1888 Deed 474/403 Piscataqua Savings Bank to George M. Ayers, it states that the property was "given to me by my father Oliver Ayers in his last will dated 1883."

84 Gates Street in 2021. Author's photo.

Searching for Oliver Ayers or just Ayers in the registry of deeds never brought up an Ayers deed before that date that could have been this house at 84 Gates Street. One day I thought what about Ayer? The search engine in the registry of deeds does not have much tolerance for a name that isn't quite right. And there it was wrongly indexed: In 1864 Deed 403/202 Joseph A. Sewall and Stephen Sewall, heirs of Susan A. Sewall sold the property to Oliver Ayers. Jonathan and Sarah's youngest daughter Susan died in December 1863. Her probate of February 1864 awards the property to Stephen Sewall of Scarborough, Maine, and Joseph A. Sewall of Bloomington, Illinois, her nephews.

The Portsmouth Advocates 1982 Historic Survey gives the historic name for 64 Gates Street as the Jonathan M. Sewall House. And so, it goes on. I am very thankful to Natalie Fenwick and Dorothy Vaughan for the wonderfully interesting articles they researched and wrote to alert the people of Portsmouth to the demolition of their colonial history. In addition, I am thankful to the people who lived in our house before 2003 and who kept the article to pass along to new owners. If it weren't for that intriguingly written piece about the house, it is unlikely I would have embarked on this biography of his life.

So, if Washington "schlept" along here, it was the neighbor's house where the Sewalls were living. Perhaps Jonathan and Sarah will thank me for letting the people of Portsmouth know that they did not live in this "modest" house at 64 Gates Street but a much larger and nicer one two doors away. And we are so pleased for Sarah Sewall. How she could have dressed for George Washington's ball and managed to get down the stairs here is hard to imagine.

> Vain Britons, boast no longer with proud indignity,
> By land your conquering legions, your matchless strength at sea,
> Since we, your braver sons incensed, our swords have girded on.
> Huzza, huzza, huzza, huzza, for war and Washington.
> —Jonathan Mitchel Sewall 1776

> Vain Hammonds, boast no longer for tradition can misguide,
> Your house was not the one, where Sewalls lived and died,
> For the deeds declare, they were not there...at all.
> Huzza, huzza, huzza, huzza for maybe he came to call.
> —Nancy Hammond 2021

Acknowledgements

My editorial team who believed in this book from the beginning and carefully read and commented on each chapter, deserve much thanks for their help and endurance: Judy Hoober from Lancaster, Pennsylvania, my sister; Bob Hammond from Highlands Ranch, Colorado, my brother; and Ann Aungle from Radlett, Hertfordshire, England, colleague and friend from my forty-five years living in England.

Others who helped and believed in the book include Tom Hardiman, Robin Silva, and Carolyn Marvin from the Portsmouth Athenaeum. James L. Garvin, the long-time New Hampshire State Architectural Historian and Valerie Cunningham of the New Hampshire Black Heritage Trail took time to read and comment positively on many parts of the book. Nicole Luongo Cloutier and Katie Czajkowski at the Portsmouth Public Library, Brian Burford at the New Hampshire Archives, and Richard Candee found an amazing amount of interesting material for me. Dennis Robinson answered all my emails with many informative and encouraging comments.

Although some information about Jonathan Mitchel Sewall was discovered easily, there was so very much more to explore with the many online sources available now including Genealogy Bank, Internet Archive, Ancestry, Find My Past, Family Search, and American Ancestors.

Continuing to write all through the pandemic would have been much more difficult if it weren't for my morning latté served up cheerfully every day by Emma Nelson and her team at Kaffee Vonsolln on Daniel Street, Portsmouth.

Many thanks to you all.

Bibliography

All newspaper articles, unless otherwise noted, are available on GenealogyBank, https://www.genealogybank.com/. An online subscription is required after a seven-day free trial.

Acts and laws of His Majesty's province of New-Hampshire. In New-England: With sundry acts of Parliament. 1771. Portsmouth, NH: Printed by Daniel and Robert Fowle.

Adams, John. 1778. *Travels, and Negotiations, 1777–1778*, part 2. Adams Family Papers. Massachusetts Historical Society. Electronic Archive.

———. 1856. *The Works of John Adams, Second President of the United States.* Boston, Little, Brown and Co.

———. (1771-1781) 1961. *Diary and Autobiography of John Adams. Volume 2: 1771–1781.* Cambridge: Harvard University Press.

Adams, Nathaniel. 1825. *The Annals of Portsmouth.* Portsmouth, NH: Nathaniel Adams.

Batchellor, Albert Stillman, ed. 1893. *Early State Papers of New Hampshire— New Hampshire State Papers,* Vol. 22. Concord: Ira C. Evans.

Belknap, Jeremy. 1637–1891. *Jeremy Belknap Papers 1637–1891.* Boston: Massachusetts Historical Society. *Belknap to Hazard*, Sept. 1, 1783; and *Plumer to Hale*, Sept. 18, 1786.

Bell, Charles H. 1894. *The Bench and Bar of New Hampshire: Including Biographical Notices of Deceased Judges of the Highest Court, and Lawyers of the Province and State, and a List of Names of Those Now Living.* Boston: Houghton, Mifflin Co.

Blackstone, William. 1765-1770. *Commentaries on the Laws of England.* Oxford: Clarendon Press.

Brewster, Charles W. (1859) 1869. *Rambles about Portsmouth.* 1st series C. W. Brewster & Son, 1859; 2nd series. Portsmouth, NH: Lewis W. Brewster.

Bryce, Robert. 2014, *Smaller Faster Lighter Denser Cheaper: How Innovation Keeps Proving the Catastrophists Wrong.* "Public Affairs."

Briggs, L. Vernon. 1927. *History and genealogy of the Cabot family 1475–1927.* Boston: Goodspeed. (Biographies of Cabot family members and Shipping letters of Bilbao).

Butterworth, Hezekiah. 1881. *Young Folks History of Boston.* Boston: Estes and Lauriat.

Celebration of the Centennial Anniversary of the Introduction of the Art of Printing into New Hampshire. 1857. Portsmouth, NH: Edward N. Fuller, Publisher.

Child, Hamilton. 1886. *Gazetteer of Grafton County, New Hampshire 1709–1866*. Syracuse, NY: Syracuse Journal Co.

Chroust, Anton-Hermann. 1957. "Legal profession in Colonial America." *Notre Dame Law Review* 33(1).

Consalus, Charles E. 1978. "Legal Education during the Colonial Period, 1663–1776." *Journal of Legal Education* 29(3), pp. 295–310.

Craig, Lawrence R. 1966. *Three Centuries Of Religious Living: A History of the South Church and Parish (Unitarian) and the Universalist Church with an Article on Early Religious Matters in Portsmouth, New Hampshire and the Glebe Land Grant*. Portsmouth, NH: Randall Press.

Crawford, Mary Caroline. 1902. *The Romance of Old New England Rooftrees*. Boston: L.C. Page & Company, p. 145.

Cunningham, Valerie. 2003. "That the name of slave may not more be heard: The New Hampshire Petition for Freedom, 1779." *Dublin Seminar for New England Folklife Annual Proceedings 2003*.

Cushing, John D. 1981. "Ezekiel Russell's Edition of Jonathan Mitchell Sewall's "War and Washington": A Bibliographical Note." *Proceedings of the Massachusetts Historical Society*, Third Series, Vol. 93, pp. 109–114.

Daniell, Jere R. 1970. *Experiment in Republicanism; NH politics and the American Revolution, 1741–1794*. Cambridge: Harvard University Press.

———. 1981. *Colonial New Hampshire; a history*. New York: KTO Press.

Davis, Joshua. 1811. *A Narrative of Joshua Davis, an American Citizen Who Was Pressed and Served on Board Six Ships of the British Navy, He was in Seven Engagements, Once Wounded, Five Times Confined in Irons, and Obtained His Liberty by Desertion*. Boston: B. True.

Dishman, Robert B. 2010. "Jeremy Belknap and Jonathan Mitchell Sewall as Abolitionists: Defining the Extent of New Hampshire's Bill of Rights." *Historical New Hampshire*, 64(2) Winter.

Dobson, Michael. 2007. "Let him be Caesar!" *London Review of Books* 29(15), 2 August.

Earle, Alice Morse. 1889. *Child Life in Colonial Days*. New York: MacMillan.

Ebel, Carol. 1988. *The Papers of George Washington: 1 April–30 September 1795*. Charlottesville: University of Virginia Press.

Eliot, John. 1809. *A Biographical Dictionary, Containing a Brief Account of the First Settlers, and Other Eminent Characters Among the Magistrates, Ministers, Literary and Worthy Men, in New-England*. Boston: Cushing and Appleton Salem, and Edward Oliver.

Ellis, George H. 1899. *The Portsmouth Book*. Boston: George H. Ellis. Assembly House description by Mrs. Ichabod Goodwin written about 1870.

Elwyn, Thomas. 1805. *A Letter to a Federalist in reply to some of the popular objections to the motives and tendency of the measures of the present administration, Feb. 1805*. Portsmouth, NH: Chronicle Office.

Essex County Probate Records. Massachusetts, U.S., Wills and Probate Records, 1635–1991. https://www.ancestry.com/.

Essex Institute Historical Collections. Vol. 37 (1901) *List of Vessels Owned Wholly or in part by Timothy Orne, Junior, 1740–1758,* p. 78; Vol. 49 (1913) *Diary for the Year 1759 kept by Samuel Gardner of Salem.* pp. 1–23. Salem, Essex Institute. https://www.hathitrust.org/.

Estes, J. Worth, and David M. Goodman. 1986. *The Changing Humors of Portsmouth: The Medical Biography of an American Town, 1623–1983.* Boston: Francis A. Countway Library of Medicine.

Federal Writers' Project, Works Progress Administration, State of New Hampshire. 1938. *New Hampshire: a guide to the granite state.* Boston: Houghton.

Felt, Joseph B. 1827. *Annals of Salem.* Salem, MA: W. & S. B. Ives.

Fenwick, Natalie (Mrs. Marston). 1958. "The Tale of a Local Poet." *Portsmouth Herald,* Dec. 13, 1958.

Foster, Sarah Haven. 1876, 1884, 1896. *The Portsmouth Guide Book.* Portsmouth, Joseph W. Foster, 1876; Joseph W. Foster, 1884; *Portsmouth Journal,* 1896.

Frink, Helen H. 2010. "Piscataqua Bridge." *Newington Neighbor,* #163.

Gagnon, Alphonse. 1913. *Questions d'hier et d'aujourd'hui.* Paris: Desclée, De Brouwer.

Garvin, James L. 2002. "Range Roads." *Old Stone Wall.* Concord, NH: New Hampshire Division of Historical Resources, Spring.

Governor Gilman's Blues Militia Record Book, 1799–1813. Archive, Portsmouth Athenaeum.

Grafton County Registry of Deeds. https://www.nhdeeds.org/grafton-home/.

Graves, Eben. 2022. *Sewall or Sewell of Coventry.* https://sewallgenealogy.com/.

Griggs, Frank Jr. 2013. "Piscataqua Bridge." *Structure,* August.

Gurney, C. S. 1902. *Portsmouth Historic and Picturesque.*

Hamilton, William. 1727, 1751. Hermes romanus anglicis Dni. Johannis Garretsoni vertendis exercitiis accommodatus: *or, A new collection of Latin words and phrases.* Dublin: George Grierson. (Illustration: London, 1727).

Hart, James D., revised by Leininger, Phillip W. 1995. *The Oxford Companion to American Literature* (6 ed.). Oxford University Press.

Heard, Patricia L. 2006. "Jonathan Mitchell Sewall." Robinson, J. Dennis, ed. *Literary Lions: Celebrating 250 years of print in the seacoast: a who's who of the seacoast literary leaders 1756-2006.* [Portsmouth: Portsmouth Athenaeum].

Hoefnagel, Dick, and Virginia L. Close. 1995. "Journey to Hanover, August 1771." *Dartmouth College Library Bulletin,* November.

Holmes, Pauline. 1935. *A tercentenary history of the Boston Public Latin School, 1635–1935.* Cambridge: Harvard University Press.

Jenks, Henry Fitch. 1886. *Catalogue of the Boston Public Latin School, established in 1635 With an Historical Sketch*. Boston: Boston Latin School Association.

Knoblock, Glen A. 2005. *Portsmouth Cemeteries*. Mount Pleasant, SC: Arcadia.

"Jay Treaty Supporters." 1796. Archival document. Portsmouth Athenaeum.

Lamikiz, Xabier. 2008. "Basque Ship Captains as Mariners and Traders in the Eighteenth Century." *International Journal of Maritime History* 20(2), December, pp. 81–109.

———. 2013. *Trade and Trust in the Eighteenth-Century Atlantic World: Spanish Merchants and their Overseas Networks*. Rochester, NY: Boydell & Brewer.

Lancaster, Daniel. 1845. *History of Gilmanton*. Gilmanton: Alfred Prescott.

Latimer, John F. 1950. "Ezekiel Cheever and His Accidence." *The Classical Weekly*. 43(12), March 6.

Littlefield, George Emery. 1904. *Early Schools and School-Books of New England*. Boston: The Club of Odd Volumes.

MacPherson, James. 1761. *Fingal, an ancient Epic Poem in six books: together with Several Other Poems composed by Ossian, the son of Fingal, translated from the Gaelic Language*. Edinburgh.

———. 1765. *The Works of Ossian*. London: T. Becket and P. A. Dehondt.

Massachusetts. 1919–1990. General Court. House of Representatives. *Journals of the House of Representatives of Massachusetts*. Boston: Massachusetts Historical Society. https://www.hathitrust.org/.

May, Ralph. 1926. *Early Portsmouth History*. Boston: C. E. Goodspeed.

Mayhew, Jonathan. 1760. *A discourse occasioned by the death of the Honourable Stephen Sewall, Esq. Chief-justice of the Superiour Court of Judicature, Court of Assize, and General-Goal-Delivery; as also a member of His Majesty's Council for the province of the Massachusetts-Bay in New-England: who departed this life on Wednesday-night, September 10. 1760. Aetatis 58. Delivered the Lord's-Day after his decease. By Jonathan Mayhew, D.D. Pastor of the West-Church in Boston*. Boston: William Draper. https://archive.org/.

McCusker, John J. 2001. *How Much Is That in Real Money? A Historical Price Index for Use as a Deflator of Money Values in the Economy of the United States*. Worcester, MA: American Antiquarian Society.

Miller, Frank W. 1872. *History of the New Hampshire Gazette, the oldest newspaper in America, 1756–1872*. Boston.

Monaghan, E. Jennifer. 1988. "Literacy instruction and the town school in seventeenth-century New England." *American Quarterly*, 40(1), March, pp. 18–41.

Moore, Sean D. 2019. *Slavery and the making of Early American Libraries*. Oxford University Press. (Cabot family transactions with Bilbao, Spain).

Morris, Richard J. 2000. "Redefining the Economic Elite in Salem, Ma, 1759–1799: A Tale of Evolution, Not Revolution." *New England Quarterly*, 73(4), Dec., pp. 603–624.

Murray, John. 1816. *The Life of Rev. John Murray*. Boston: Munroe and Francis.

New England Historic Genealogical Society (NEHGS). 1871. Biographical sketch William Plumer, Sr. *Register and Antiquarian Journal* (NEHGR 25(1).

New England Historic Genealogical Society (NEHGS). 2005. *Colonial collegians: biographies of those who attended American colleges before the War for Independence*. Boston: Massachusetts Historical Society, New England Historic Genealogical Society. https://www.americanancestors.org/.

New Hampshire Committee of Safety. 1775. Founders Online, National Archives. founders.archives.gov/documents/Washington.

New Hampshire Department of State. Division of Archives and Records Management. Petitions: 6/12/1781 for Mary Traill; 5/31/1793(3) for the Universalist Society; June 1801(6) for Jonathan M. Sewall.

New Hampshire State Papers. https://www.sos.nh.gov/archives.

New Hampshire Wills and Probate Records, 1643–1982. 2020. Image #290. https://www.ancestry.com/.

Office of the United States Historian. *John Jay's Treaty, 1794–95*. https://history.state.gov/milestones/1784-1800/jay-treaty.

Oliver, Fitch Edward, ed. 1890. *The Diary of William Pynchon of Salem. A Picture of Salem Life, Social and Political, a Century Ago*. Boston: Houghton Mifflin.

Owen, Marie Bankhead. 1911. "No Pent-up Utica Contracts Your Powers. - J. M. Sewall." Talks with Girls, *Montgomery Advertiser*. Montgomery (Alabama) June 22, 1911.

Page, Elwin L. 1932. *George Washington in New Hampshire*. Portsmouth, NH: Portsmouth Marine Society.

Patterson, Adoniram J. 1873. *Centennial Anniversary of the Planting of Universalism in Portsmouth, New Hampshire Nov. 16 & 17, 1873*. Portsmouth, NH: Wm. A. Plaisted.

Perley, Sidney. 1889. *The Poets of Essex County, Massachusetts*. Salem: S. Perley.

———. 1926. *The history of Salem, Massachusetts,* Vol. 2: 1638–1670. Salem: Sidney Perley.

———. 2022. *Salem in 1700*. Extracts from the Essex Antiquarian, 1898–1910, Vol. 2–13. Phillips Library at The Peabody Essex Museum. archive.org. (Deed and drawing of Stephen Sewall House, Salem).

Phillips, James Duncan. 1937. *Salem in the Eighteenth Century*. Boston: Houghton Mifflin.

Pichierri, Louis. 1960. *Music in New Hampshire 1623–1800*. New York: Columbia University Press.

Plumer, William, Jr. 1857. *Life of William Plumer*. Boston: Phillips, Sampson.

Ricks, Thomas E. 2012. *First Principles*. New York: Harper Collins.

Rorabaugh, W. J. 1986. *The Craft Apprentice: from Franklin to the Machine Age in America*. New York: Oxford University Press.

Sammons, Mark J., and Valerie Cunningham. 2004. *Black Portsmouth Three Centuries of African American Heritage*. Durham, NH: University of New Hampshire Press.

Sewall, Jonathan Mitchel. 1776. *A favorite song at the Columbian camp, in the late glorious and victorious struggle for liberty; To the tune of the British grenadier*. [Salem, Mass.], [Ezekiel Russell], 1 sheet ([1] p.) Collection of the Massachusetts Historical Society.

———. 1777. *Washington: a favorite new song in the American camp, broadside*. Danvers, [Mass.], [Ezekiel Russell], 1 sheet ([1] p.) Collection of the Massachusetts Historical Society.

———. c. 1778. *A new epilogue to Cato, spoken at a late performance of that tragedy*. [Portsmouth, N.H.]: [Daniel Fowle], Early American imprints. First series; no. 43372.

———. 1788. *An oration, delivered at Portsmouth, New-Hampshire, on the Fourth of July, 1788: being the anniversary of American independence. By one of the Inhabitants*. Portsmouth, NH: George Jerry Osborne.

———. 1798. *A Versification of President Washington's excellent Farewell-Address, to the Citizens of the United States*. Portsmouth, NH: Charles Peirce. Published under the pseudonym of "A Gentleman of Portsmouth, N.H."

———. 1799. *Eulogy on the Late General Washington; Pronounced at St. John's Church, in Portsmouth, Newhampshire, on Tuesday, 31st December, 1799, at the Request of the Inhabitants*. Portsmouth, NH: William Treadwell.

———. c. 1800. Sewall, Jonathan Mitchell. Manuscript poetry volume. Portsmouth, NH: Portsmouth Athenaeum, Portsmouth Historical Society Collection.

———. 1801. *Miscellaneous Poems*. Portsmouth, NH: William Treadwell.

———. 1805. *A parody on some of the most striking passages in a late pamphlet entitled "A Letter to a Federalist": with large additions & improvements*. Portsmouth, NH: Oracle Press. Published under the pseudonym of Vernon H. Quincey.

Sewall, Samuel. 1700. *The Selling of Joseph: A Memorial*. Boston: Bartholomew Green and John Allen.

Sewall, Stephen. 1808. "Elegy on the Death of J. M. Sewall, Esq." *The Literary Mirror*, April 9.

Spicer, Richard C. 2001. "Popular Song for Public Celebration in Federal Portsmouth, New Hampshire." *Popular Music and Society*.

Stearns, Ezra B. 1906. *History of Plymouth, New Hampshire.* Cambridge, MA: University Press.

Strawbery Banke Museum website. Winn-Yeaton House.

Suffern, Richard Winslow. 1972. *From Graces to Gargoyles: a social essay on the theater in Portsmouth, New Hampshire, 1762–1850.* Portsmouth, NH: Seacoast Arts Council.

Tuer, Andrew White. 1897. *History of the Horn-Book.* London: Leadenhall Press.

Upham, George B. 1920. "The Province Road." *The Granite Monthly,* Vol. 52, November, p. 440.

Uriarte, Aingeru Zabala. 1998. "The Consolidation of Bilbao as a Trade Centre in the Second Half of the Seventeenth Century." Janzen (ed.) *Merchant Organization and Maritime Trade.* Liverpool University Press.

Waldo, Albigence. 1897. "Life at Valley Forge 1777–1778." *Pennsylvania Magazine of History and Biography,* Philadelphia. Jan.

Walsh, James Leslie. 1996. *Friend of government or damned Tory: The creation of the loyalist identity in revolutionary New Hampshire, 1774–1784.* University of New Hampshire Scholars' Repository.

Washington, George. 1861. *The Diary of George Washington 1789–1791.* Richmond, VA: Press of the Historical Society.

Watson, Henry C. 1888. *Noble Deeds of Our Fathers as Told by Old Soldiers of the Revolution Gathered around the Old Bell of Independence.* Boston: Lee and Shepard, 1888.

———. 1889. *The Boston Tea Party and Other Stories of the Revolution relating many Daring Deeds of the Old Heroes.* Boston: Lee and Shepard.

Wentworth, Frances. 1775. Historical marker Governor John Wentworth House, Pleasant St., Portsmouth, NH.

Wetherbee, Fritz. 2016. "John Pickering of Newington." *New Hampshire Chronicle,* WMUR, Nov. 29.

Whitcher, William F. 1919. *History of the Town of Haverhill, New Hampshire.* Concord, NH: Rumford Press.

Willis, Eola. 1924. *The Charleston Stage in the XVIII Century.* Columbia, SC: The State Co.

Wilson, James Grant and John Fiske (eds.) 1900. *Appleton's Cyclopædia of American Biography,* 5:473–474. New York: D. Appleton.

Index

Page numbers in italics indicate illustrations.

A

Adams, John
  birthday celebrations in Portsmouth, 63, *63*, 147
  Edmund Burke and, 67–68
  friendship with cousin Jonathan Sewall, 54–55, 57
  friendship with David Sewall, 61
  friendship with John Pickering, 62–63
  Massachusetts constitution and, 100
  Ossian poetry and, 60
  Pickering connections and, 62–63
  presidential election, 144–145
  Stephen Sewall and, 41
  visit to Bilbao, Spain, 50
Adams, Joseph, 62
Addison, Joseph, 86–87, 104–105
Aesop's Fables, 34, 36–37
Aler, Paul, 36
Allenstown, N.H., 85, 128
The Annals of the Times, 156, 163
"Anniversary Song" (Sewall), 63, 155
Apothecaries, 46–47, *47*
Argus, 119
Ark Tavern, 169
Assembly Room (Portsmouth)
  civic celebrations and, 126, 130, 144–147
  eulogy for Washington and, 15–16
  Federalist meetings at, 168–169
  Fourth of July celebrations and, 167
  Republican meetings at, 150–151
  theater and, 104–105
  Washington's visit to Portsmouth and, 12
Atherton, Joshua, 141
Atkinson, George King, 61, 99, 102, 116, 118
Atkinson, Susannah Sparhawk, 61, 99, 116, 118
Atkinson, William K., 141
Ayers, George M., 182
Ayers, Oliver, 182

B

Barnard, John, 96
Barnes, Thomas, 156
Bartlett, Joseph, 22
Bartlett, Sarah Price. *See* Price, Sarah
Bartlett, Walter Price, 22
Barton, Samuel, 23
Batchellor, Albert Stillman, 41
Battle of Bunker Hill, 77
Belknap, Jeremy, 11, 99–100
Bell, Charles, 64
Bench and Bar of New Hampshire (Bell), 64, 66, 69, 85
Benjamin (schooner), 44
Benjamin, Park, Sr., 88
Berry, Thomas, 24
Bilbao, Spain, 47, 49–50
Biographical Dictionary of New England (Eliot), 39
Bishop, A., 119
Black Petition, 89–93
Blackstone, William, 56–57
Bochacheco (ship), 76

195

INDEX

Boston, Mass.
    1728 map of, *31*
    Back Bay, 30
    Boston style of writing and, 38
    early schools in, 32, *32*, 33–38
    enslaved petition for freedom in, 92
    population of, 50
    Sewall Mansion in, 30–32
    Boston Evening Post, 70
    Boston Gazette, 40, 47
    Boston Post Boy, 40–41
Boston Public Latin School
    Boston style of writing and, 38
    curriculum at, 34–37
    Ezekiel Cheever and, 35
    fees and, 32–33
    J.M. Sewall and, xiv, 30, 34, 36
    John Lovell and, 33
    map of, *31*
    school day at, 33
    Stephen Sewall and, 30, 34, 36
    students admitted to, *34*
    textbooks for, 34–37
Boston State House, *31*
Boston Tea Party, 75
Bouton, Nathaniel, 102
Bow, Samuel, 85
Bow Street Theatre (Portsmouth), 104, 118, *118*, 119–121
Bradford, William, Jr., 87
Brewster, Charles W., 14, 64–65, 98, 124, 138, 171, 178
Brewster, Nero, xv, 91
Brewster, William, 8
Brewster's Tavern, 8, 10, 12, 115, 117
"The British Grenadiers," 2, 80
Brown, Henry, 80
Buckminster, Joseph, 9, 119
Burke, Edmund, 67, *67*, 68, 175

C

Cabot, Anna Orne, 44
Cabot, Elizabeth. *See* Higginson, Elizabeth Cabot
Cabot, Francis
    as guardian to Sewall daughters, 24–26, 43
    home of, *25*
    merchant trade and, 25, 44–45, 47
    voyages to Bilbao, Spain, 47, 49
Cabot, John, 25
Cabot, Joseph, 25, 44–45, 47
Cabot, Mary, 21, 24
Caesar's Commentaries, 37
Captain Daniel Fernald House, 115
Carey, Henry, 120
Caesar (schooner), 46
The Catalogue of the Boston Public Latin School established in 1635 with an Historical Sketch (Jenks), 34
Cathedral-Church of Bilbao, 50
Cato (Addison), 86–87, 104–105
Chadwick, Capt., 130
Chamberlain, Nathaniel, *72*
Chase, Mr., 133
Cheever, Ezekiel, 35
Cheever's Accidence, 34–35, 37
Chroust, Anton-Hermann, 58
Cilley, Joseph, 8
Civil, Mr., 120
Clark, Thomas, 181
Clarke, John, 36–37
Colonial Collegians, 42, 57
Columbian Centinel, 153, 159, 166
Columbian Phenix, 172
Commentaries (Blackstone), 57
Committee of Correspondence, 75
Concord, N.H., 54, 99, 102, 108, 127–129
Confiscation Act, 97
Congregational Church (Portsmouth), 9
Congress of New Hampshire, 81
Connecticut Courant, 86

Continental Journal and Weekly Advertiser in, 86
Coos County, 66
Corderius' Colloquies, 34, 36–37
Cordier, Mathurin, 36
Coriolanus (Shakespeare), 104–105
Cotton, Henry, 181
Cotton, Leonard, 116
Coues, Peter, 74
Cunningham, Valerie, 91
Cutter, Ammi Ruhamah, 10–11, 99, 103
Cutter, Dorothy, 103
Cutts, Samuel, 75

D

The Diary or Loudon's Register, 121
Dame, William, 3, 5–6, 8
Davenport, John, 169
Dearborn, Benjamin, 109
Delphi (Horace), 37
Democratic-Republican Party, 163, 165–166, 168
Derby, Richard, 45, 47–48
Dishman, Robert B., xii, 91, 100
Dobson, Michael, 104
Dolbeare, Benjamin, Jr., 37
Drown, Mr., 74
Durand, John, 76
Durham, N.H., 70, 128–129, 150

E

Early Portsmouth History (May), 65
Early Schools and School-Books of New England (Littlefield), 35
Early State Papers of New Hampshire (Batchellor), 41–42, 46–47, 53, 81–82, 173, 181
Education. *See also* Boston Public Latin School; Salem Latin School
  arithmetic, 34, 39
  boys and breeching, 27
  classical studies and, xiv, 30, 37
  handwriting and, 33–34, 38–39

  home instruction and, 27–28
  hornbooks, *27*, 28
  New England Primer, 28, *28*
"Elegy on the death of J. M. Sewall, Esq." (S. Sewall), 19, 172–173, *173*
"An Elegy on two female Steeds" (Sewall), 83
Eliot, John, 39
Elliot, Samuel, 157
Elwyn, Elizabeth Langdon, 165
Elwyn, Thomas, 165–166
Enslaved people
  ads for sales and runaways, 124–125, *125*
  death notices and, 122, *122*
  J.M. Sewall anti-slavery writing and, 90–91
  Jonathan Sewall legal defense for, 56, 90
  legal representation and, 91–92
  New Hampshire Bill of Rights and, 102
  petitions for freedom, 91–92, 102
"Epilogue" (Sewall), 107
"Epilogue to Cato" (Sewall), 86–89
"Epilogue to Coriolanus" (Sewall), 104
Epistles (Tully), 37
"Epitaph on the Death of Primus" (Sewall), 93, *93*, 122–123
"Epitaph to a QUACK who died of an Asthma" (Sewall), 144
Essex Journal and New Hampshire Packet, 106
Eulogy on the Late General Washington (Sewall), 15–17, *17*, 18, 149, 179
Eutropius, 36–37
Ewen, Alexander, 128

F

The Farmer's Cabinet, 155
Farmer's Weekly Museum, 165
Federal Observer, 15, 148–149

INDEX

Federal Republicans, 168
Federalists, 135, 159, 161, 163, 165, 169
Fenton, John, 69, 71, *71*, 76–77
Fenwick, Natalie, xi, xiv, 177, 182
Fernald, Amos, 181–182
Fernald, Beulah Nichols, 115
Fernald, Daniel, 115
Fingal, an ancient Epic Poem in six books (MacPherson), 58
First Church of Salem, 21, 39
First Continental Congress, 75
First Principles (Ricks), xiv
First School House (Boston), 32, *32*
Fisher, Anna Wentworth, 96–97
Fisher, John, 96–97
Flagg, Major, 113
Flying Stagecoach, 65
Folsom, Nathaniel, 75, 102
Formulae Oratoriae (Clarke), 36
Fort William and Mary (New Castle Island), 75
Foster, Sarah H., 178
Fowle, Daniel, 4, 66, 89, 93, 122, 124, *124*
Fowle, Primus, 4, 93, 122, *122*, 123–125
Fowles Printing Office, 115
Francis (schooner), 44
Francis Cabot House (Salem, Mass.), *25*
Franklin, Benjamin, 167

G

Gage, Thomas, 80
Gagnon, Alphonse, 80
Gardner, Samuel, 47–49
Garretson, John, 35–36
Garretson's Hermes romanus, 35, *35*, 36–37
Garvin, James, 114
Gee, Mary, 61
Gerrish, Cesar, xv
George III, King, 68, 75–76, 87, 131

George Washington in New Hampshire (Page), 10
Gilman, John Taylor, 144, 157, 165
"God save the King", 6
Goat Island (Newington), 129, 150, 159
Goodale, Mary Sewall
  birth of, 21
  education of, 27
  guardianship of, 24, *24*, 25–26
  inheritance from grandfather, 25
  marriage to Nathan Goodale, 43, 100
Goodale, Nathan, 43, 100–101, 103–104
Goodwin, Ichabod, 105
Goodwin, Sarah Parker, 105
Gookins, Nathaniel, 16, 36
Goss, Dorothy, 117
Grace, Charles Bellamy, 116
Grace, Joseph, 178
Gradus Ad Parnassum (Aler), 36–37
Grafton, Joshua, 46
Grafton County
  Eleventh Regiment in, 69
  Haverhill in, 70–73
  J.M. Sewall as register of probate in, 66, 69–71, *71*, 72–73
  J.M. Sewall law practice in, 71
  Plymouth in, 70–71, *71*
  population of, 70
Grafton County Registry of Deeds, 66
Granite Monthly, 92
Green Mountain Patriot, 167
Greenland, N.H., 63, 84
Greenleaf's New York Journal and Patriotic Register, 131
Griggs, Frank, Jr., 128, *128*
Gullager, Christian, 12
Gurney, C. S., 178

H

"Hail Independence" (Sewall), 168
Hale, John, 143

Hale, Jonathan, 72
Hale, Samuel, 4
Hall, Seneca, xv
Hamilton, Alexander, 135
Hamilton, William, 35–37
Hammond, Otis, 92, 102
Hancock, John, 38, 55
Hannah (brigantine), 44
Harvard College, 26, 30, 42, 47, 57
Haven, Samuel, 96, 111, 115
Haverhill, N.H., 70–73, 76
Hawthorne, Nathaniel, 23
Hazard, Ebenezer, 99
Hazen, John, 73
Heathen Gods (King), 37
Higginson, Elizabeth Cabot, 25, 43
Higginson, John, 25, 27, 36, 53–54, 137
Higginson, Margaret Sewall, 25
Higginson, Stephen, 24–25, 43
Hill, Col., 109
Hill, Joseph Sherburne, 143
History of Concord (Bouton), 102
History of Gilmanton (Lancaster), 99
History of Plymouth (Stearns), 71
Hobart, David, 69
"The Hobbies Parodied" (Sewall), 167–168
Holbrook, Abiah, 33, 38, *38*
Holmes, Mary, 181
Holt, William, 128
"Homer" (Sewall), 37
Horace, 37
Hornbook, *27*, 28
House of Seven Gables, 22–23
Hull, Hannah, 30–31
Humphries, Daniel, 141
Hurd, John, 72

I

Incarnation Church (Bilbao, Spain), 50
Independent Chronicle, 81
"The Inflexible Patriot" (Sewall), 138

Intelligencer, 170, 173
"Introductory Prologue on opening the Theatre in this town" (Sewall), 118–119
Isaac, Abraham, 143, 157–158
"It Comes" broadside (Sewall), 110, *110*

J

Jackson, Hall, 133
Jackson, William, 9
James vs. Lechmere, 56, 90
Jay, John, 131–132
Jay Treaty, 131–133, *133*, 134, 137
Jefferson, Thomas, 163, 165
Jefferson Hall, 160–161, 168
"Jefferson Hall" (Wentworth), 160
Jenks, Henry F., 34
Jenk's Portland Gazette, 153
Johnson, Samuel, 101
Jonathan M. Sewall House, *55*, 182, *182*
Jones, John Paul, 117
Journal of the House, 97

K

King, William, 37
King's Chapel, 32
Knoblock, Glenn A., 142–143

L

Lancaster, Daniel, 99
Langdon, John
    attack on Fort William and Mary, 75
    governor of New Hampshire, 99, 109, 165–166, 169
    Grafton County land ownership and, 66
    Great Parade Fire and, 158
    J.M. Sewall and, 12
    ratification of the U.S. constitution, 113

Washington's visit to Portsmouth and, 4, 8–9, 11
Langdon, Mary, 156
Larkin, S., 16
Latimer, John F., 35
Leahy, Patrick J., 140
Lear, Mary, 12, 115, 179
Lear, Tobias, 9, 12, 15, 115
Leopard (brigantine), 44
Libbey, Jeremiah, 74, 128
Libbey, John, 180–181
The Literary Mirror, 19, 171, *171*, 172–173
Little, Stephen, 169
Littlefield, George Emery, 35–36
Livermore, Samuel, 132
Lives of the English Poets (Johnson), 101
Long, E. J., 16
Long, Peirse, 116
Lovell, James, 33
Lovell, John, 33, *33*, 34
Lowd, Benjamin, 117
Lowd, Benjamin, Jr., 117
Lynde, William, 26
Lyon and Mortar, 47

M

Mackey, Benjamin, 180
MacPherson, James (Ossian), 58–60
Madison, James, 135
March, Angier, 153–154
March, Clement, 84–86
March, Eleanor Veasey, 84–85
March, Elizabeth. *See* Salter, Elizabeth March
March, Martha, 84–85
March Farm, 84
Margaret vs. Muzzy, 56, 90
Marshall, John, 116
Marshall, Nathaniel, 116
Marshall Estate, 116
Massachusetts Historical Society, 63
Massachusetts Mercury, 153

Massachusetts Spy, 78
May, Ralph, 65
Mayhew, Jonathan, 40
McCusker, John J., 24
McIntire, James, 116
Medicines, 46–47, *47*
Melcher, John, 4, 122, 126–127
Melcher, Nathaniel, 181
Mercantile business
  apprenticeships in, 42–45
  in Salem, Mass., 44–45
  ship ownership and, 44–45
  trading goods and, 46, 49–50
  trans-Atlantic voyages, 46–49
Metamorphoses (Ovid), 37
Militia, 66, 69–70
Miller, Frank W., 89
Miscellaneous Poems (Sewall), 58, 83, 103, 142, 151, 153, *153*, 154, 156, 171
Mitchell, Jonathan, 22, 42
Montgomery Advertiser, 89
Murray, John, 73, *73*, 74

N

Narrative of Joshua Davis, 78
New England Historic Genealogical Society, 140
New England Primer, 28, *28*
New Hampshire
  center of government in Portsmouth, 65
  constitution and bill of rights, 98–102
  Coos County, 66
  Democratic-Republican Party, 165–166
  Federalists and, 159, 161, 165
  First Continental Congress delegates from, 75
  Grafton County, 66, 69–73
  independent government in, 81
  land grants in, 66
  lawyers in, 140–141

Portsmouth newspapers in, 122, 124, *124*, 125–126
ratification of the U.S. Constitution, 108–109, *109*, 110–111
Republicans and, 151, 159–161
road construction in, 65–66
Rockingham County, 66–67
Second Constitutional Convention, 99, *99*, 100
state capital in Concord, 129
Strafford County, 66
New Hampshire Committee of Safety, 80
New Hampshire Fire & Marine Insurance Company, 157
New Hampshire Gazette, 65, 71, 86, 90, 97, 108, *109*, 110, 122–123, 127, 131, 142, 160, 166
New Hampshire Mercury, 108
New Hampshire Patriot and State Gazette, 99
New Hampshire Sentinel, 153, 159
New Hampshire Spy, 108, 112–113, 118–119, 121–122, 127
New World, 88, *88*
New York Historical Society, 80
Newington, N.H., 61–63, 113, 128–129, 150
Newington Town Church, 62
Newmarch, Cato, xv
Nomenclature (Hamilton), 35, 37
North Cemetery (Portsmouth), xiii, 158, 172
North Church (Market Square, Portsmouth), 9
North Meeting House (Portsmouth), 119, 169
Nutting, John, 23

O

"Ode for the celebration of American Independence, 1788" (Sewall), 112
"Ode to Independence" (Sewall), 146
Odiorne, Samuel, 113–114
Odiorne, Samuel, Jr., 114
Ogden, John C., 9
Olcott, Simeon, 71–72
Old South Meeting House (Portsmouth), 115
"On Fanaticism; A Parody" (Sewall), 74
"On Music and Poetry; addressed to a Lady" (Sewall), 57–58
"On the Death of an Ox who died suddenly in Portsmouth Street July 1798" (Sewall), 143–144
"On the gloomy prospects of 1776" (Sewall), 81
Oracle of the Day, 15, *15*, 131–132, 146
Oracle Press, 166
An oration delivered at Portsmouth, New-Hampshire, On the Fourth of July, 1788 Being the Anniversary of American Independence by One of the Inhabitants (Sewall), 112, *112*
Orations (Tully), 37
Orne, Josiah, 48
Orne, Timothy, 44–47, 49
Osborne, George Jerry, 112, 122
Ossian. *See* MacPherson, James (Ossian)
"Ovid" (Sewall), 37

P

Page, Elwin L., 10
"Paraphrase of the 80th Psalm" (Sewall), 77
Parish Church of St. John, 50
Parker, John, 8–10, 66
Parker, Mary. *See* Sewall, Mary Parker
Parker, Noah, 98, 128
Parker, Ray, 178
Parker, Samuel, 94–95
Parker, William, 60, 94, 141
Parker House Hotel, 32

INDEX

"Parody on Marseilles-Hymn" (Sewall), 147
A Parody on some of the most striking passages in a late pamphlet entitled "A letter to a Federalist" with large additions and improvements (Sewall), 166, *166*
Parry, Edward, 76
Pascal, Elisabeth, 114, 180
Peabody, A. P., 63, 175
Peabody, Oliver, 141
Pearce, Peter, 128
Pearse, Mr., 3
Peirce, Andrew, 116
Peirce, Charles, 13, 137
Peirce, Daniel, 116
Peirce, John, 114
Peirce, Joshua, Sr., 116
Peirce, Nathaniel, 161
Peirce, Washington, 161
Penhallow, A., 181
Pepperell, Elizabeth, 61
Pepperell, William, 61
Perley, Sidney, 168
Petition of Nero Brewster and friends 89–93
Philadelphia Repository and Weekly Register, 154
Pickering, Abigail Sheafe, 62–64, 161, 163
Pickering, Deborah, 61
Pickering, John (1640-1721), 58
   Gates Street area and, 114, 116
Pickering, John (1737-1805), *64*
   connection with J.M. Sewall, 4, 61–62
   death of, 163
   drinking and, 162–164
   friendship with John Adams, 62–63
   friendship with March family, 84, 86
   Harvard College and, 58, 62–63
   home of, 64–65
   impeachment of, 162–163
   J.M. Sewall study of law with, 60, 63–64, 84, 124
   as lawyer and jurist, 64, 141
   loss of home in fire, 161
   marriage to Abigail Sheafe, 62–63
   New Hampshire constitution and, 99–102
   petition on behalf of, 163, *163*
   pro bono work, 64, 91–92
   religion and, 64
   "Scituation" in Portsmouth and, 95
   Washington's visit to Portsmouth and, 4, 10–11
Pickering, John (1740-1811), 62
Pickering, Joshua, 61, 163
Pickering, Thomas, 61, 80
Pickering, Timothy, 62, 135, 137, *137*, 138
Pickman, Benjamin, 45
Pierce, Joseph, 84
Piscataqua Bridge Tavern, 150
Piscataqua River, 75
Piscataqua River Bridge, 128, *128*, 129, *129*, 150, 161
Pittsburgh Post, 88
Plumer, William, Jr., 163
Plumer, William, Sr., 11, 64, 86, 94, 140, 163
Plymouth, N.H., 69–71, *71*
"A Poem, On the burning of Charlestown" (Sewall), 77
Poet Laureat to the Muses acrostic, 170, *170*, 171
The Poets of Essex County, Massachusetts (Perley), 168
Pompey, *90*
Pope, Alexander, 111, 166
Porter, Asa, 72
Portsmouth, NH. *See also* Assembly Room (Portsmouth)
   armed resistance to Great Britain in, 75
   birthday celebration for Washington, 145–147

202

INDEX

birthday celebrations for John Adams, 63, *63*, 147
Bow Street fire, 169–170
British flour and, 80
celebration for John Adams election, 144–145
civic celebrations, 126–127, 130
Democratic-Republicans and, 168
Federalists and, 159, 161, 168–169
Fourth of July celebrations, 110–112, 158–161, 166–167, 169–170
Gates Street, 114–117, 128, 177–178, *178*, 179–180, *180*, 181–183
General Court in, 95, 106
Goat Island, 129, 150, 159
Great Parade Fire, 157–158, 161, 169
historical buildings in, 177–183
Howard Street, 180, *180*
Hunking Street, 115
Maudlin Lane, 115, 180
Muddling Street, 115, 180
newspapers in, 122, 124, *124*, 125–126
observations of Washington's death, 15–16
opposition to Wentworth in, 76–77
Paul Revere's ride to, 75
Peirce's Lane, 116, 179
petition for freedom of enslaved in, 91–92, 102
Piscataqua River Bridge, 128, *128*, 129, *129*, 150, 161
Pleasant Street, 115
raid on Fort William and Mary, 75–76
ratification of the U.S. constitution, 108–112
report on "Scituation" in, 95
Republicans and, 151, 159–161
Rev. John Murray and, 73–74
rioting against the Jay Treaty, 131–133
as seat of N.H. government, 65
Sewall connections in, 60–61
ship building and trade in, 65
Social Library and, 103
theater in, 104–107, 118, *118*, 119–121
Washington Street, 31–32, 113, 117, 122, 178, 180
Washington's visit to, 3–4, 7–14, 105, 115–117
Water Street, 115
Portsmouth Athenaeum, 13, 17, 38, 60, 92, 114, 177
Portsmouth Cemeteries (Knoblock), 142
The Portsmouth Guide Book (Foster), 178
Portsmouth Herald, xi, xiv, 177
Portsmouth historic and picturesque (Gurney), 178
Portsmouth Historical Society, 60
Portsmouth Journal of Literature and Politics, 89
Portsmouth Livery Company, 178
Portsmouth Oracle, 162, 166, 169, 172
Portsmouth Public Library, xiv
Portsmouth State House, 3, *3*, 4, 8
Portsmouth Times, 113, 178
Pray, Sarah, 114
Prentice, John, 141
Price, Elizabeth. *See* Sewall, Elizabeth Price
Price, Sarah, 22
Price, Walter, 22, 27
Primus. *See* Fowle, Primus
Prince George (ship), 80
"Profiles of Eminent Men" (Sewall), 37, 101, 103, 141–142, *142*, 154
"Prologue to Portsmouth Plays" (Sewall), 105–106
Proscription Act of 1778, 97

INDEX

The Protestant Tutor, 28
Provincial Congress, 80
Putnam, James, 54
Pynchon, Catherine Sewall
   birth of, 21
   education of, 27
   family visits in Salem, 100
   friendship with David Sewall, 60
   guardianship of, 24, *24*, 25–26
   inheritance from grandfather, 25
   marriage to William Pynchon, 43
Pynchon, Elizabeth, 44
Pynchon, William
   Diary, 43, 49, 51, 60–61, 78
   family visits in Salem, 100–101, 103–104
   friendship with David Sewall, 60–61
   marriage to Catherine Sewall, 43
   Mitchel Sewall and, 43
   Salem literary club and, 101
   Timothy Pickering and, 62

Q

Questions d'hier et d'aujourd'hui (Gagnon), 80
Quincey, Vernon H., 166, *166*
Quincy, Dorothy, 55
Quincy, Esther, 55
Quincy, Mary, 55, 62

R

Rambles about Portsmouth (Brewster), 14, 64–65, 98, 124, 138, 171, 178
Register and Antiquarian Journal, 140
Republican Ledger, 161
Republican Ledger and Portsmouth Price Current, 148
Republican or Anti-Democrat, 159
Republicans, 88, 135, 151, 159–161
Revere, Paul, 75
Reynolds, Joshua, *67*

Ricks, Thomas E., xiv
Rindge, Romeo xv
Robie, Thomas, 57, *57*
Rockingham, Lord, 67
Rockingham County, 66–67
Russell, Chambers, 54
Russell, Ezekiel, 1

S

Salem, Mass.
   early schools in, 27, 29
   first school board in, 27
   literary club in, 101
   mercantile business in, 44–45
   population of, 44, 50
   Sewall family in, 20–26
Salem First Church, 61
Salem Gazette, 63
Salem Latin School, 29–30, 42–43, 53
Salter, Elizabeth March, 84–85
Salter, John, 85
Salter, John, Jr., 85
Salter, Joseph March, 85
San Nicolás of Bari Church, 50
Sandemanian meeting-house, 98
Sargent, Epes, 23
Scarborough (man-of-war), 97
Seaward, John, 180
Sebastian (schooner), 44
Second Constitutional Convention, 99, *99*, 100
The Selling of Joseph (Samuel Sewall), 90
Sewall, Caroline Storer, 4, 103, 117, 156
Sewall, Catherine. *See* Pynchon, Catherine Sewall
Sewall, David, 60–61, 90, 92, 95, 104, 156
Sewall, Elizabeth Price (mother), 21–24, 26
Sewall, Elizabeth (sister), 21, 26, 43
Sewall, Esther, 55

INDEX

Sewall, Henry, 22
Sewall, Jane, 22
Sewall, John (1654-1699), 60
Sewall, John Barnard, 4, 96, 117, 157, *157*, 158, 161, 169
Sewall, Jonathan (1693-1731), 53
Sewall, Jonathan (1729-1796) (cousin)
    Attorney General of Massachusetts, *53*, 55–56, 94
    defense of enslaved people, 56, 90
    friendship with John Adams, 54–55, 57
    Harvard College and, 42, 57
    home of, *55*
    J.M. Sewall study of law with, 53–54, 56–58
    law practice and, 53–54
    marriage and family of, 55
    poetry of, 57, *57*
    return to England as Loyalist during Revolution, 55
    Salem Latin School master, 29, 43, 53
Sewall, Jonathan (1766-1839), 55
Sewall, Jonathan Mitchel (b.1779), 94–95
Sewall, Jonathan Mitchel. *Apprenticeships and training*
    impact of illness on, 51–52
    malignant fever and recuperation in Bilbao, 46–47, 49–51
    mercantile business and, 42–47
    study of law with cousin Jonathan, 53–54, 56–58
    study of law with John Pickering, 60, 63–64, 84, 124
Sewall, Jonathan Mitchel. *Early years and education*
    birth in Salem, 2, 21
    Boston Public Latin School and, xiv, 30–34, 36, 39
    classical education and, xiv, 30
    death of father, 21, 26
    death of mother, 39
    death of Uncle Stephen, 39–41
    early education in Salem, 27–29
    extended family and, 22–23, 26
    guardianship and influence of Uncle Stephen, 26, 30, 39–41
    South Writing School and, 33–34
Sewall, Jonathan Mitchel. *Later years*
    admiration for George Washington, 1, 4, 83, 136, 138, 179
    David Sewall family and, 60–61
    death of, 168, 172–176
    defense of enslaved people, 91–92, 102
    denouncement of slavery, 89–93
    drinking and, 52, 85, 123, 164
    friendship with March family, 84, 86
    friendship with Primus, 123–124
    John Wentworth and, 66–67
    land grants in Jefferson, 66
    law practice and, 76, 81–82, 86, 91–92, 97–100, 117, 140–141
    as lawyer in Plymouth, 71, *71*
    as major in the militia, 66, 69–70
    nervous affections and, 51–52, 85, 102–104
    New Hampshire constitution and bill of rights, 98–102
    nominated as Attorney General, 12, 86, 94
    obituaries for, 172–176
    Pickering connections and, 61–62
    pro bono work, 91–92
    as register of probate for Grafton County, 66, 69–73, *73*, 76
    resemblance to Edmund Burke, 66–68, 175
    Rev. John Murray and, 74
    "Scituation" in Portsmouth and, 95
    Social Library and, 103
    Universalist Church and, 98

INDEX

Universalist Meeting House petition, 127, *127*, 128
Washington's visit and, 3–7, 10, 12–13, 117
Sewall, Jonathan Mitchel. *Marriage and family*
  birth of Caroline, 103
  birth of John Barnard, 96
  birth of Stephen, 76
  birth of Susan Atkinson, 117
  death of Sarah Wood, 82
  family visits to Salem, 100–104
  first son with Sarah March, 94
  Gates Street home, xiii, 113–117, 128, 177–178, *178*, 179–180, *180*, 181–182, *182*, 183
  marriage to Sarah March, xi, 86
  marriage to Sarah Thurston Wood, 73, 75–76
  second son with Sarah Wood, 82
  Wentworth House and, 97, 114
Sewall, Jonathan Mitchel. *Writings*
  "Anniversary Song", 155
  Bow Street Theatre Prologue, 120–121, *121*
  celebration for John Adams, 144–145
  civic celebration of 1793, 126–127
  civic celebration of 1795, 130–131
  denouncement of slavery in, 90–93
  "An Elegy on two female Steeds", 83
  "Epilogue to Portsmouth Plays", 107
  "Epilogue to Cato", 86–89
  "Epilogue to Coriolanus", 104
  "Epitaph on the Death of Primus", 93, *93*, 122–123
  "Epitaph to a QUACK who died of an Asthma", 144
  epitaphs for animals, 143–144
  epitaphs for friends, 142–143, 158
  Eulogy on the Late General Washington, 15–17, *17*, 18, 148, *148*, 149, 179
  "On Fanaticism; A Parody", 74
  "On the gloomy prospects of 1776", 81
  "Hail Independence", 168
  handwriting and, 39, *39*
  "The Hobbies Parodied", 167–168
  "The Inflexible Patriot", 138
  instrumental and vocal music performances, 119, *119*
  "Introductory Prologue on opening the Theatre in this town", 118–119
  "It Comes" broadside, 110, *110*
  Jay Treaty and, 133–134
  Miscellaneous Poems, 58, 83, 103, 142, 151, 153, *153*, 154, 156, 171
  "On Music and Poetry; addressed to a Lady", 57–58
  "Ode for the celebration of American Independence, 1788", 112
  "Ode to Independence", 146
  Odes to Washington, 3, 5–7
  "On the Death of an Ox who died suddenly in Portsmouth Street July 1798", 143–144
  An oration delivered at Portsmouth, New-Hampshire, On the Fourth of July, 1788 Being the Anniversary of American Independence by One of the Inhabitants, 112, *112*
  "Paraphrase of the 80th Psalm", 77
  A Parody on "A letter to a Federalist", 166, *166*
  "Parody on Marseilles-Hymn", 147
  patriotic songs, 150

INDEX

"A Poem, On the burning of Charlestown", 77
Poems of Ossian and, 58–59, *59*, 60
Poet Laureat to the Muses acrostic, 170, *170*, 171
poetry of, xiv, xv, 38–39, 57–58, 70, 77, 83
"Profiles of Eminent Men", 37, 101, 103, 141–142, *142*, 154
"Prologue to Portsmouth Plays", 105–106
proposals for printing poems, 151, *151*, 152, *152*, 153
on the ratification of the U.S. constitution, 110–113
"Sewall's Poems", *154*, 155–156
"Shout, Shout America 1777", 83
"Song for President Adams' Birth-Day", 63, 147
"A Song for the Anniversary of Independence, July 4, 1805", 167
"A Song Written in 1776—in imitation of the "Watry God"", 81, 91
Songs for Washington's Birthday, 145–147
"To S. S. Esq. on joining the American Army in 1777", 83
"Two excellent Songs from the elegant and ingenious pen of", 167
"Verses Written in a Summer-House", 105
Versification of Washington's Farewell Address, 13, *13*, 14, 136–137, *137*, 138–140
"War and Washington", xiii, 1, *1*, 2, 78–79, *79*, 80, 179
"Washington Hall", 159–160, 162
Sewall, Joseph A., 182
Sewall, Katherine, 22
Sewall, Margaret. *See* Higginson, Margaret Sewall
Sewall, Margaret Mitchell, 20, 22, 41
Sewall, Margaret (Peggy), 21, 24, *24*, 25–27, 43
Sewall, Mary (b.1698), 25
Sewall, Mary Parker, 60, 92, 95
Sewall, Mitchel (1699-1748) (father)
 death of, 21, 23
 education and law practice of, 21, 43
 estate of, 23, *23*, 24, 26
 guardianship of children, 25–26
 marriages and family of, 21, 53
Sewall, Nabby Lee, 95, 100
Sewall, Nicholas, 60
Sewall, Samuel (1652-1730), 20, 30, 90
Sewall, Samuel (1688-1769), 60
Sewall, Samuel (b.1689), 21–22
Sewall, Sarah March
 Allenstown property of, 85, 128
 birth of John Barnard, 96
 first son with J.M., 94
 friendship with Storers, 103–104
 Gates Street home, 114, 179–183
 inheritance from father, 84–85
 on J.M.'s drinking, xi, 85
 marriage to J.M., xi, 86
 Washington's visit and, 4, 12, 117
Sewall, Stephen (1657-1725), 20, *20*, 21, 27, 41, 60
Sewall, Stephen (1702-1760) (uncle)
 adoption of Jonathan and Stephen, 26, 30, 39–40
 as Chief Justice of Massachusetts, 26, 30, 40, *40*, 41
 death of, 39–40
 estate of, 41
 friendship with John Barnard, 96
 funeral of, 40–41
 Harvard College and, 26, 42
 influence on J.M. Sewall, 41
 Mitchel Sewall's estate and, 26, *26*

INDEX

property in Boston, 22, 31
Sewall, Stephen (1746-1799) (brother)
  adoption by Uncle Stephen, 26, 30, 39–40
  Boston Public Latin School and, 31–32, 34, 36
  death of father, 21
  death of infant Jonathan Mitchel, 95
  death of mother, 39
  death of Uncle Stephen, 39–41
  early education in Salem, 29
  mercantile business and, 43
  wife Nabby and, 95, 100
Sewall, Stephen (1775-1844) (son)
  birth of, 76
  brother John Barnard and, 96
  "Elegy on the death of J. M. Sewall, Esq.", 19, 172–173, *173*
  family visits to Salem, 101
  The Literary Mirror, 19, 171, *171*
  newspaper publishing and, 125, 156, 162–163
  obituary for father, 176
  Washington's visit to Portsmouth and, 3–4, 117
  working as a printer, 3, 19, 125–126, 156
Sewall, Stephen (grandson), 182
Sewall, Susan Atkinson, 117, 156, 182
Sewall Mansion (Boston), 30–32
"Sewall's Poems" (Sewall), *154*, 155–156
"Shakespeare" (Sewall), 142
Shakespeare, William, 104–105
Shannon, R. Cutts, 163
Sheafe, Abigail. *See* Pickering, Abigail Sheafe
Sheafe, Jacob, IV, 55, 62, 66, 133
Sheafe, James, 74
Sherman, James S., 88
Shillaber, Jonathan, 117, 122
Shillaber, Joseph, 117

"Shout, Shout America 1777" (Sewall), 83
Smith, John, 97
Snell, John, 116
Snell, Lucy, 116
Snell, Lucy Marshall, 116
Snell, Nabby, 116
Snell, Reuben, 116
Snell, Sarah, 116
"Song for President Adams' Birthday" (Sewall), 63, 147
"A Song for the Anniversary of Independence, July 4, 1805" (Sewall), 167
"A Song Written in 1776—in imitation of the "Watry God"" (Sewall), 81, 91
South Meeting House (Boston), *31*, 32
South Writing School (Boston), 33–34, 38
Sparhawk, George, 3, 5–6, 8
Sparhawk, Jane, 61
Sparhawk, John, 21, 61
Sparhawk, Nathaniel, 61
Sparhawk, Susannah. *See* Atkinson, Susannah Sparhawk
Sparhawk, T., 16
Sparhawk, William Pepperell, 61
Sparhawk Hall, 61
Spicer, Richard, 110
St. John's Church (Portsmouth), 9, 16, 148, 169, 179
Stanwood, Mr., 16
State Papers, 102
Staver, John, 65
Stavers Tavern, 12
Stephen Sewall House (Salem, Mass.), 20, *20*
Storer, Clement, 103
Storer, Hannah March, 103–104
Storer, Joseph, 103
Storer, Joseph, Jr., 103
Strafford County, 66
Strawbery Banke Museum, 114, 134

Sullivan, John, 8–9, 12, 75, 141

T

Tetherly, George, 181
Thurston, Sarah. *See* Wood, Sarah Thurston
Titcomb, Moses, 72
"To S. S. Esq. on joining the American Army in 1777" (Sewall), 83
Tragedy of Chrononhotonthologos (Carey), 120
Traill, Mary, 97–98, *98*
Treadwell, Daniel, 157
Treadwell, William, 149
Tully, Richard, 37
Turner, Edward, 23
Turner, Elizabeth, 22
Turner, Freestone, 22
Turner, John, 22–23
Turner, John, III, 23, 44
Turner, John, IV, 23
Turner, Mary, 23
Turner, Mary (dau.), 23
"Two excellent Songs from the elegant and ingenious pen of J. M. Sewall, esq.", 167

U

Union (ship), 109
United States Constitution, 108–111
United States Oracle of the Day, 15–16, 18, 159–160
Universalist Church (Portsmouth), 82, 98
Universalist Meeting House (Portsmouth), 127, *127*, 128
Universalist Society, 127

V

Vaughan, Dorothy, xi, xiv, 177, 182
Veasey, Eleanor. *See* March, Eleanor Veasey
"Verses Written in a Summer-House" (Sewall), 105

Versification of Washington's Farewell Address (Sewall), 13, *13*, 14, 136–137, *137*, 138–140
Virginia Gazette, 78

W

Waldo, Albigence, 78
Walker, Jacob, 114
"War and Washington" (Sewall), xiii, 1, *1*, 2, 78–79, *79*, 80, 179
Ward's Latin Grammar, 36
Warner, Cato, xv
Warner, Jonathan, 11, 132
Washington, George
 appointment as Commander in Chief, 77–78
 British flour and, 80
 Cato drama and, 86–87
 classical plays and, xiv, xv
 death of, 15, 148–149
 declining candidacy, 135, *135*
 "Farewell Address" and, 13–14, 135–136, *136*, 138, 140
 Federalists and, 135
 Jay Treaty and, 131, 133–134
 Jeffersonian Republicans and, 135
 Piscataqua River excursion, 10
 Portsmouth birthday celebration for, 145–147
 Portsmouth church visits, 9–10
 Portsmouth observation of death, 15–16, 148–149
 public approval for, 135
 Sewall's admiration for, 1, 3, 10, 136, 138, 179
 Sewall's eulogy for, 15–18, 148, *148*, 179
 Sewall's poetry on, 4–7, 77–78
 stay at Brewster's Tavern, 8
 Timothy Pickering appointment as postmaster general, 62
 visit to Portsmouth, 3–4, 7–13, 105, 115–117

INDEX

Washington, Martha, 9
Washington Hall, 162
"Washington Hall" (Sewall), 159–160, 162
Watson, Henry C., 155
Watts, Mr., 120
Weeks, Eleanor March, 104
Weeks, George, 104
Wentworth, Anna. *See* Fisher, Anna Wentworth
Wentworth, Benning, 10, 67
Wentworth, Charles, 67
Wentworth, Daniel, 114
Wentworth, Frances, 77, 96–97
Wentworth, George, 180
Wentworth, John
   flight from Portsmouth, 76–77, 97
   friendship with English Wentworths, 67
   home of, 96–97, *97*
   J.M. Sewall appointments and, 65, 69
   road construction in New Hampshire and, 65–66
   as royal governor of New Hampshire, 10, 61, 65
   as Surveyor General of the Woods, 76
Wentworth, John (son of Thomas), 160–161
Wentworth, Joshua, 11, 66, 109, 112–114
Wentworth, Mark Hunking, 96
Wentworth, Martha Hilton, 10
Wentworth, Michael, 10, 67
Wentworth, Thomas, 160
Wentworth Mansion, 114–115, 123
Wentworth Senior Living, 96
Wentworth-Woodhouse, Mary, 77
Wesley, Charles, 6
Wetherbee, Fritz, 164
Wetmore, Catherine, 100
Wetmore, William, 100
Whidden, Capt., 144, 146
Whidden, Samuel, 170
Whipple, William, 98, 162
Willard, Rev. Mr., 16
William (brigantine), 44
William Pynchon's Diary, 43, 49, 51, 60–61, 78
"Windsor-Forest" (Pope), 111
Wood, Daniel Gerrish, 72, *72*
Wood, Sarah Thurston, 72–73, 75, 82
Woodward, Capt., 109, 112
The Works of John Adams, Second President of the United States, 54
The Works of Ossian (MacPherson), 59

Y

Yeaton, Phillip, 116
Yeaton, Thales, 134

About the Author

Nancy Hammond graduated from Miami University in Oxford, Ohio with a BA in French and from Western Reserve University with an MS in Library Science. She worked as a cataloguer at the Harvard University School of Higher Education and completed the coursework for an MA in Education. While working as Head of Circulation at Baker Library Harvard Business School she exchanged jobs with a British librarian and then moved to England in 1972. There she worked as Tutor librarian at Hatfield Polytechnic, Library Education Officer at the Polytechnic of North London, and Lecturer at Brighton Polytechnic Library School. While living in Northumberland after retirement she was involved with the Bailiffgate Museum in Alnwick researching houses and the people who lived in them in that town.

She bought a house jointly with her sister in Portsmouth, N.H. in 2003, moved there permanently in 2018 and became involved with a committee researching local properties for Portsmouth's 400th anniversary in 2023. She is a volunteer at the Portsmouth Athenaeum where she is now a Proprietor, and at the Strawbery Banke Museum. Also, she is a member of the Portsmouth Historical Society, the New Hampshire Historical Society, and the New England Historical Society and subscribes to American Ancestors, Genealogy Bank, Ancestry and Find My Past. Her research into the life of Jonathan Mitchell Sewall began with the purchase of the house in 2003 and she has written his biography during the pandemic as well as creating a Google Site of historic properties in the South End of Portsmouth.

www.ingramcontent.com/pod-product-compliance
Lightning Source LLC
Chambersburg PA
CBHW071157160426
43196CB00011B/2108